Publisher and Creative Director:
B. Martin Pedersen

Chief Visionary Officer:
Patti Judd

Design Director:
Hee Ra Kim

Designers:
B. Martin Pedersen
Hee Ra Kim
Hiewon Sohn

Associate Editor:
Colleen Boyd

Publisher's Assistant /Designer:
Claire Yuan Zhuang

Writer:
Maxim Sorokopud

Interns:
Maggie Herrera
Eli Hiscott
Sam Mayer

Japanese Advisors:
USA: Toshiaki & Kumiko Ide
Japan: Taku Satoh
Sakura Nomiyama

Chief Executive Officer:
B. Martin Pedersen

Cover Image:
On a wing, 2023
Illustration By Craig Frazier

Published by:
Graphis Inc.
389 5th Ave., Suite 1105
New York, NY 10016
Phone: 212-532-9387
www.graphis.com
help@graphis.com

ISBN 13: 978-1-954632-31-8

Dear Graphis Readers,

Welcome to Graphis Journal 382. This edition continues our tradition of celebrating the extraordinary work in Design, Advertising, Photography, Art/Illustration, and Education. Inside, discover exclusive interviews with leading creative talents in the industry, offering insights into their innovative processes and philosophies. Each story in this issue showcases the enduring power of creativity and our commitment to documenting and honoring exceptional work in the visual arts.

DESIGN: Graphis Master **Michael Vanderbyl** (US) is a true design master with a portfolio that spans identity, interiors, textiles, and product design. His ability to seamlessly integrate 2D and 3D design demonstrates their profound influence on each other.

Byoung il Sun (KR), a graphic designer and professor at Namseoul University, considers posters the "flowers of graphic design." His work, driven by social engagement, has earned numerous accolades for its powerful visual narratives.

At **Xiaomi** (CN), creative director Lu Chen leads the way in product design, blending functionality with aesthetic appeal. She shares insights into Xiaomi's three creative initiatives and the importance of listening to customer feedback in shaping top-tier products.

ADVERTISING: Duncan Channon (US) emphasizes a "feelings first" approach across five disciplines. The firm's dedication to building relationships through emotionally resonant work sets it apart.

PHOTOGRAPHY: Graphis Master **Patrick Molnar** (US) has made a name for himself with striking photoshoots for the USMC, Army, and Homeland Security, bringing attention to the lives of military personnel.

Graphis Master **Lindsey Drennan** (CA), the first international student to intern at *Vogue*, has pushed the boundaries of beauty and fashion photography with her glamorous images, making her a standout talent in the industry.

ART/ILLUSTRATION: Meanwhile, another Graphis Master, **Craig Frazier** (US), reflects on his 40+ year career, his latest book *Drawn*, and how his work blurs the lines between illustration and design.

EDUCATION: Natasha Jen (US), a Graphis Master, a co-partner at Pentagram, and an educator at the School of Visual Arts, emphasizes the importance of research and progressive learning to her students, preparing them for successful careers in design.

PRODUCTS: My Falco Moscata Superyacht (UK, FR, IT) is an international collaboration resulting in a stylish and durable vessel. Paradoxal Surfboards's **3D-Printed Surfboard** (FR) is eco-friendly and made from refined algae, combining sustainability with performance. JMB Aircraft's **Evo** (BE, CR, US) features a custom cabin, a powerful 750-horsepower engine, and an impressive fuel capacity. Quicksilver Aircraft's **MXL II Sport Light Service Aircraft** (US) is an easy-to-build and fly kit reminiscent of the iconic Wright Flyer.

ARCHITECTURE: Inspired by a French folk tale, **Mr. Plocq's Caballon** (FR) uses the Golden Ratio to create a unique glamping pod with curved wooden ribs. **Dune Villa West aan Zee** (NL) by 2by4-architects appears as a natural sand dune but reveals a sustainably built home with mid-century and Scandinavian design elements upon closer inspection.

Thank you for your continued support and passion for the visual arts and creative excellence. We hope you enjoy this edition of Graphis Journal and look forward to bringing you more exceptional stories in the next issue.

Best regards,

B. Martin Pedersen
Publisher & Creative Director

Contents

(Opposite page) Woman Life Freedom, Iran Poster, 2022. Design by Michael Vanderbyl

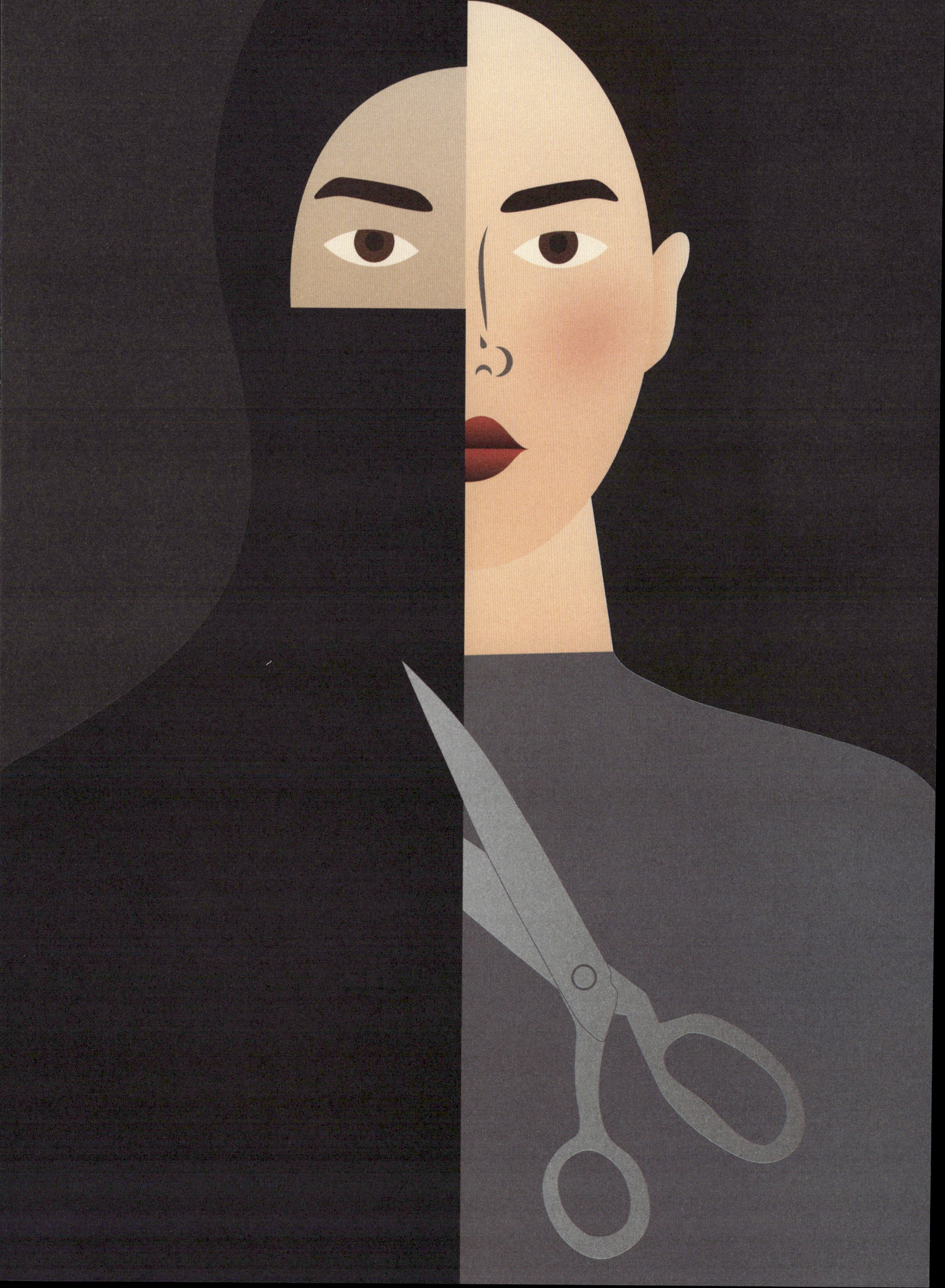

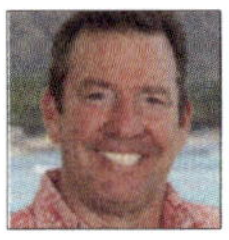

Introduction by Sean Dee

Sean Dee is responsible for developing and deploying global marketing, brand, revenue management, and sales strategies for the Outrigger Hospitality Group global portfolio. He joined Outrigger from Anschutz Entertainment Group (AEG) Worldwide, where he was executive vice president, chief marketing officer, and, subsequently, president of global branding for its live music division. Prior to AEG, Mr. Dee was the first EVP–chief marketing officer for Hard Rock International, directing the company's worldwide brand, sales, marketing, and merchandising initiatives for its global portfolio of restaurants, hotels, casinos, and live venues. His expertise in digital marketing and traditional media was honed early in his career as global marketing director–digital and vice president of brand marketing at Levi Strauss & Company, where he led the pioneering teams that launched the company into the e-commerce marketplace in the mid-1990s.

PHOTOGRAPHY:

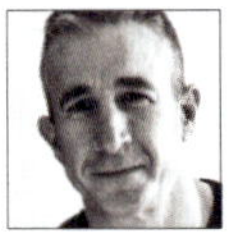

62 Patrick Molnar (Graphis Master) / USA

Based in Atlanta, Georgia, Pat is a passionate visual storyteller whose work embodies the authenticity of real-life moments. With a no-nonsense approach and unwavering commitment, he consistently brings his A-game to every production. From portraits and lifestyle to sports and military, Pat has worked with clients all over the globe, including Disney, the Marines, Allstate, USAA, Wells Fargo, and more.

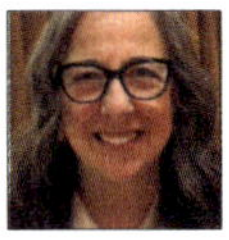

Introduction by Donna Grossman

Donna Grossman is an NYC-based casting director who casts coast-to-coast and worldwide. With over 20 years of experience, Donna has been at the forefront of commercial and print casting, as well as casting for both feature films and shorts. Utilizing her background in acting and teaching, Donna brings her skills as a director to every project and prides herself on making her casting studio and sessions a safe environment for actors to practice their craft. Donna is a proud recipient of several CLIO awards for her commercial work in some of the most memorable advertising campaigns. A sampling of Donna's work can be seen on her website at www.donnagrossmancasting.com, and she has credits on IMDB.

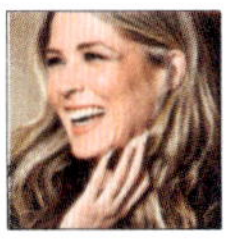

76 Lindsey Drennan (Graphis Master) / Canada

Lindsey is a commercial photographer from Toronto, Canada, represented by Coup&Co. Highlighting a photography career spanning over 19 years, she has curated a portfolio with an extensive array of Canada's premier brands, esteemed publications, leading agencies, and prominent production houses. Her career started in 2005; while pursuing her studies, she became the first-ever international student to secure an internship at the iconic *Vogue* in New York City. Since then, Lindsey has dedicated her expertise to commercial product and beauty photography, setting unparalleled standards of creativity and excellence.

Introduction by Ashley Barth

Ashley Barth is an artist rep and producer at Coup&Co. Established in 2014, Coup&Co. is a gathering of image makers and a full-service, Toronto-based agency working towards the ultimate creative goal: do what you love, love what you do. They exist to support each artist's individual growth, and in turn, each artist is here to support their clients' individual vision. Their roster of photographers, directors, and DOPs aims to produce exceptional advertising, commercial, and artistic content in photography and video. They love to create in any form, seeking inspiration and beauty in their everyday.

ART/ILLUSTRATION:

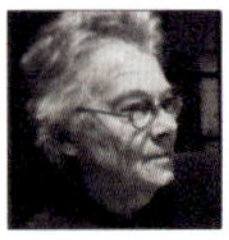

92 Craig Frazier (Graphis Master) / USA

Craig Frazier has been an illustrating designer since 1978. His work is recognized internationally for its wit, surprise, and simplicity. He is a frequent contributor to *The New York Times* and publications like *Time Magazine*, *Fortune*, *Bloomberg Business Week*, *Harvard Business Review*, and *The Wall Street Journal*, to name a few. His corporate clients include Adobe, American Express, Boeing, Chevrolet, Deloitte, MasterCard, Mohawk Paper, Navigant, the Royal Mail, the U.S. Postal Service, and United Airlines. Craig has created eight postage stamps, including the 2006 Love stamp and the 2010/11 commemorative Scouting stamps. Craig published his second monograph, *Drawn* (Goff Books), in January 2024; his first is a 176-page monograph titled *The Illustrated Voice* (Graphis Press, 2003). He is also the author and illustrator of ten children's books.

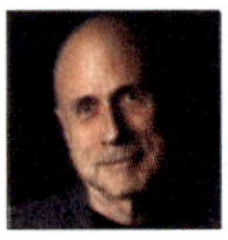

Introduction by Ken Segall

Born in Detroit, Ken Segall pursued a higher education before breaking away to pursue drumming; this did not pan out how he intended. He found himself flipping burgers along the Jersey Shore and later assumed the role of a bank teller. He eventually transitioned to a file clerk position at an LA ad agency. Seeking to refine his skills, Ken enrolled in a copywriting course and eventually relocated to New York. Despite initial setbacks, including relying on his girlfriend for support, he secured his first copywriting gig with Smirnoff Vodka. However, his second job ended abruptly after just four weeks. Ken discovered his true calling in the tech advertising arena, spending 12 years as Steve Jobs' ad guru. Along the way, he penned a *New York Times* best-seller, embarked on an international speaking career, and authored a second book. Though content with his accomplishments, a part of Ken still wishes the drumming panned out.

(Opposite page) Spaghetti Road, 2020. Illustration by Craig Frazier

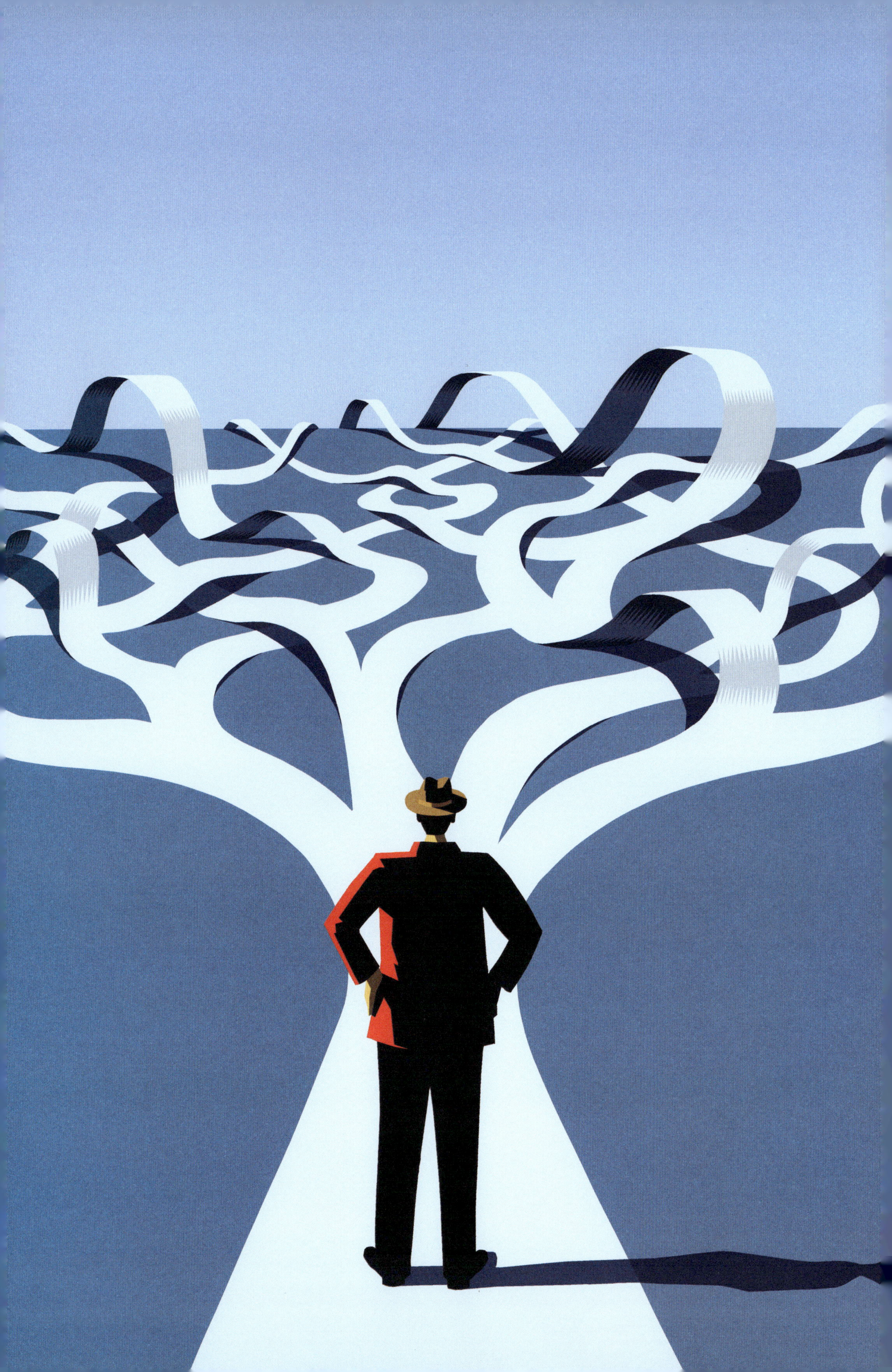

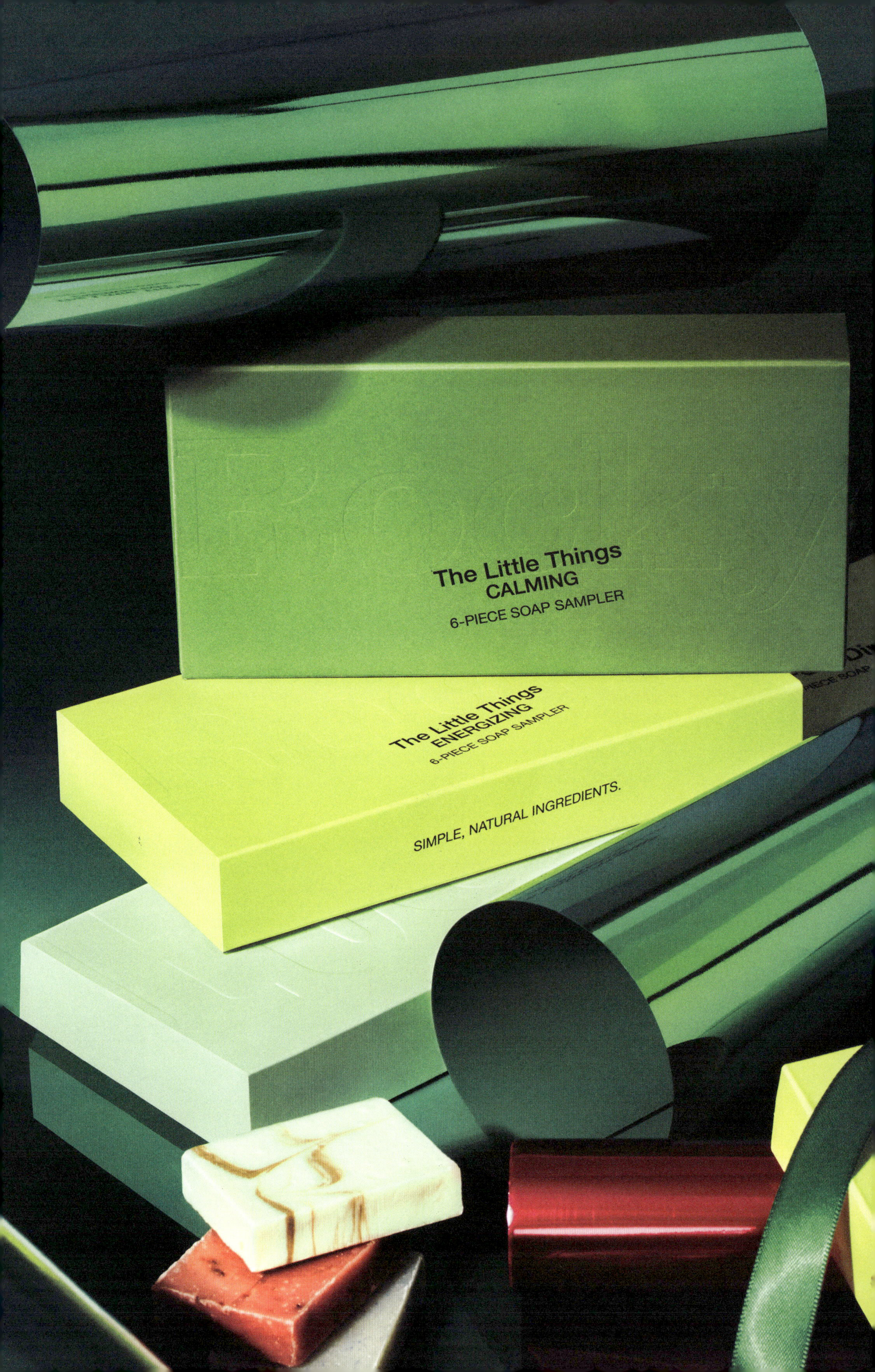
The Little Things
CALMING
6-PIECE SOAP SAMPLER
The Little Things
ENERGIZING
6-PIECE SOAP SAMPLER
SIMPLE, NATURAL INGREDIENTS.

(Opposite page) ROCKY MOUNTAIN. Photo by Lindsey Drennan

D

DESIGN

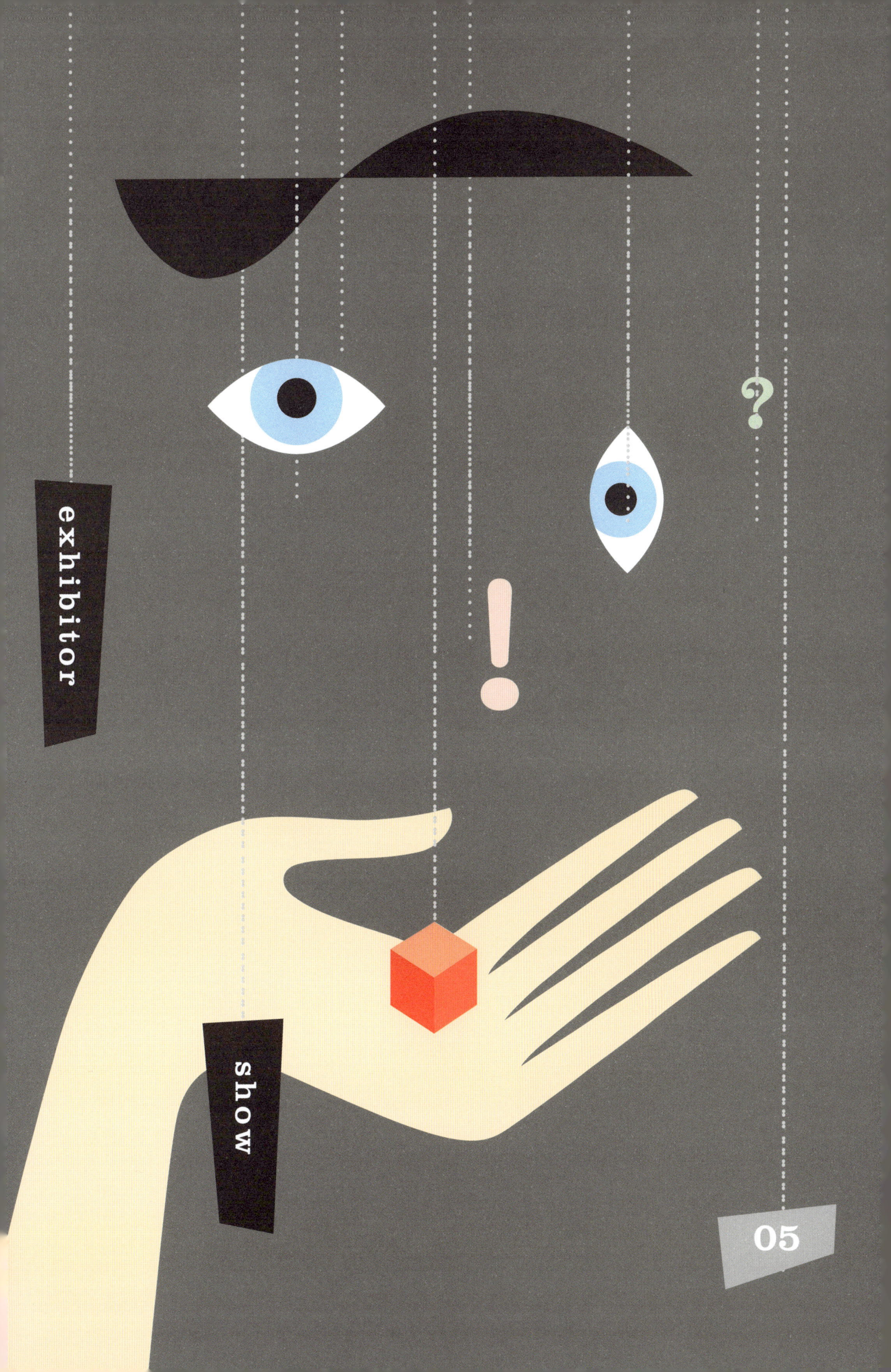
exhibitor
show
05

MICHAEL'S CREATIVE DESIGN SOLUTIONS ARE THE ESSENCE OF PROFOUND ELEGANCE AND MINIMALISM. THEY ARE PERFECTLY APPROPRIATE, SEEMINGLY EFFORTLESS, AND ENDURING.
HE IS A TRUE VISIONARY AND A TREASURE.

Bret Lopez & Mimi DeBlasio, *Co-founders, Scarecrow Wine*

MICHAEL VANDERBYL HAS LONG BEEN KNOWN FOR HIS CREATIVITY, REFINEMENT, AND ELEGANCE IN DESIGN. MICHAEL IS A MASTER OF DESIGN AND GRAPHICS, AND WE LOOK TO HIM FOR HIS MAGNIFICENT AND CLASSIC INSPIRATION.

Ralph Rudin, *Owner, A.Rudin*

MICHAEL WAS MY GRANDEST DREAM AND PRIVILEGE TO WORK FOR, LEARN FROM, AND BE INFLUENCED BY, AND HIS IMPACT STILL CONTINUES TO THIS DAY. HE IS A WELL OF BRILLIANCE!

Terrie Myers, *Artist, Terrie Myers Representational Fine Art*

MICHAEL VANDERBYL WAS ONE OF MY EARLY IDOLS IN DESIGN, AND HE STILL IS.
HIS WORK HAS BEEN CONSISTENTLY TASTEFUL, ELEGANT, AND TIMELESS.

B. Martin Pedersen, *Designer*

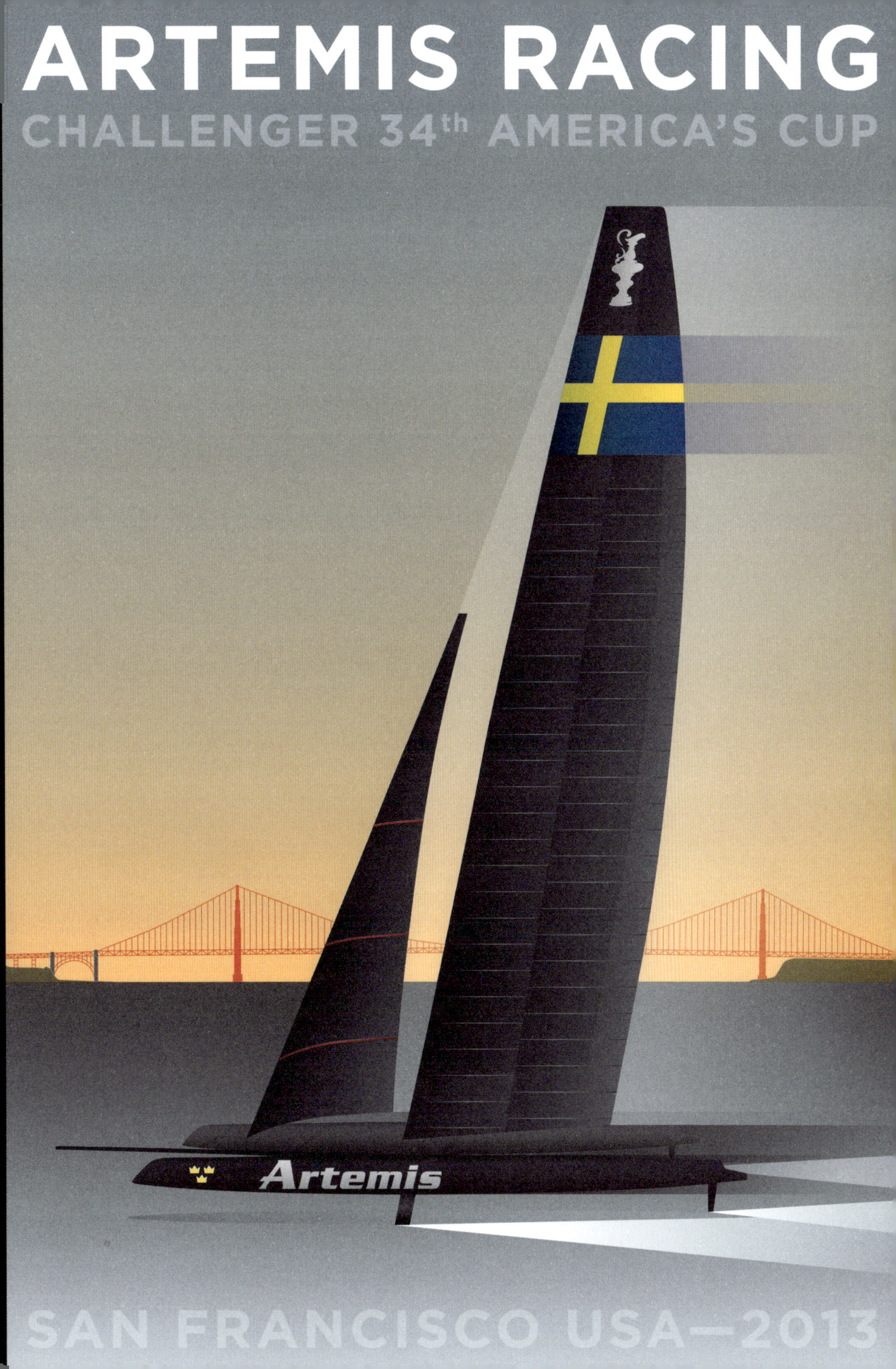
ARTEMIS RACING
CHALLENGER 34th AMERICA'S CUP
Artemis
SAN FRANCISCO USA—2013

Introduction by **Kathy and Jim Barbour** *Vintners & Owners, Barbour Vineyards*

Michael Vanderbyl is one of perhaps eight or nine pioneers who helped create the luxury (cult) wine market niche in Napa Valley. Each pioneer brought fresh ideas to their area of expertise. Michael's contribution was recognizing the need for more creativity in wine label design and packaging, which essentially lacked branding. Michael's approach, which was novel then, was to portray the brand's story on the label. It isn't easy to imagine now, but back then, wine labels typically featured lots of text, government-mandated language, and maybe a pen-and-ink drawing of a building. Michael has this unmatched ability to quickly grasp the brand story and translate it in an elegant and minimalistic way that exudes sophistication. If not for him, I don't think the luxury wine market would be where it is today.

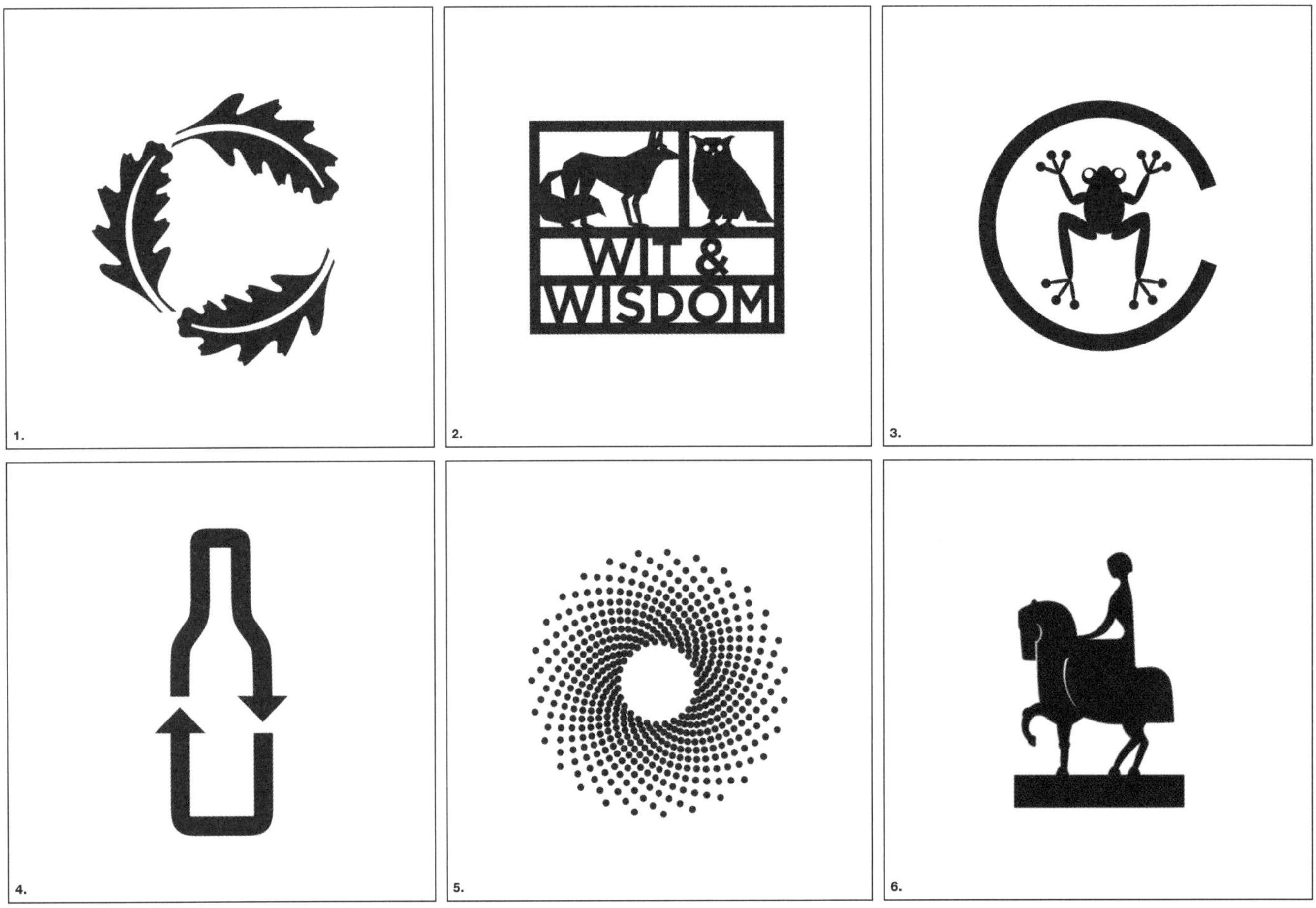

1. *Carmel Valley Ranch Logo, 2005* / **2.** *Michael Mina Restaurant Wit & Wisdom Logo, 2011* / **3.** *Coqui Water Park Logo, Blackstone Group, 2008*
4. *Loop Line Food & Wine Logo, 2022* / **5.** *Sunset Beach Resort Logo, Blackstone Group, 2011* / **6.** *Bedford Property Logo, 1986*

I LIKE THEM ALL BECAUSE EVEN THOUGH THEY ARE DIFFERENT FORMS, THEY INFLUENCE EACH OTHER... 2D INFLUENCES THE 3D AND VICE VERSA.

Michael Vanderbyl, *Designer & Educator, Vanderbyl Design*

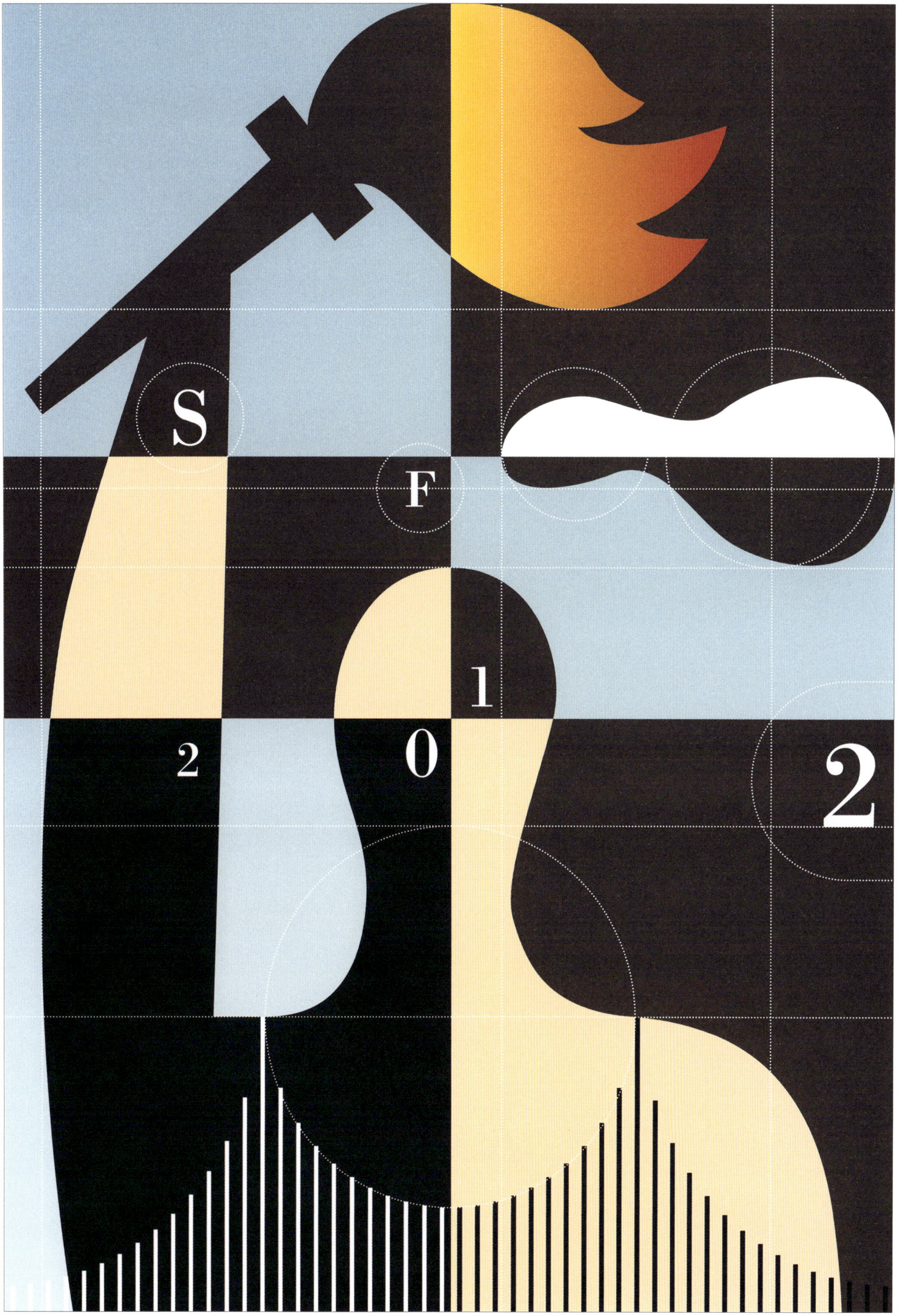

San Francisco Olympic Bid Poster, 2012

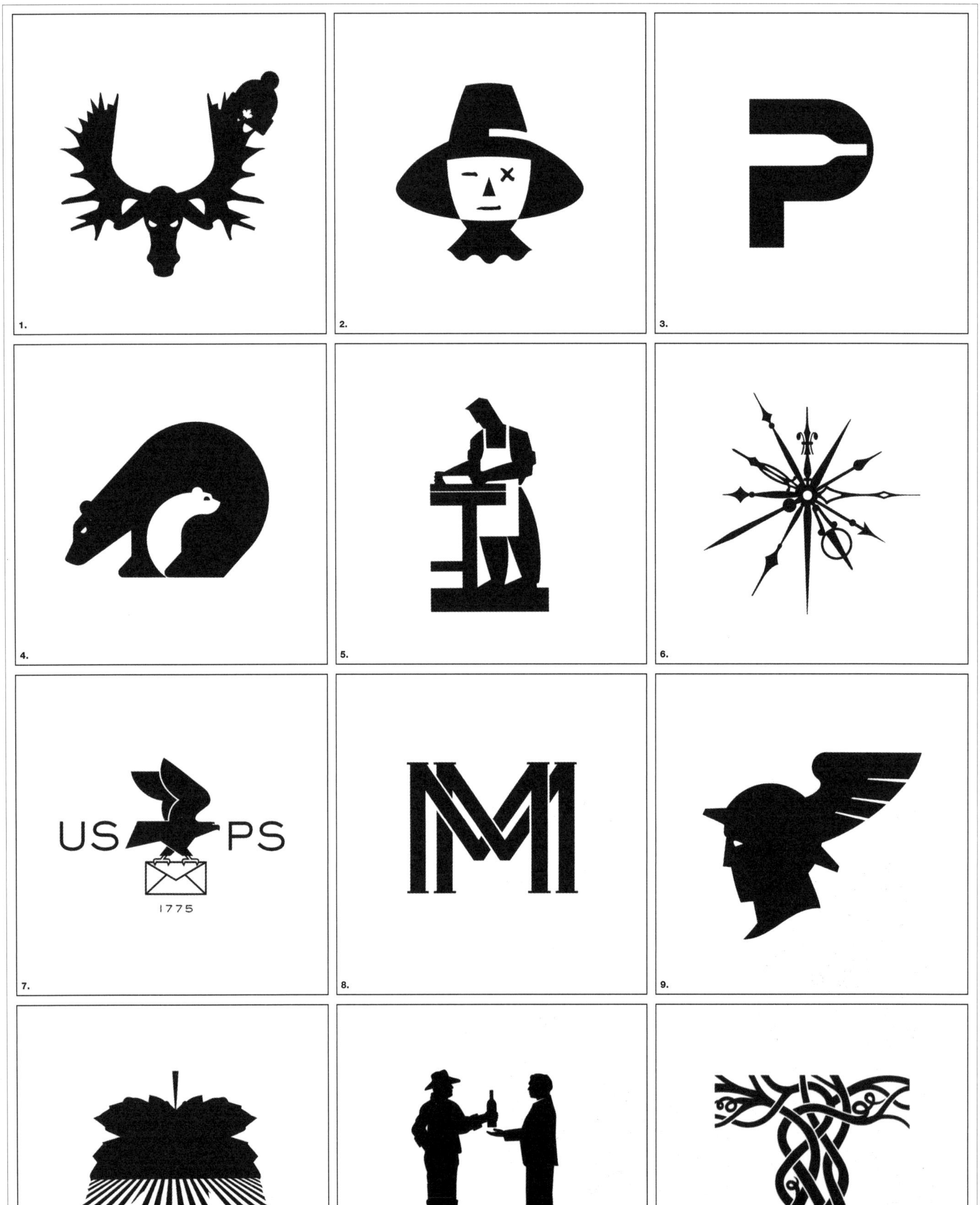

1. *Loose Toque Canadian Spirits, 2021* / **2.** *Scarecrow Wine Logo, 2003* / **3.** *Proof Loyalty Logo, 2019*
4. *California Conservation Corps, 1979* / **5.** *Rob Murray Silkscreen Printer Logo, 1992* / **6.** *Michael Mina Clock Bar Logo, 2008*
7. *United States Postal Service Logo, 2007* / **8.** *Michael Mina Restaurant Group Logo, 2008* / **9.** *Windquest Sailing Team Logo, 2003*
10. *Gary's Wine & Marketplace Logo, 2021* / **11.** *Emmisary Wine Group Logo, 2012* / **12.** *Terrano Logo, Napa Valley Development, 2008*

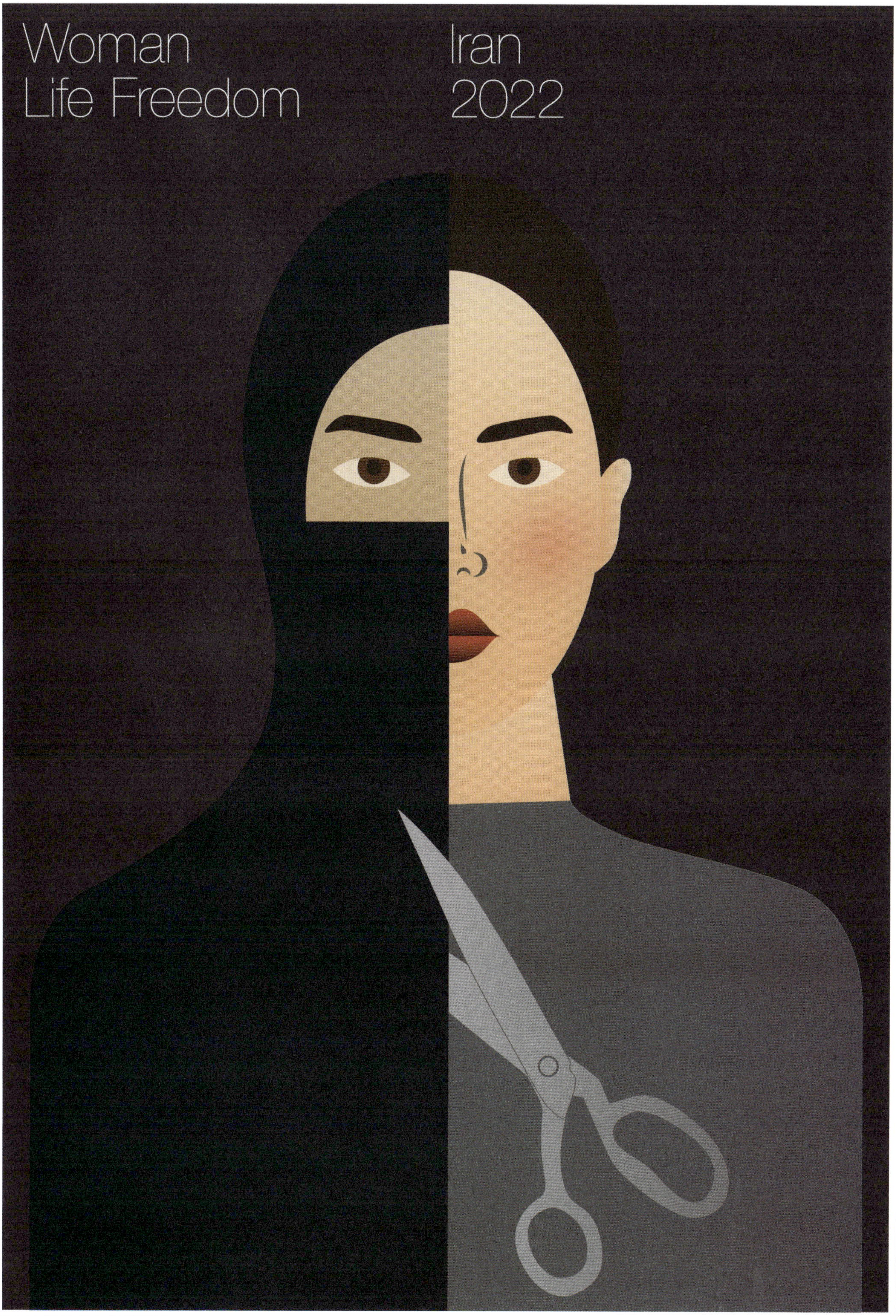

Woman Life Freedom, Iran Poster, 2022

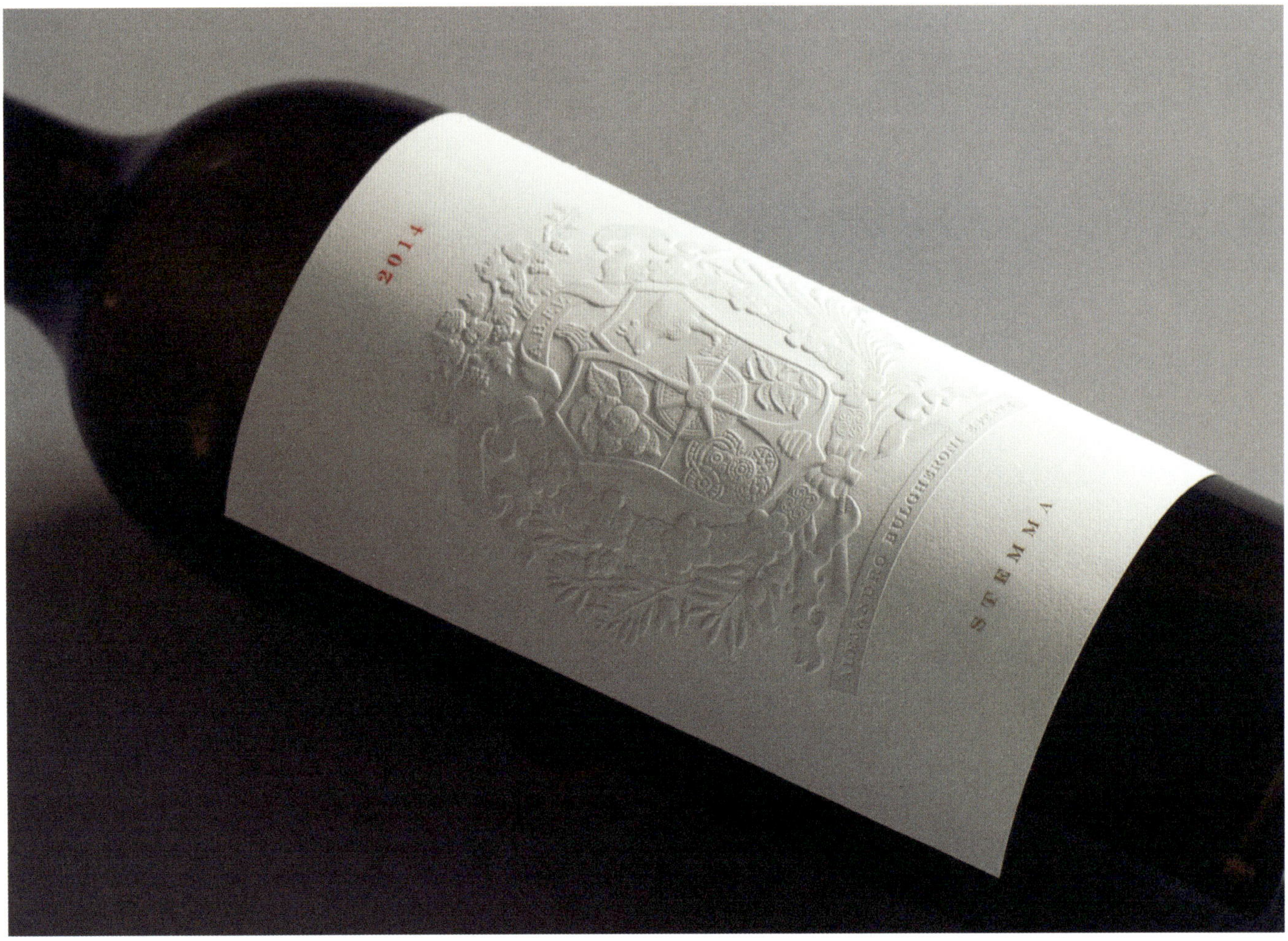

Alejandro Bulgheroni Wine Label, 2017

You have worked with many types of design, from identity and interiors to textiles and product design. What is your favorite type to work with?
I like them all because even though they are different forms, they influence each other… 2D influences the 3D and vice versa.

Who is or was your greatest mentor?
Massimo Vignelli and G. Dean Smith. G. Dean Smith was my first employer in San Francisco. He was a great designer and a great businessman. Massimo Vignelli was my sponsor for AGI.

Who were some of your most significant past influences?
Past influences would be the Bauhaus and Push Pin Studios: an odd combination, almost polar opposites.

Who among your contemporaries today do you most admire?
I have many, but the designers that blow me away the most are Paprika out of Montreal, Canada. The breadth of their work is powerful and elegant.

Who have been some of your favorite people or clients you have worked with?
It's a long, ongoing career, but Doug Tompkins, who was the head of Esprit, and David Feldberg, the head of Teknion and a client for nearly 30 years, for whom I'm still doing work.

You are also an educator who has worked as a visiting instructor at many national universities. Which school is the most memorable and why?
I spent many years as dean of the School of Design at CCA (California College of the Arts in San Francisco), where I helped develop the design curriculum in graphic design, fashion, industrial, digital design, and illustration.

As a member of AGI, how did you become a member? What does being part of that organization mean to you?
Massimo Vignelli was my sponsor; the organization has been very influential in my life and career. You become friends with people who are your heroes.

How do you define success?
I think happiness is the definition of success.

What would you change if you had to do it all over again?
Nothing. The path has been a fantastic adventure.

Michael Vanderbyl www.vanderbyl.com
See his Graphis Master Portfolio at graphis.com.

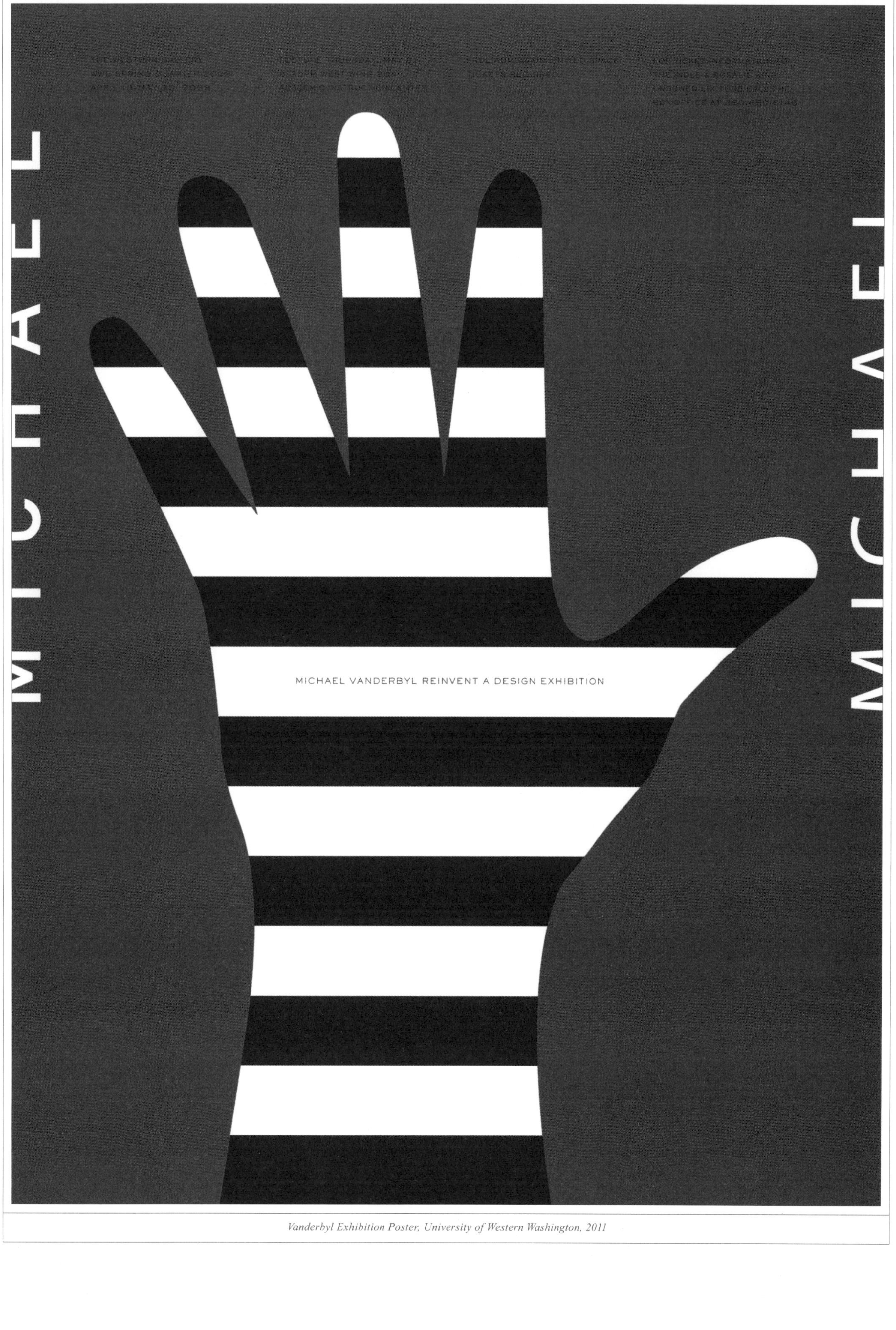

Vanderbyl Exhibition Poster, University of Western Washington, 2011

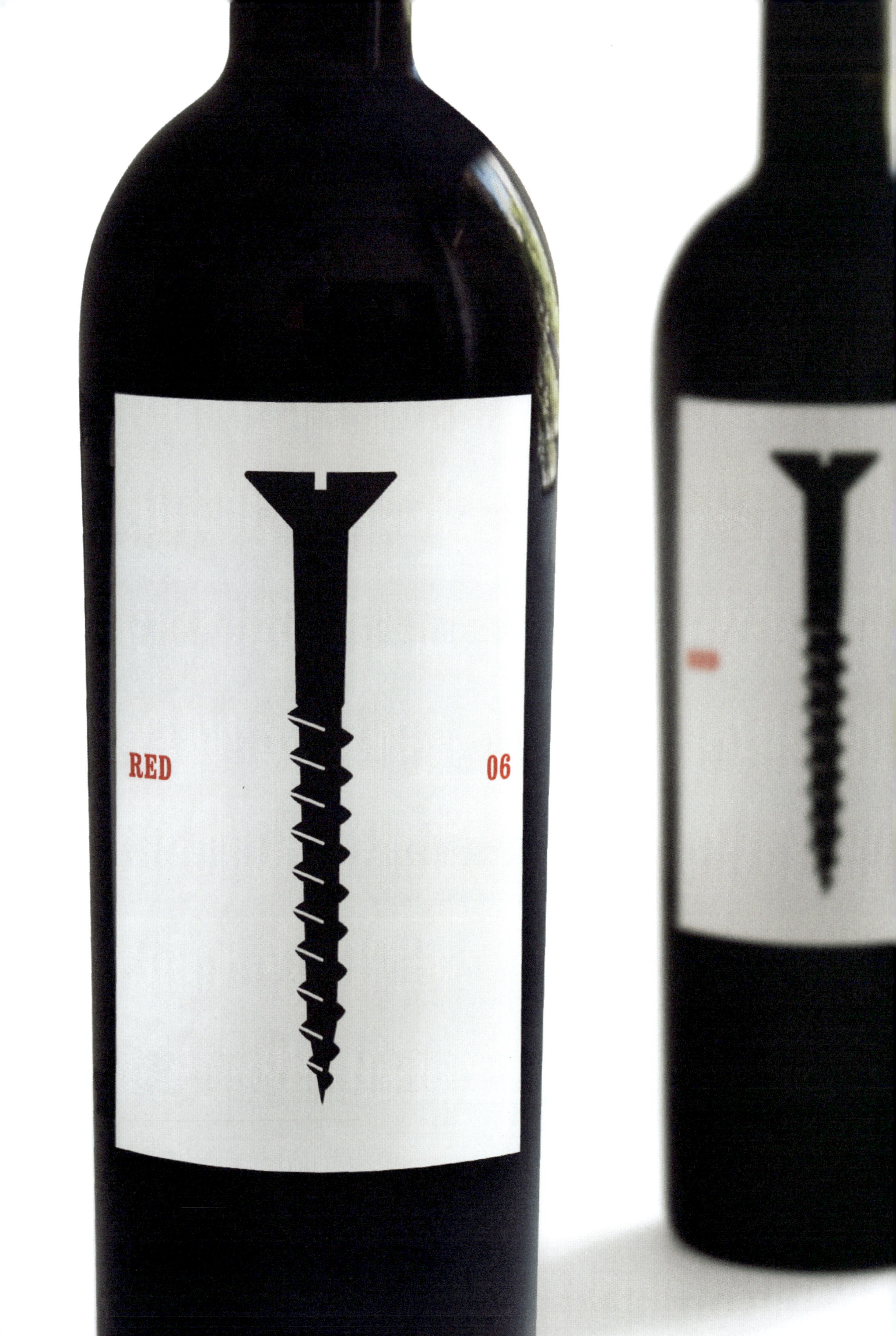
RED
06

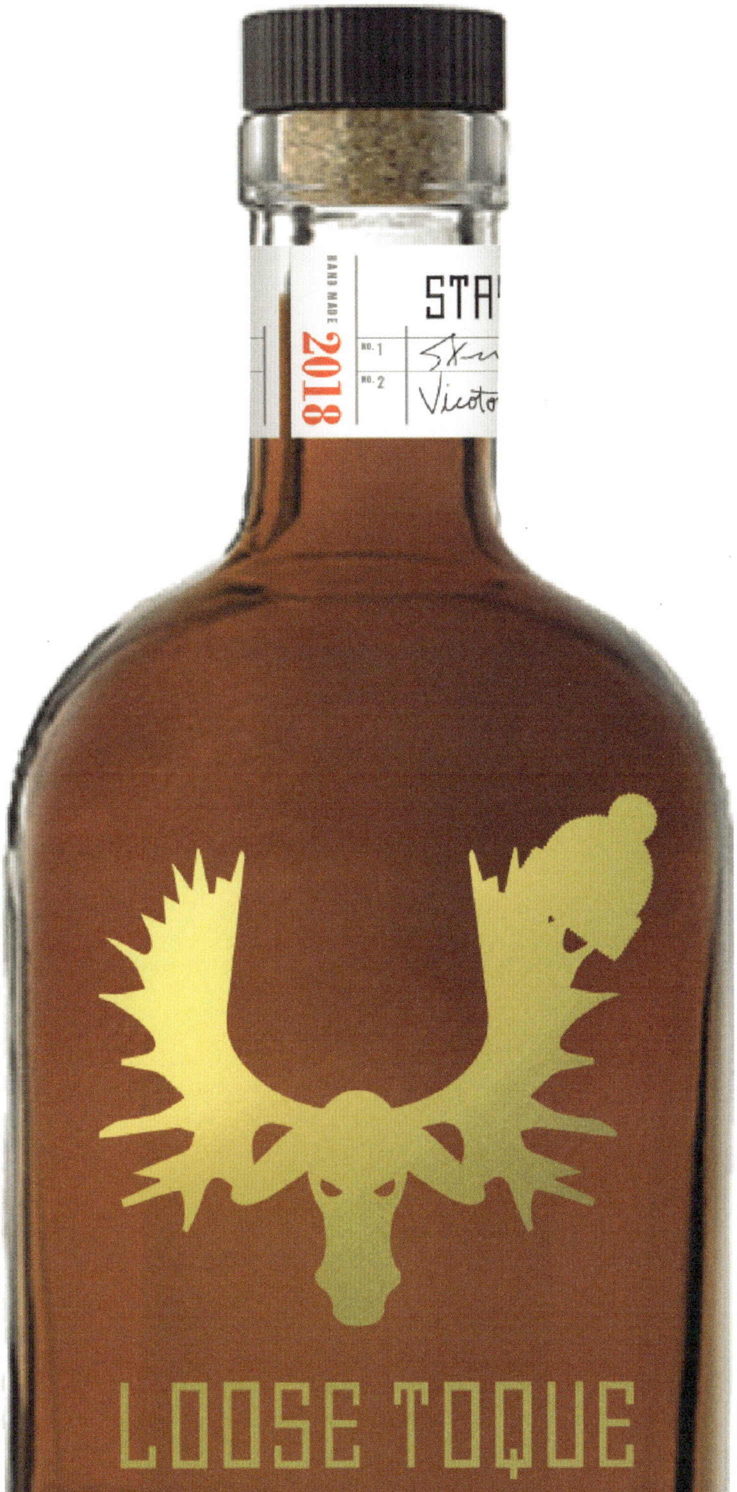

(Above) Loose Toque Canadian Whiskey, 2021 / (Opposite page) Stratus Vineyards Screw Wine Label, 2010

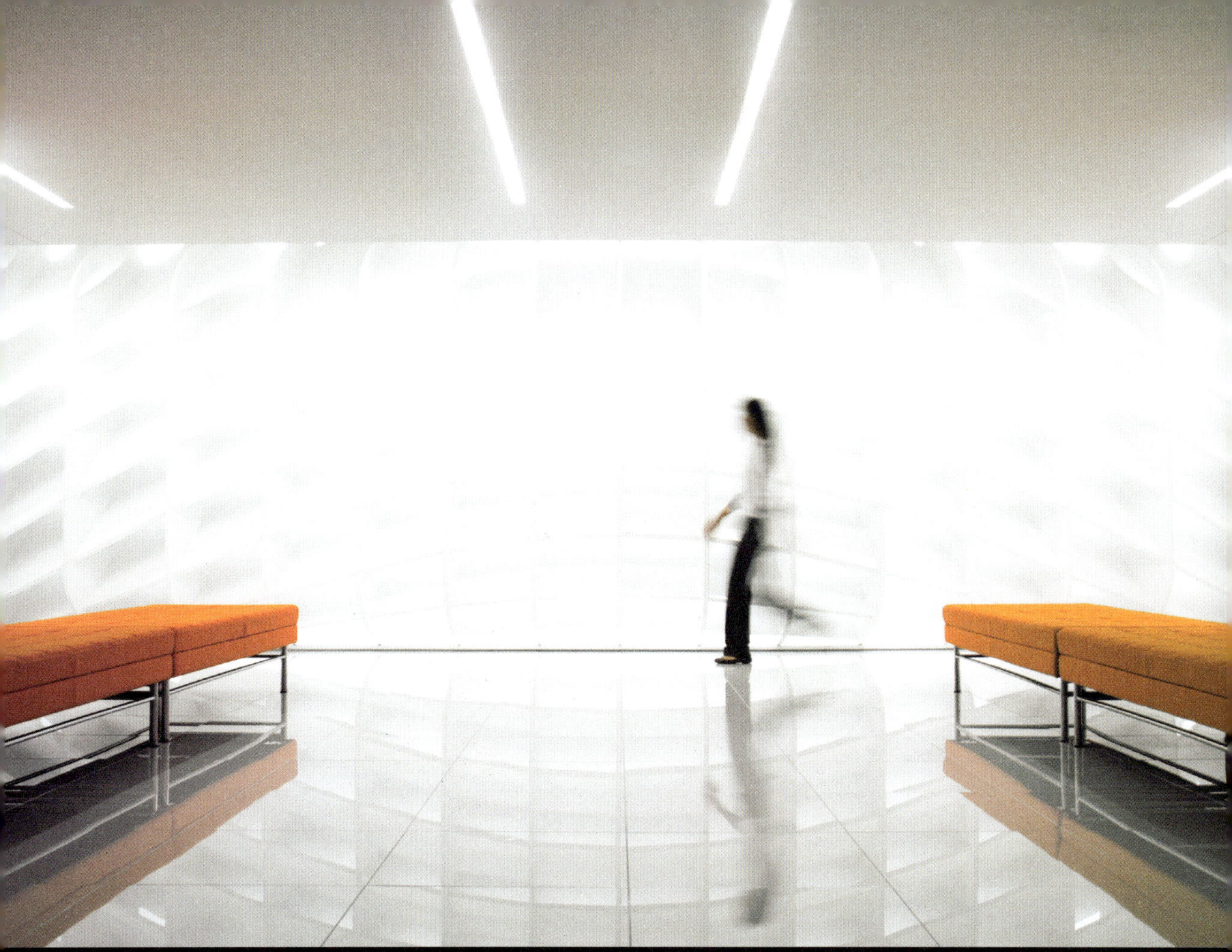

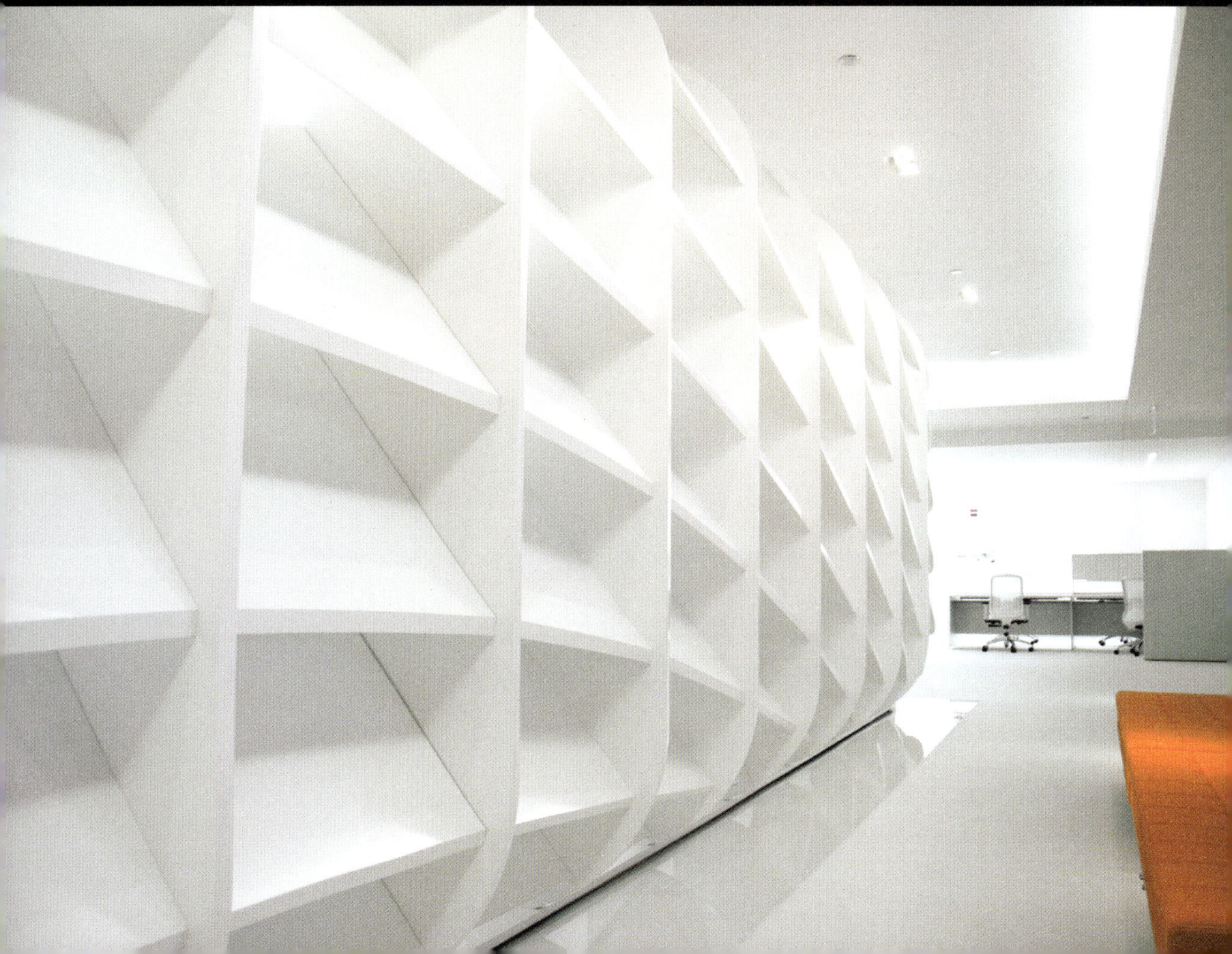

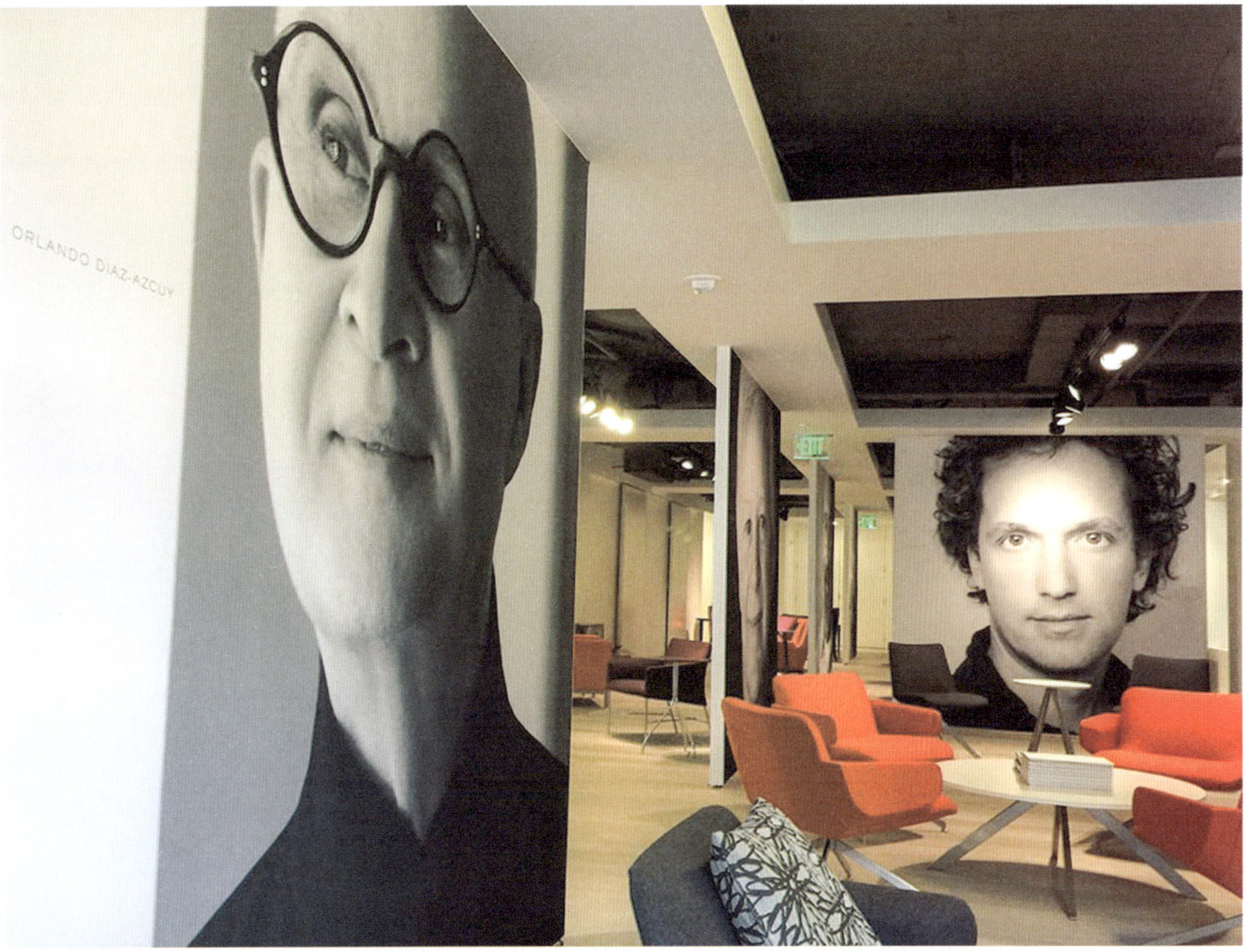

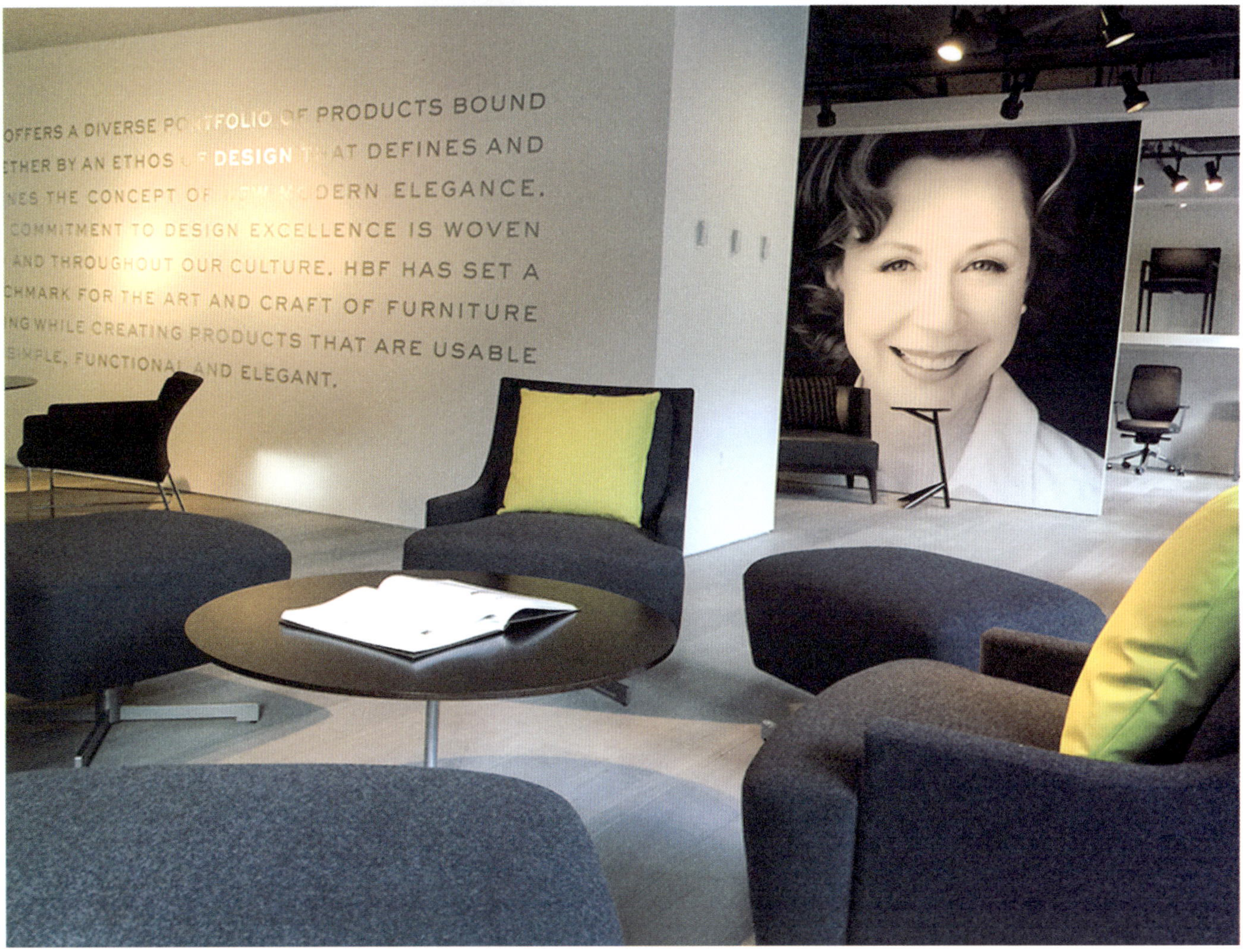

HBF Washington, DC Showroom, 2014

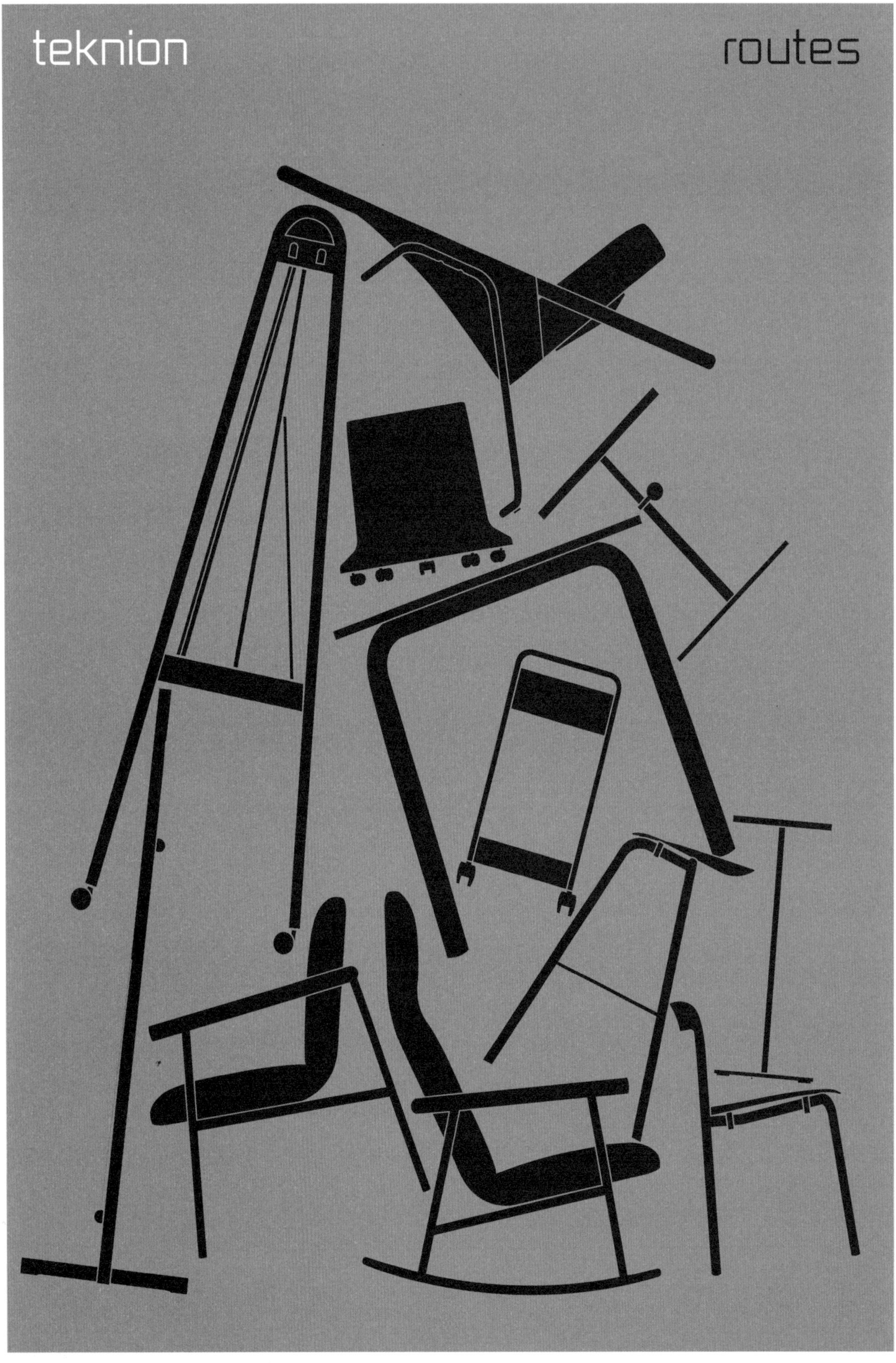

Teknion Routes Collection Poster, 2023

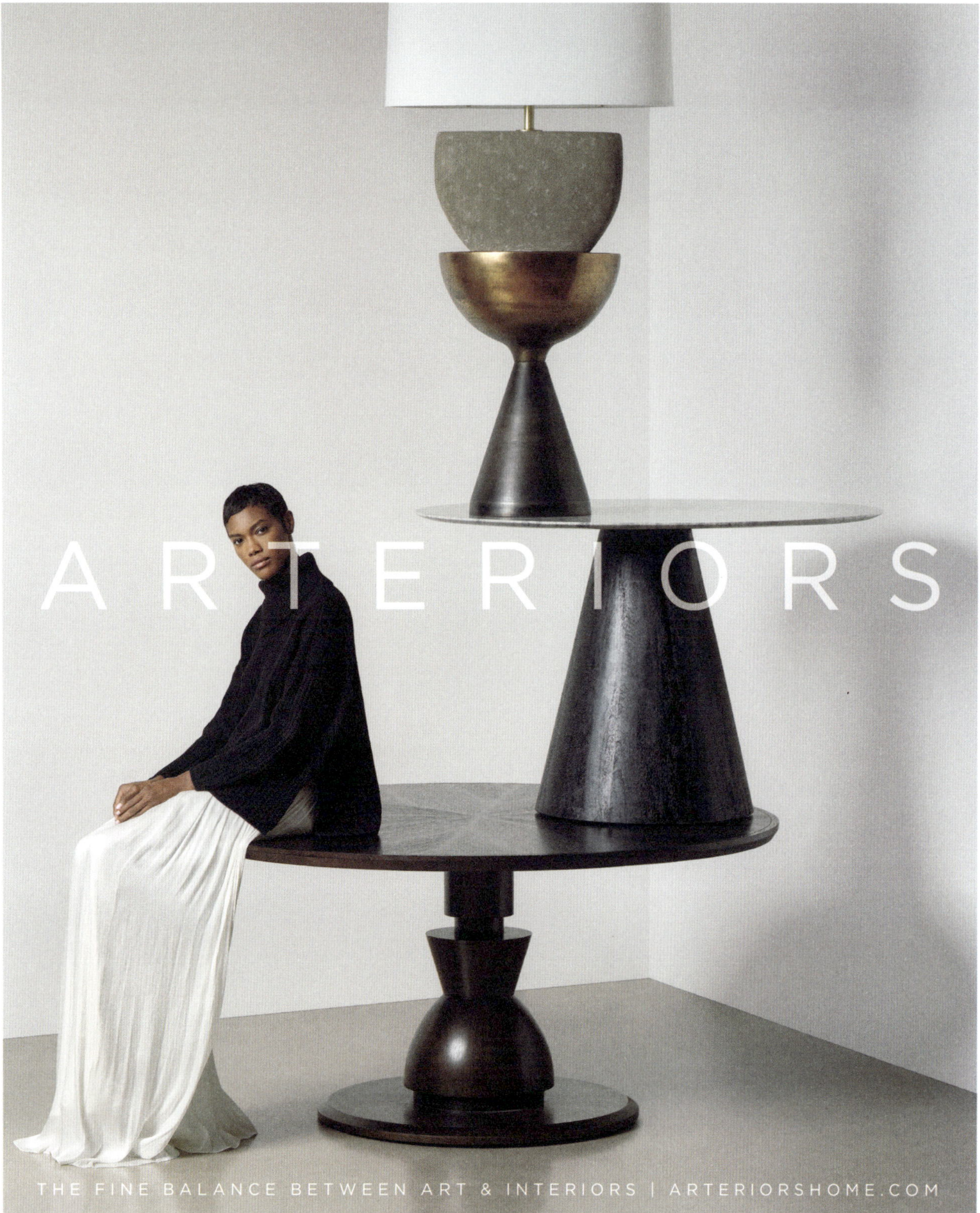

Arteriors Advertising, 2021

MR. SUN IS A RESPECTED MENTOR WHO GIVES ME PASSIONATE AND EDUCATIONAL ADVICE ON POSTER DESIGN. HIS BRILLIANT IDEAS AND EXPERIMENTATION IN POSTER DESIGN RESULT FROM HIS IMAGINATION AND CONVICTION.

Mi-Jung Lee, *Designer & Assistant Professor, Namseoul University*

WITH HIS COMMUNICATION DESIGN, HE CREATES POSTERS THAT INSPIRE REFLECTION. HIS UNCONVENTIONAL AESTHETIC SOLUTIONS STICK IN THE MEMORY, ACHIEVING A STRONG EFFECT.

Stephan Bundi, *Designer, Atelier Bundi AG*

BYOUNG IL SUN HAS A UNIQUE ABILITY TO PUSH THE BOUNDARIES OF TRADITIONAL GRAPHIC DESIGN AND CREATE VISUALLY STUNNING AND INTELLECTUALLY STIMULATING POSTERS.

Agnieszka Ziemiszewska, *Professor, Polish-Japanese Academy of Information Technology*

BYOUNG IL SUN'S INNOVATIVE DESIGNS BLEND TRADITIONAL KOREAN AESTHETICS WITH MODERN ELEMENTS, CREATING VISUALLY STRIKING AND CULTURALLY RICH POSTERS.

Rikke Hansen, *Designer, Wheels & Waves*

I BELIEVE THAT A GOOD DESIGNER IS ALWAYS A GOOD PERSON. THE VALUE AND BEAUTY ARE VISIBLE WHEN VIEWED IN PERSONAL COMMUNICATION WITH HIS WORK. I AM UTTERLY DELIGHTED WITH ITS DESIGN.

Peter Bankov, *Designer, Bankov Posters*

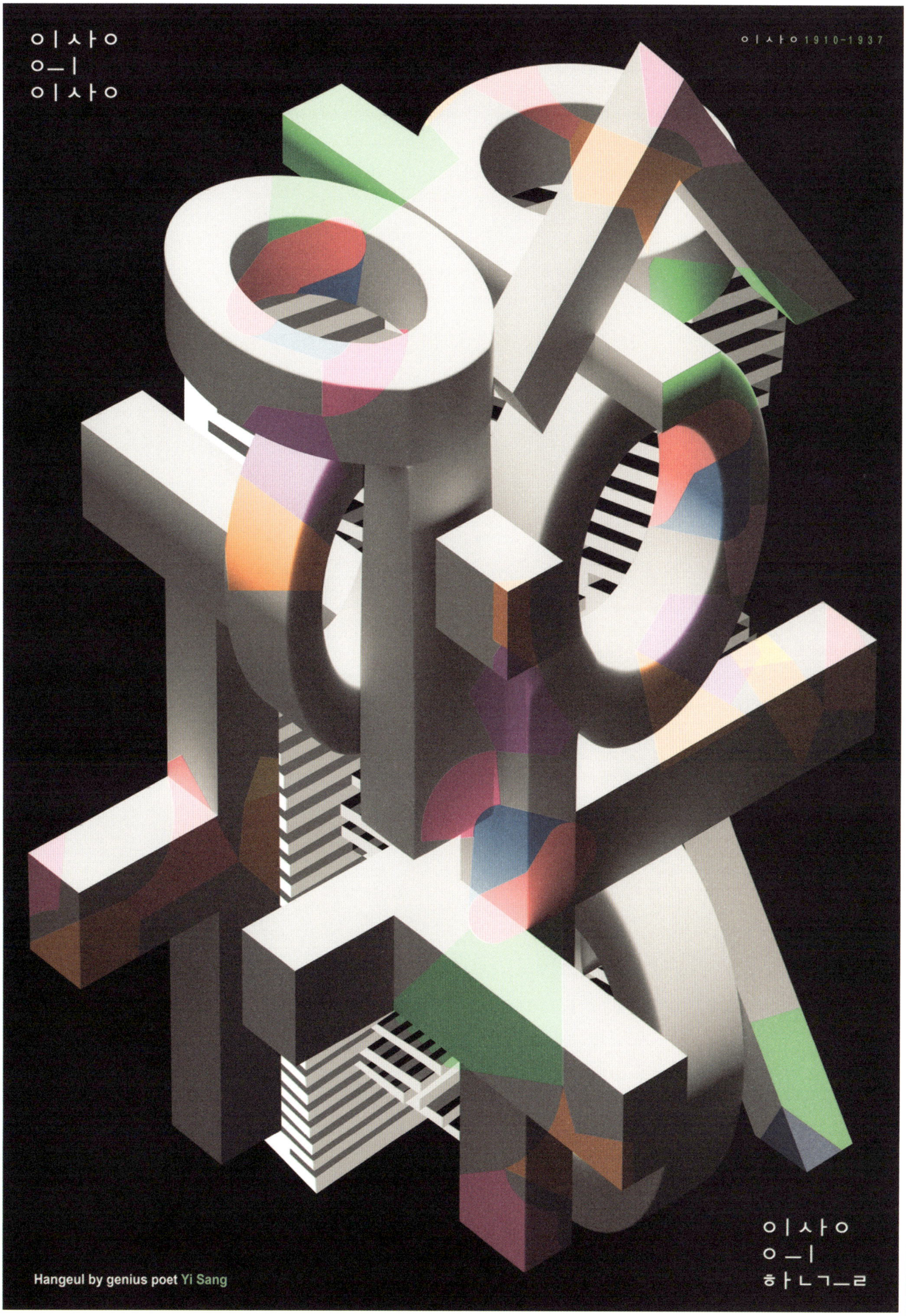

Hanguel by genius poet Yisang. Digital print, 70x100cm, 2022

Introduction by Antonio Castro H. *Professor, University of Texas at El Paso*

Besides being a great designer and design educator, Byoung il Sun also organizes the well-regarded BI International Poster Art Biennale in South Korea, an event where I have had the honor to participate twice. The event is beautifully organized and produces very handsome catalogs. He has made significant partnerships with other design organizations and schools, such as the Polish-Japanese Academy, the Moholy-Nagy University of Art and Design, Hungary's Metropolitan University, Canakkale Onsekiz Mart University, Untar University, Pradita University, Poster Blog, and Poster Territory. These partnerships have led to the 100 best posters from the biennale traveling to other venues, such as Purdue University. I commend Byoung for taking on such a massive task and making poster design appreciated and cherished worldwide.

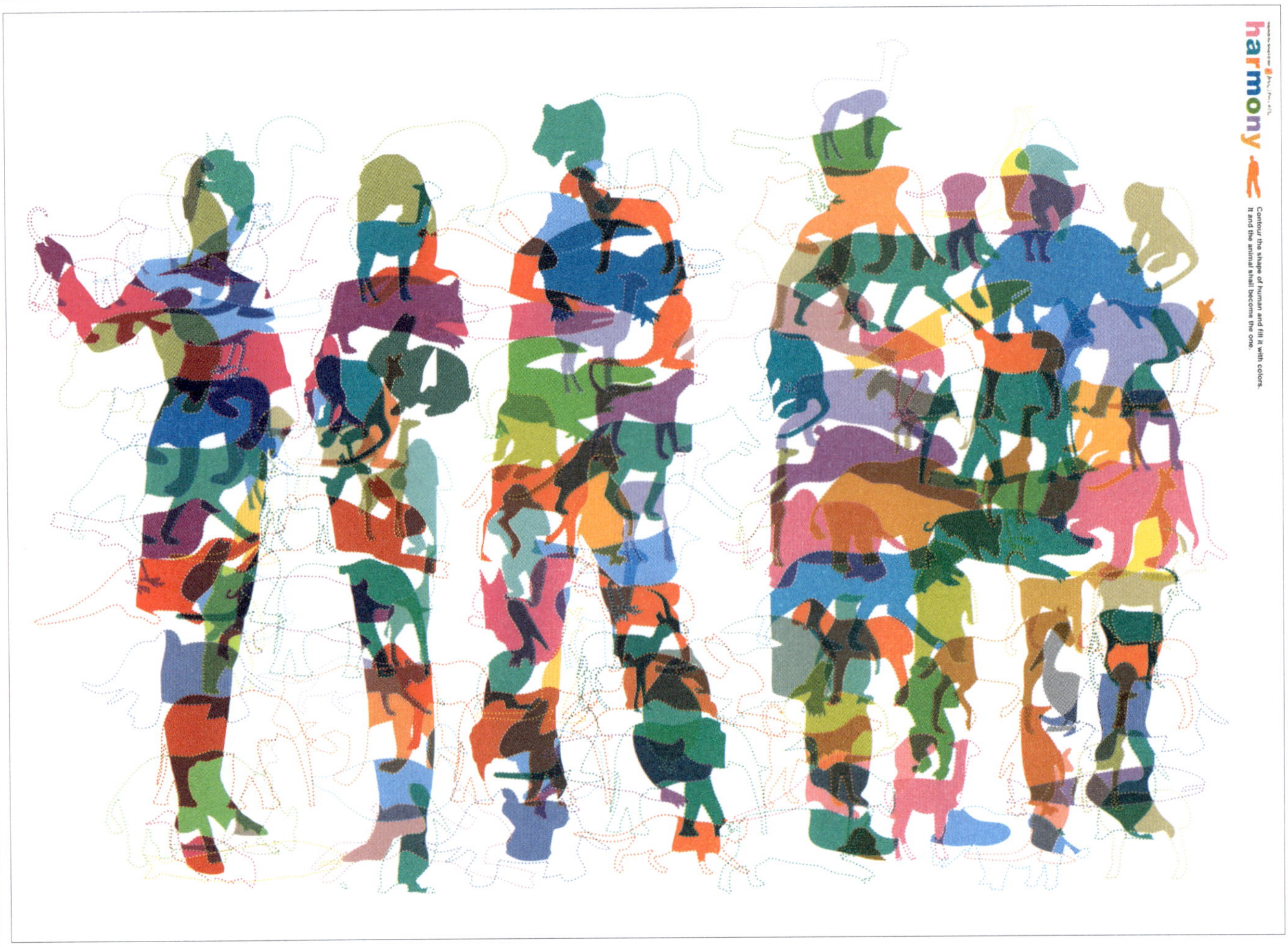

Harmony Serious. Offset print, 100x70cm, 2009

A POSTER IS A DREAM.
TELL YOUR DREAMS ON A POSTER.

Byoung il Sun, *Professor Emeritus, Namseoul University, & President & Founder, BI International Poster Art Biennale*

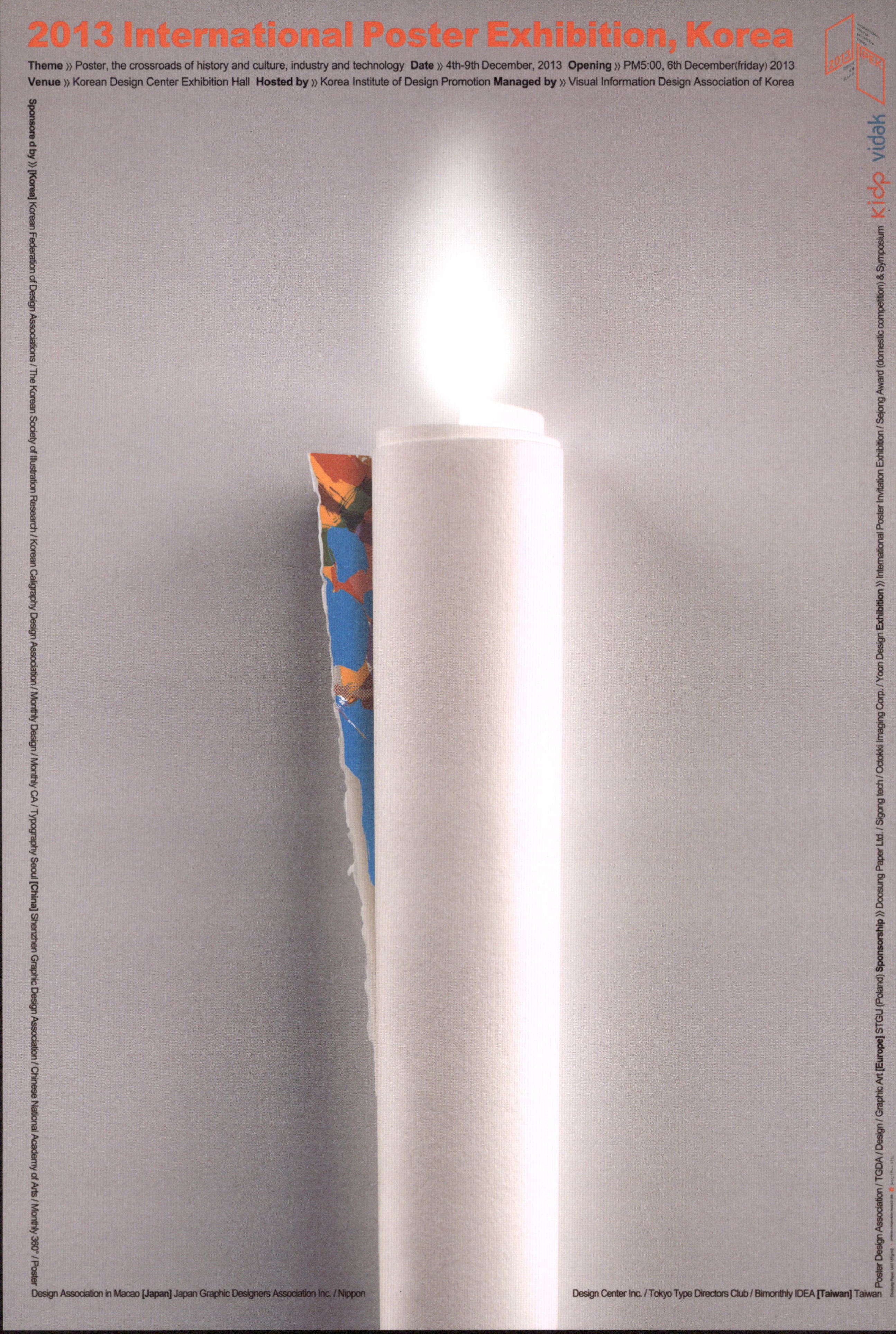

2013 Int'l Poster Exhibition Offical Poster. Offset print, 70x100cm, 2013

What has inspired or motivated you in your career?
I usually find inspiration in my life. As a poster designer, I am motivated by social engagement through posters.

What is your work philosophy?
To speak to the world through images.

Who is or was your greatest mentor?
1,817 Four Character Idioms.

What is it about design that you are most passionate about?
Poster design.

You are primarily known for your poster designs. What draws you to designing them?
Posters replace language with images. Posters are the flower of graphic design.

What is the most difficult challenge you've overcome to reach your current position?
My biggest challenge has always been the fight against time because I've always been short on it.

Who have some of your most significant past influences been?
Bruno Munari.

Who among your contemporaries today do you most admire?
Uwe Loesch.

What would be your dream assignment?
To turn a poster into a sculpture.

Who have been some of your favorite colleagues or clients?
My favorite colleague is A. Ziemiszewska, and my favorite client is the Ministry of Culture and Tourism of South Korea.

What are the top things you need from a client to do successful work for them?
I need them to recognize and believe in professionals.

What do you consider your most outstanding professional achievement so far?
When one of my students whom I coached and taught became a professor.

Having won multiple awards, is there a particular award that means the most to you?
The Ekoplakat Award from Slovakia.

What about your work has given you the greatest satisfaction?
When I finished a three-hour special lecture on posters in China.

What part of your work do you find the most demanding?
When the client doesn't understand the design image for a project due to a lack of awareness.

What professional goals do you still have for yourself?
I would like to open up design education to overseas students who have not achieved much in design and provide them with opportunities.

You are both a designer and a professor at Namseoul University. How do you balance your two careers?
It requires absolute self-management and sufficient time management. The most important things are a sense of mission as a professor and passion as a designer.

What advice do you have for students starting out today?
A poster is a dream. Tell your dreams on a poster.

What interests do you have outside of work?
Poetry and music. I play guitar and sing.

What do you value most in life?
I value a constant passion for the things I love and my goals.

What would you change if you had to do it all over again?
I would open a poster design school.

Where do you find inspiration?
I get it before I sleep or when I wake up.

How do you define success?
I define success as being satisfied with what you do.

Where do you see yourself in the future?
I see myself following through with my beliefs and actions.

How do you balance your work with your personal life if there is a distinction between the two?
I spend a lot more time on work, so my life is always unbalanced.

In what ways do you see your field changing over the years?
It is becoming more mechanized and losing its warmth and human touch.

Byoung il Sun www.gallerybi.com

I USUALLY FIND INSPIRATION IN MY LIFE.
AS A POSTER DESIGNER, I AM MOTIVATED BY SOCIAL ENGAGEMENT THROUGH POSTERS.

Byoung il Sun, *Professor Emeritus, Namseoul University, & President & Founder, BI International Poster Art Biennale*

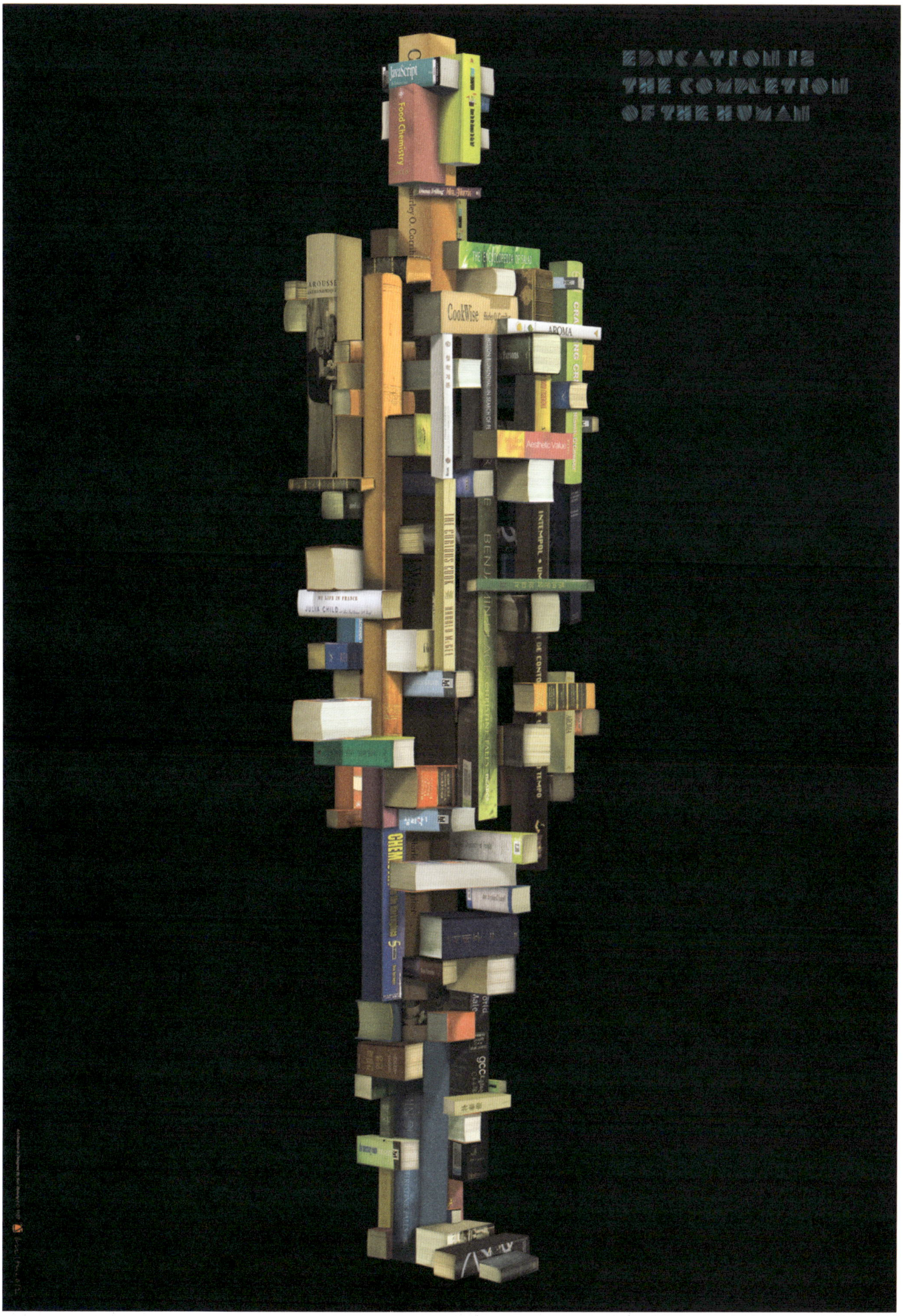

Education is the Completion of the Human. Digital print, 841x1189cm, 2011

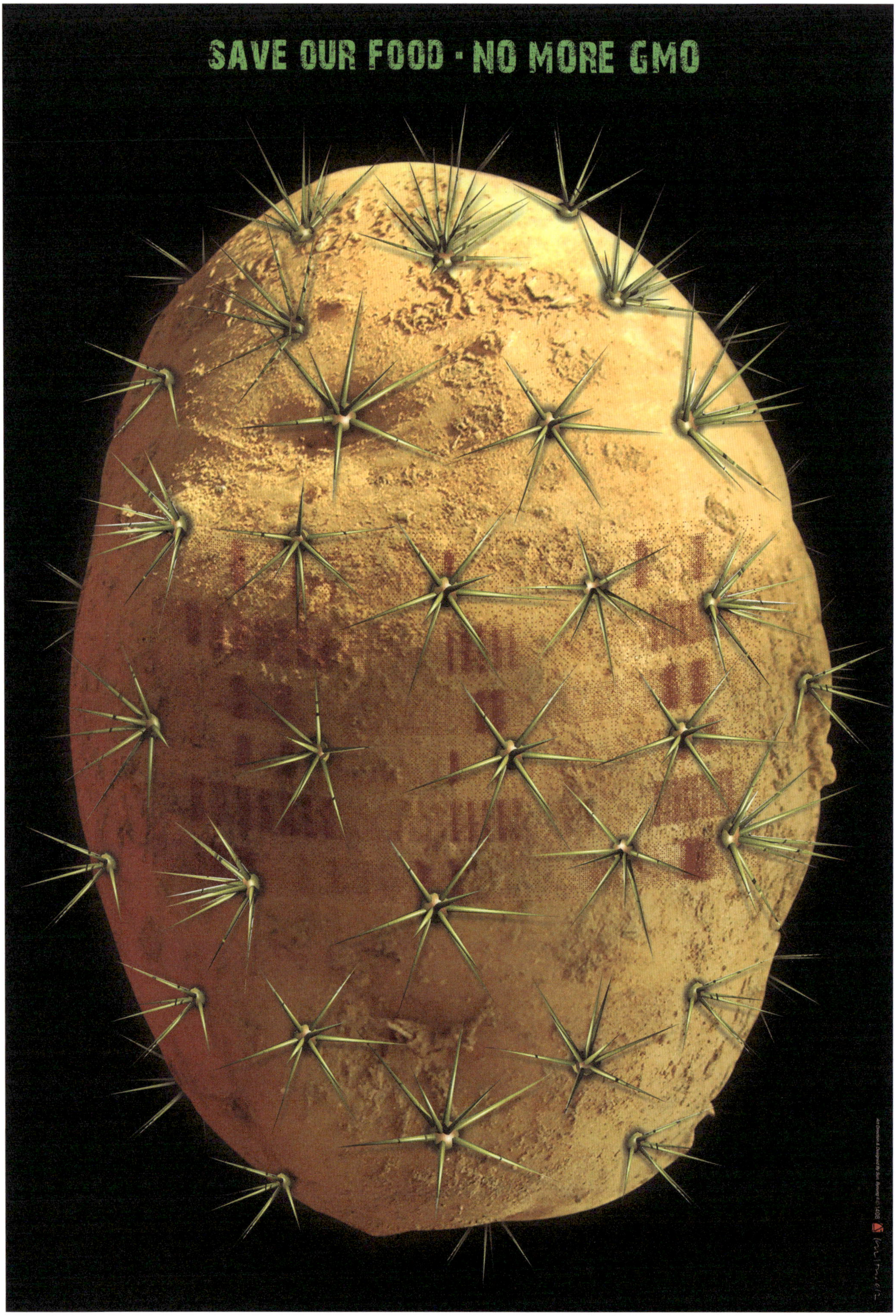

Save Our Food. Digital print, 70x100cm, 2015

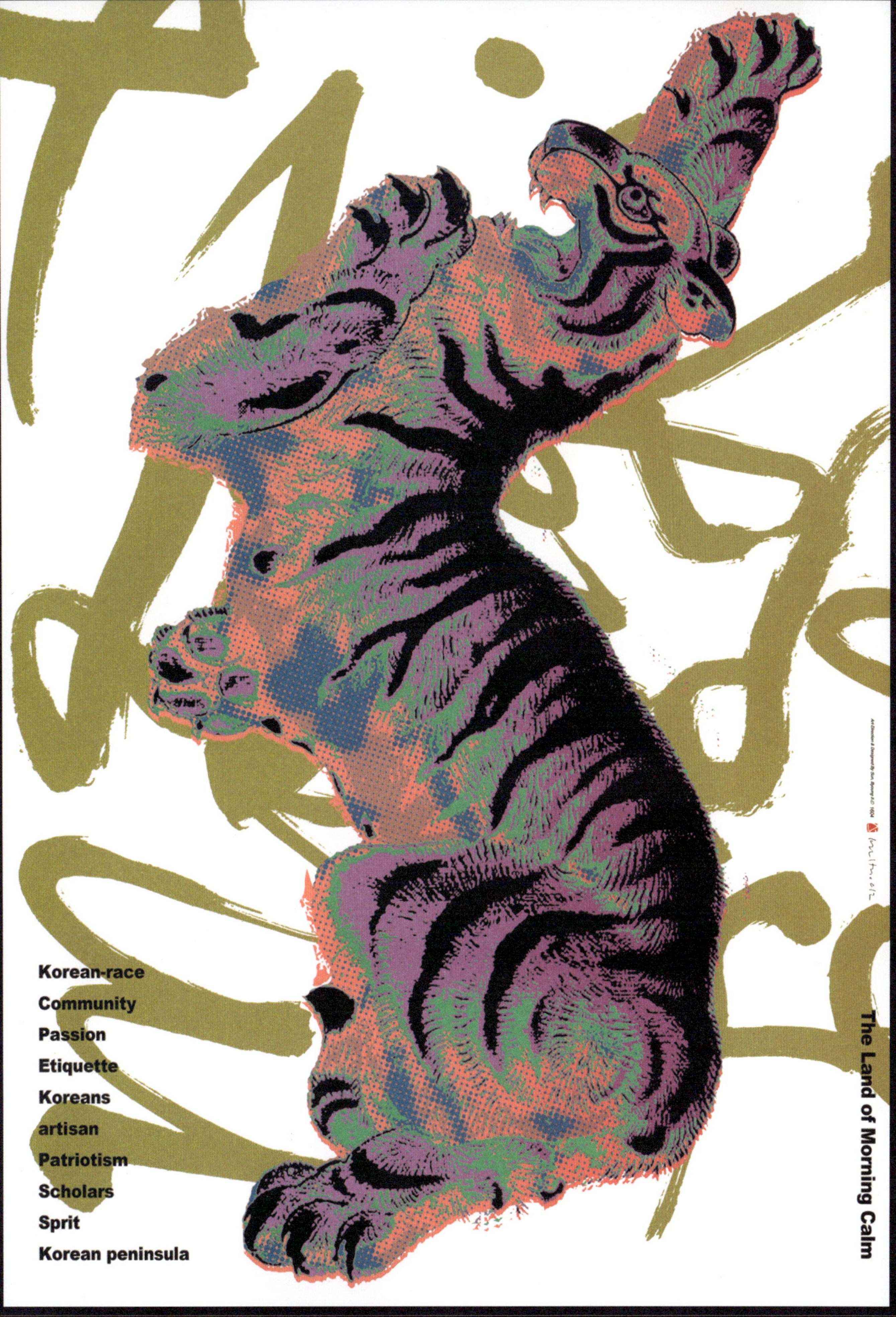

Korean Spirit, Digital print, 70x100cm, 2016

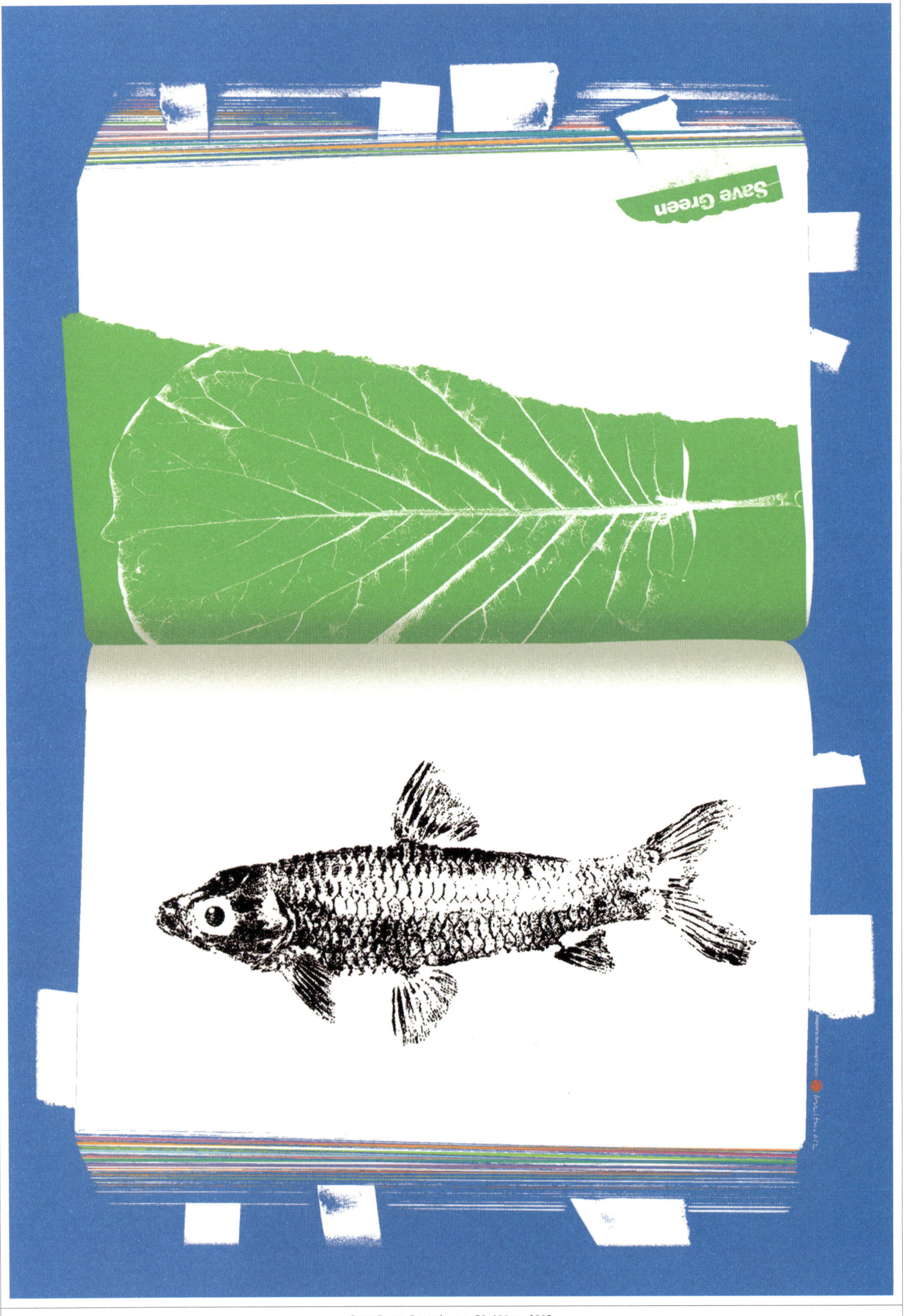

Save Green. Digital print, 70x100cm, 2007

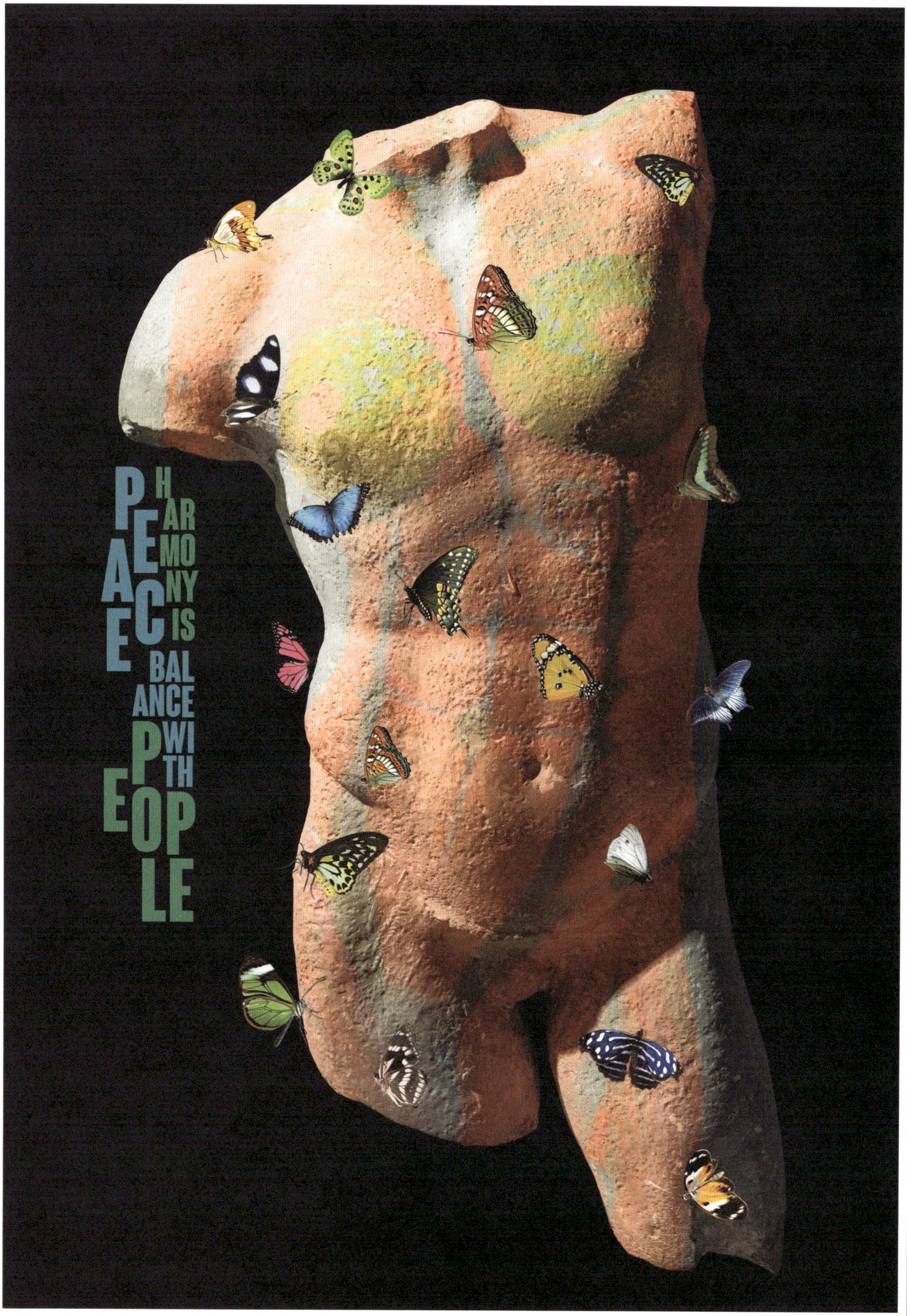

Harmony is Peace. Digital print, 70x100cm, 2018

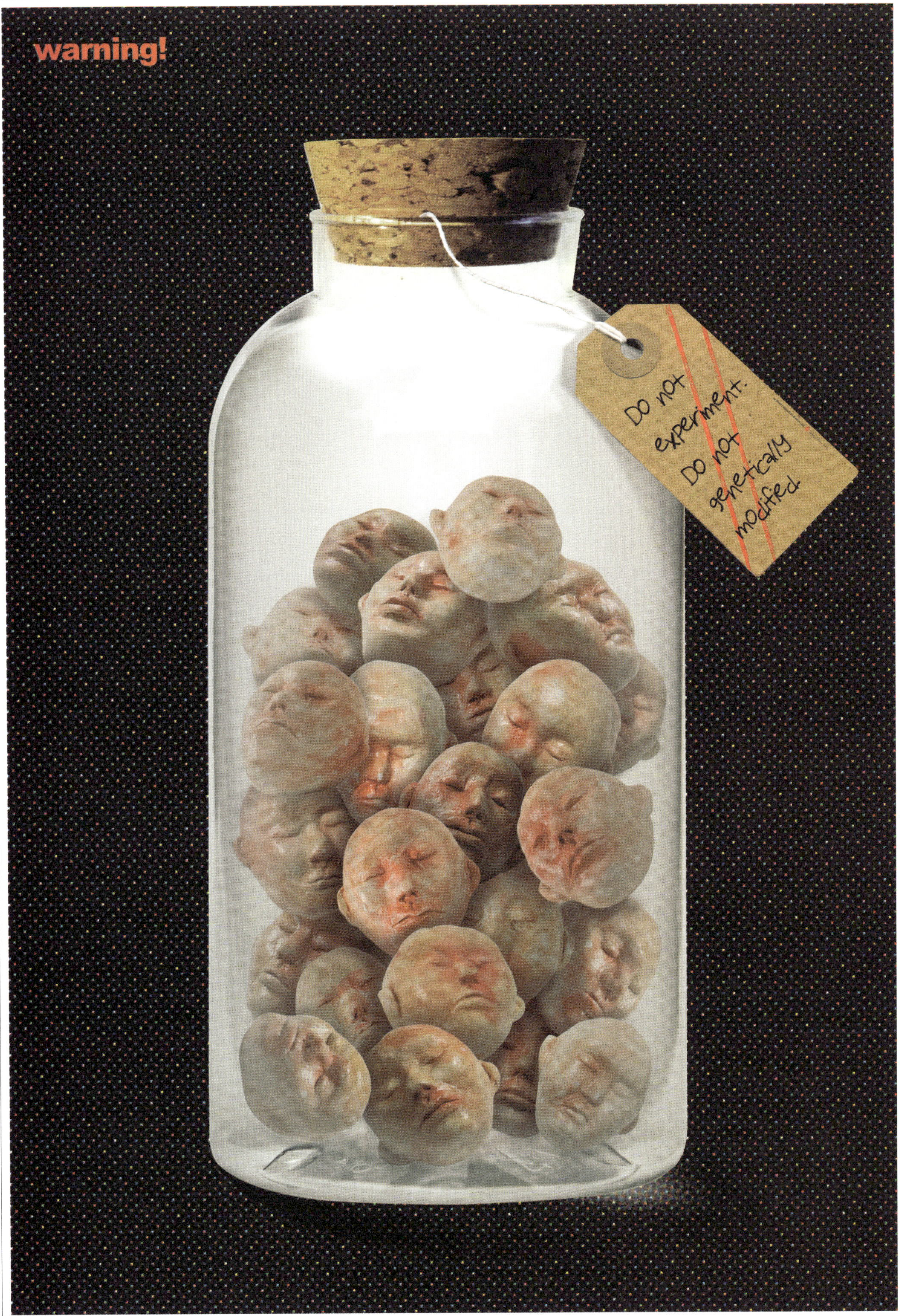

Warning! Digital print, 70x100cm, 2012

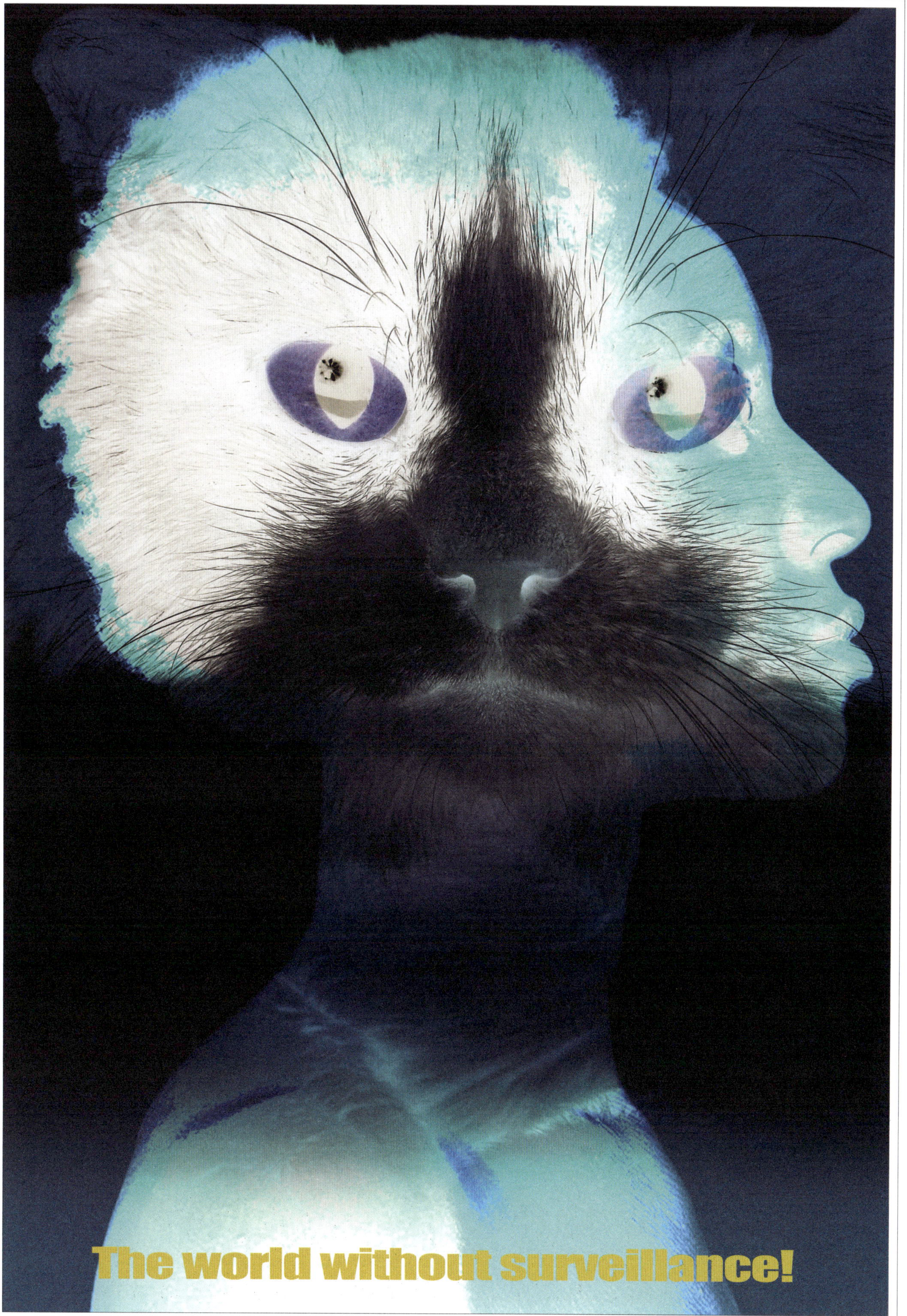

The world without surveillance! Digital print, 70x100cm, 2018

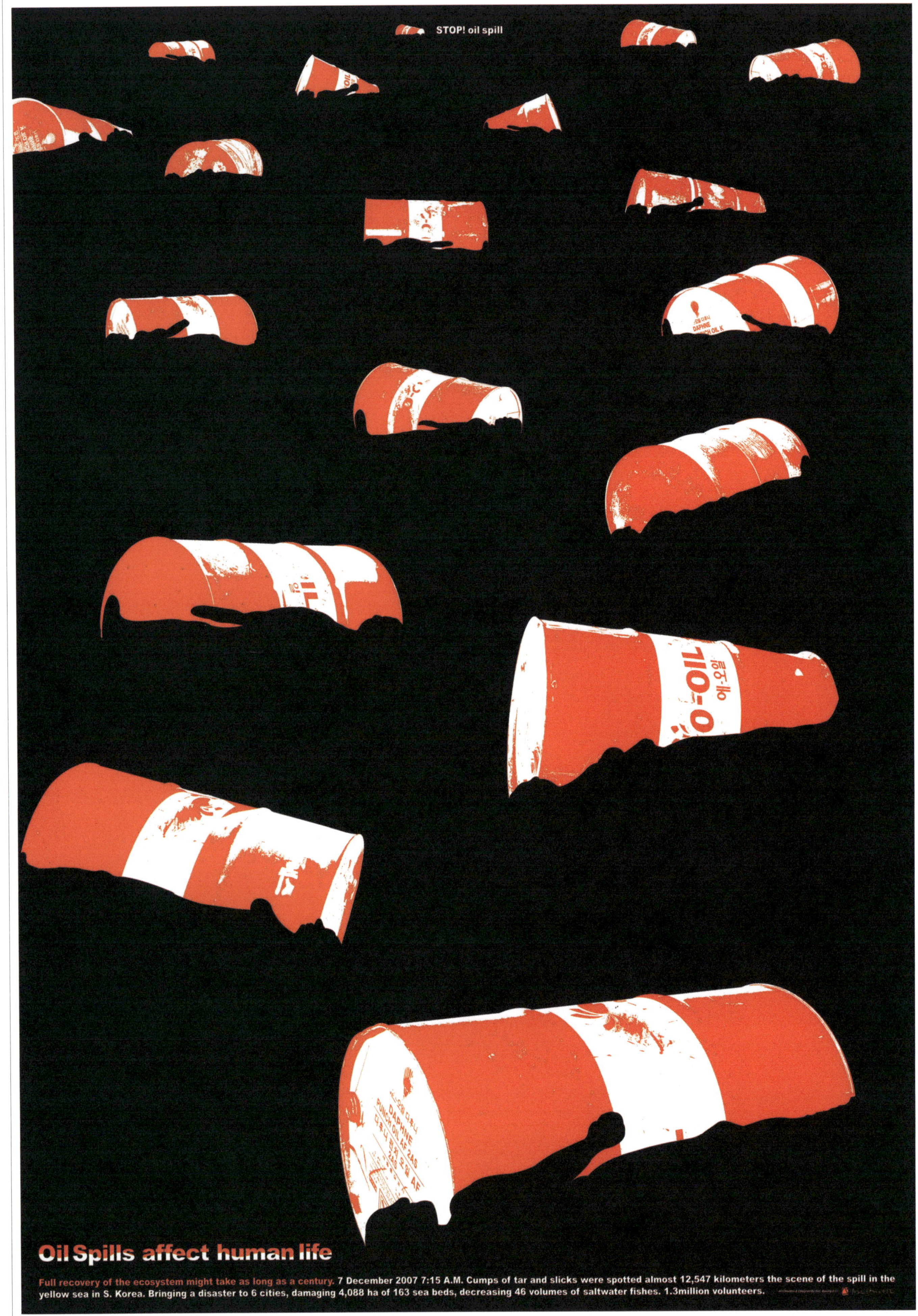

Stop! Oil Spill. Offset print, 70x100cm, 2007

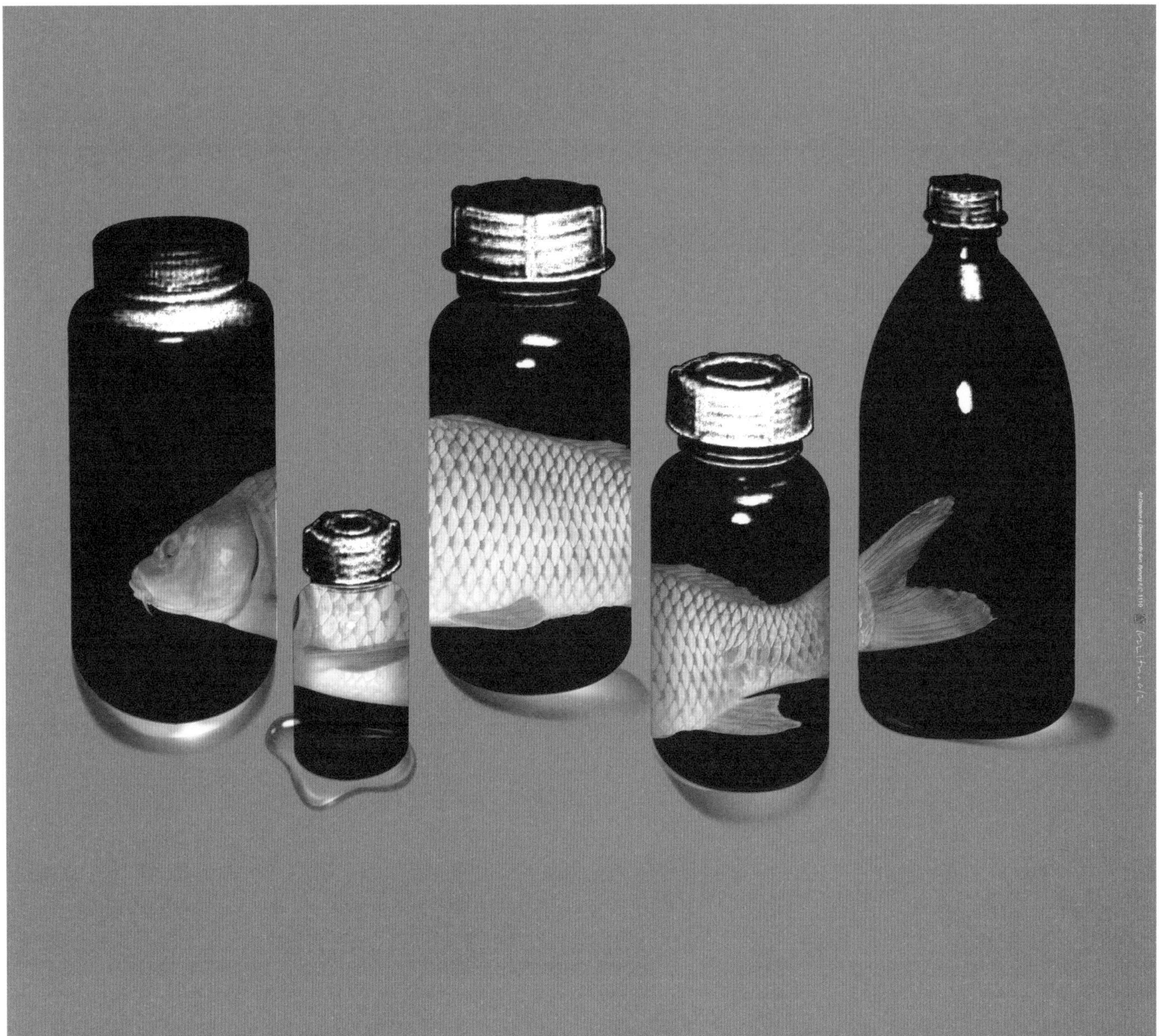

help me! Digital print, 70x100cm, 2012

HAVING LED THE DESIGN OF NEARLY 1,000 PRODUCTS AND THEIR PACKAGING OVER THE PAST 14 YEARS, LU CHEN SHOWS HER AMAZING DESIGN TALENT, RICH MARKETING EXPERIENCE, AND GREAT SENSE OF RESPONSIBILITY TO SOCIETY.

Suxia Rhonda Jiang, *Editor-in-Chief, Package & Design Magazine*

XIAOMI IS ALWAYS MINIMAL, PRACTICAL, AND SUSTAINABLE. AT THE HEART OF EACH DESIGN IS A SIMPLE IDEA THAT IS BEAUTIFULLY EXECUTED AND IS ALWAYS THE RIGHT ANSWER FOR THE RELEVANT PRODUCT LINE.

Clem Halpin, *Design Lead, Taxi Studio*

XIAOMI IS AN EXCELLENT ENTERPRISE AS IT IS RATHER COMPETITIVE AND CARING FOR SOCIETY. AND THE MOST REMARKABLE THING ABOUT THEM IS THEY LITERALLY DO CARE.

Tiger Pan, *Founder & Chief Designer, Shenzhen Tigerpan Design Co.*

THE XIAOMI PACKAGING DESIGN TEAM MAINTAINS A CLEAN AND CONSISTENT LOOK ACROSS A WIDE VARIETY OF PRODUCTS. THEIR ATTENTION TO DETAIL AND CARE FOR LEGIBILITY SHOULD BE A ROLE MODEL FOR OTHER COMPANIES!

José Scaglione, *Type Director, TypeTogether*

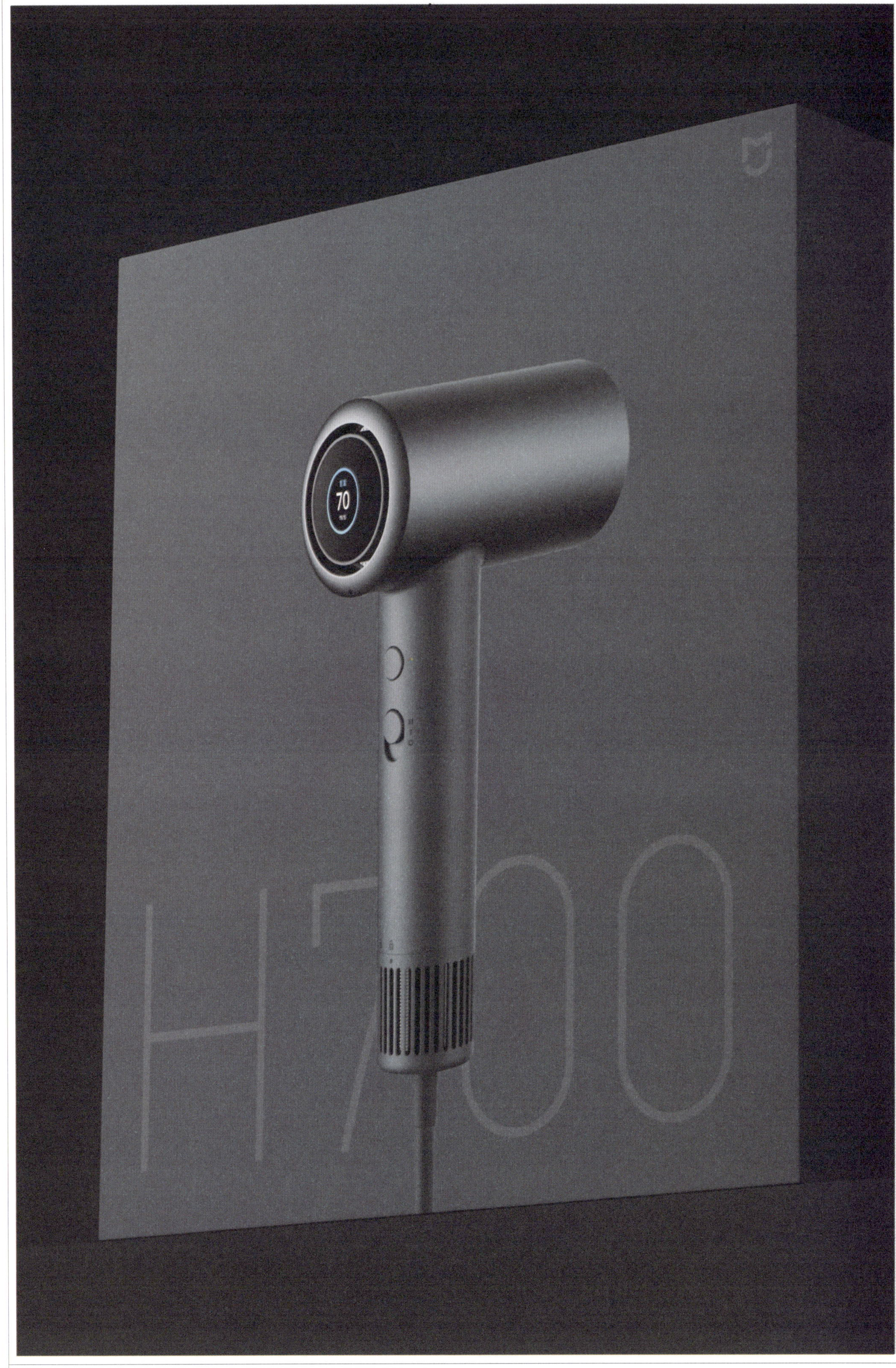

Mi Ionic Hair Dryer H700

Introduction by Eric C. Yim *MPhil, B.Arch, RIBA Chairman, Hong Kong Design Centre*

Xiaomi has emerged as a trailblazer in the realm of inimitable and innovative design, offering a wide range of affordable products that enhance our daily lives and have a profound societal impact. With a focus on minimalistic design, Xiaomi has transformed even the simplest household items, like a socket board, into objects of beauty. While initially known for its smartphones, Xiaomi has expanded its reach to include wearables and a vast ecosystem of smart devices that support its core business. What truly sets Xiaomi apart is its dedication to building a community around its brand. Xiaomi has created a loyal following beyond just selling products by engaging with customers, hosting events, and seeking feedback. With diverse offerings, from fitness bands to air purifiers and TVs, Xiaomi welcomes customers into its ecosystem with open arms, showcasing that design is not just about aesthetics but about creating a meaningful connection with the people who use its products.

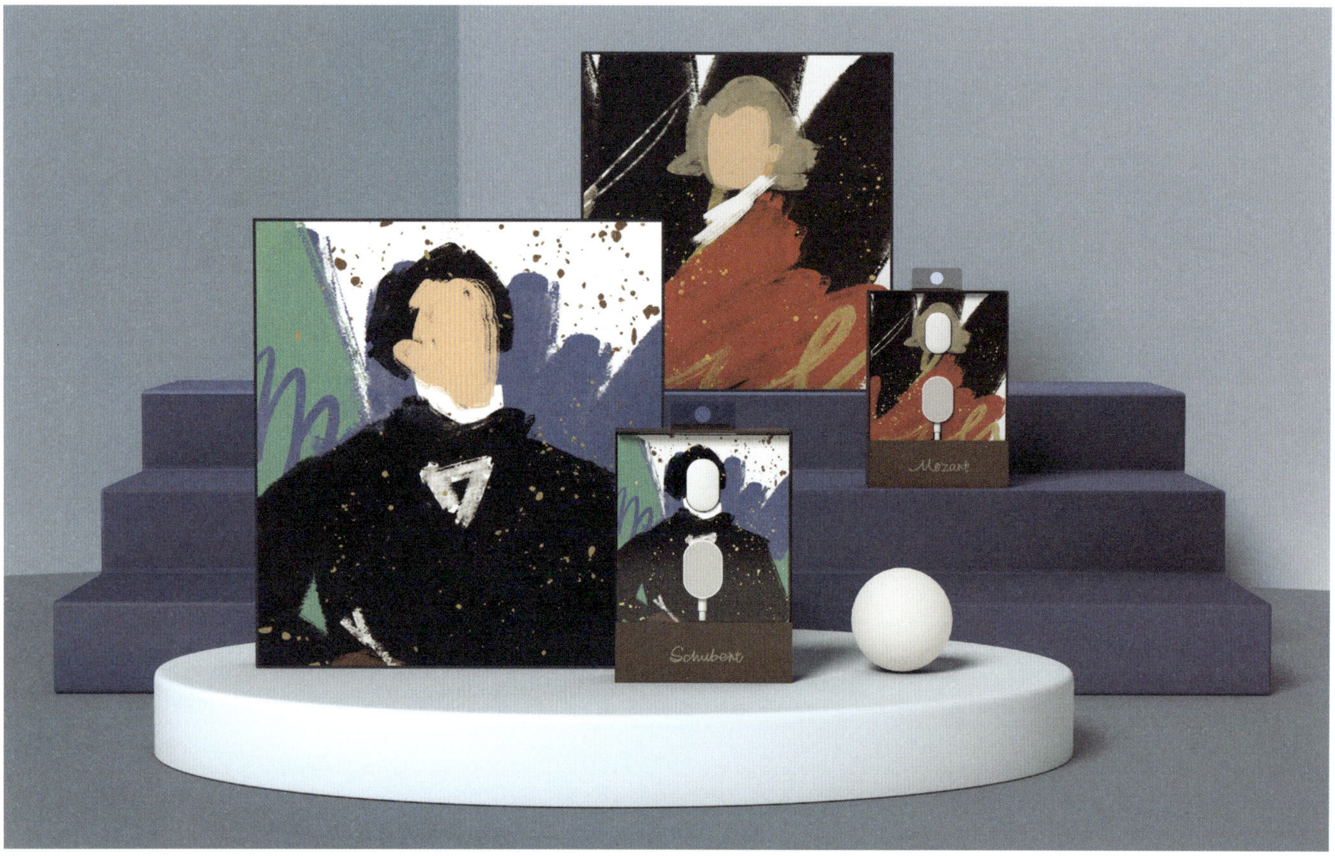

Mi Bluetooth Headset Mini

Q&A: Lu Chen, Senior Director, Xiaomi

What is your work philosophy?
Design aesthetics, creativity, responsibility, learning ability, communication, and teamwork.

Who is or was your greatest mentor?
De Liu, the senior VP of Xiaomi. He is an alumnus of mine from the ArtCenter College of Design and introduced me to Xiaomi. He is a great designer himself, as well as a great product manager and entrepreneur. He taught me the relationship between design and business and how to use design's power to help companies succeed. As one of the founders of Xiaomi's design style, he has profoundly influenced Xiaomi's industrial design and packaging design.

What is it about design that you are most passionate about?
It is the ability to solve practical problems through creativity and make an impact on the environment, design, or humanity.

What is the most difficult challenge you've overcome to reach your current position?
Continuously learning new areas of knowledge, communication skills, and having synergy with different teams.

Who have some of your most significant past influences been?
My mother. She taught me hard work, sheer tenacity, responsibility, and never giving up.

Who among your contemporaries today do you most admire?
I admire Elon Musk the most because he led his team in making innovative and groundbreaking products and because he has gone through many lows and emerged from them. That conviction is what I admire most.

What would be your dream assignment?
A chance to design an Olympic medal.

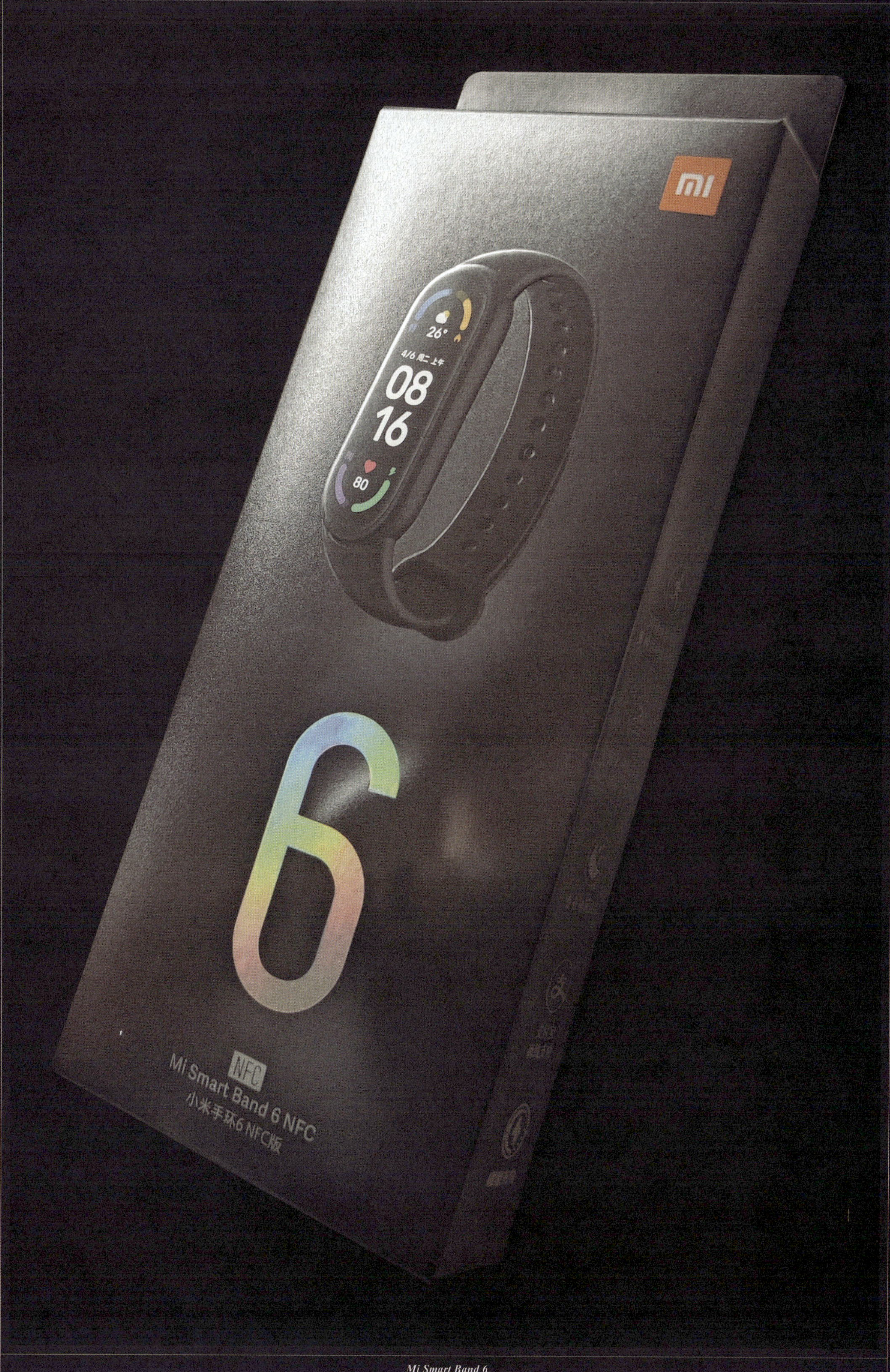

Mi Smart Band 6

Who have been some of your favorite colleagues or clients?
My favorite colleague is Ningning Li, Xiaomi's industrial design director. We are both ArtCenter College of Design alums and were former roommates.

What are the top things you need from a client to do successful work for them?
I want to gain their trust, communicate openly with them, and share the joy of their success.

What do you consider your most outstanding professional achievement so far?
I am more than satisfied with the design of the One Paper Box. This design method is not for a single product but for all product packaging in a small size. I cognitively changed the packaging structure design so that electronic product packaging is no longer a simple stack. Through precise design, I can reduce the amount of raw materials. This is also a simple idea that, I hope, improves the environmental awareness of both designers and the public and reduces the pressure of packaging products on the environment.

What about your work gives you the greatest satisfaction?
I like that my work, which I love, can help society and make users happy.

What part of your work do you find the most demanding?
Being creative is not only about being different but also about solving a problem, which may be budget, structure, mass production, sales, etc. The most demanding part of my job as a designer is how to cleverly use design to solve problems.

What professional goals do you still have for yourself?
I want to be a teacher and pass on some of my design and project experience to other designers.

What advice do you have for students starting out today?
Keep your enthusiasm for learning and be curious about everything.

What interests do you have outside of work?
I love cooking and teaching my seven-year-old son to cook. He is excellent at cooking fried rice and fried eggs.

What do you value most in life?
Inner peace, health, and the company of family and friends.

What would you change if you had to do it all over again?
I would start learning painting skills at a younger age, learn more about type design in college, and do an internship in a printing house to learn printing techniques.

Where do you find inspiration?
Fine art, sculpture, photography, books, and stories.

How do you define success?
I define success as contributing to the development and survival of society, the environment, and human beings, as well as improving the inner self and maintaining inner peace.

Where do you see yourself in the future?
As a designer, I hope to create more work. As a mentor, I hope young designers can make more creative works with my help.

How do you balance your work with your personal life if there is a distinction between the two?
I think work and life go hand in hand. Work is fun for me, and I enjoy the challenges of work. My daily life often inspires me to design.

In what ways do you see your field changing over the years?
Sustainable design has become the design trend for packaging. Consumers are also paying more attention to the reuse of packaging, consumer electronic products are more intelligent, and the IoT (the Internet of Things) has become the mainstream of product development.

Xiaomi is a consumer electronics and intelligent manufacturing company. For those unfamiliar with product design, what kind of work goes into designing a product compared to other types of design?
For Xiaomi, product design is given specific definitions of features and functions. Our product designers work on the outside look of a solid product (form, style, color, material, and surface finish), its insides (hardware layout and assembly), and its interaction with users (ergonomics and interface, including a display, button, switch, or even light and sound), always keeping the feasibility of mass-production in mind and finalizing the proposals to make the product real.

What have been some of your favorite Xiaomi products to work on?
I like the earphone series. Every time we make earphone packaging, it is the most exciting moment for our team. Packaging for earphones is full of challenges, imagination, and possibility. In addition, there is the Xiaomi watch packaging, which is the accumulation of our packaging technology, collaboration, and creativity and is also one of my favorite designs.

One of Xiaomi's core company beliefs is "Just for Fans." What does that mean to you? How does that affect your design work?
Embracing our vision to "make friends with users and be the coolest company in the users' hearts," Xiaomi continuously pursues technological innovations, compelling user experience, and operational efficiency. It relentlessly develops unique products to let everyone enjoy a better life through innovative technology.

Xiaomi focuses on listening to users' feedback in product development and creating the ultimate user experience beyond expectations. Users inspire the company to keep innovating and pursuing technological progress all the time. In fact, the company started out by building its first-ever product, our operating system MIUI, by working closely with users to enrich and improve its product design and features.

Therefore, we must consider the user's feelings at the beginning of the design, take the user as the center, and start from the user experience.

Xiaomi has three creative initiatives: Xiaomi Studios, Xiaomi Creators, and Xiaomi Fan Stories. How were they started, and what is their purpose?
Xiaomi Studios is a filmmaking initiative created by Xiaomi International. It was founded in 2019 as one of Xiaomi International's first IP projects. With Xiaomi Studios, we aim to build on our company's mission of "innovation for everyone" and provide filmmakers an opportunity to unleash their inner

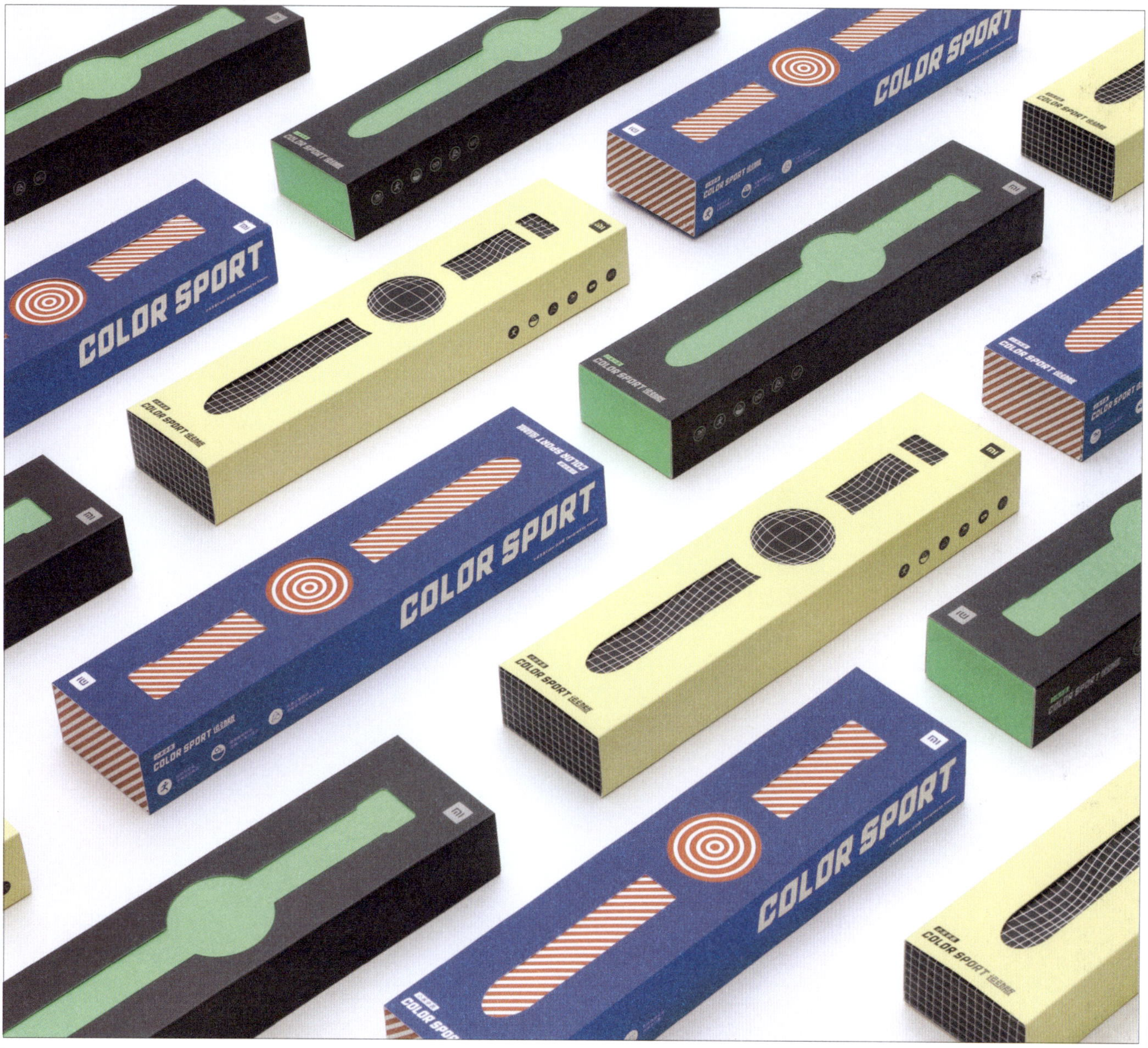

Mi Watch Color Sport

creativity with the Xiaomi smartphones in their pockets: "creativity for everyone." Xiaomi Studios is both a platform for our talented creators to show off their notable creative films and a community for people worldwide looking to unleash their creativity with their Xiaomi smartphones. Xiaomi Studios has produced over 60 short films entirely shot on Xiaomi smartphones in cooperation with filmmakers and creators worldwide, collaborating with renowned filmmakers and institutions such as Academy Award-winner Chris Overton and the Sundance Film Festival.

Xiaomi Creators is Xiaomi International's official talent program that provides filmmakers and photographers opportunities to share their creativity in different visual-related projects like Xiaomi Studios and Xiaomi Imagery. With the Xiaomi Creator program, we aim to share our creators' works globally and provide the Xiaomi Creators with a global stage to grow as creators and share their unique stories and knowledge with people worldwide. The Xiaomi Creator program officially launched in 2021 as part of the Xiaomi 11T Pro Global Launch. The program currently features over 25 creators from over ten markets worldwide.

Xiaomi Fan Story is a documentary series portraying the real lives of our international Xiaomi fans. By providing our fans with a platform to share their unique stories with the world, we aim to emphasize the core value of Xiaomi: being friends with our users. There are currently ten episodes of Xiaomi Fan Story. The guests for each episode come from different regions and have different occupations and personalities. However, one thing in common is that they all believe in and tie back to the underlying spirit of Xiaomi—"innovation for everyone." Their wonderful, moving, and touching stories inspire us as a brand, and we want to share these exciting stories worldwide. Xiaomi fans are a core part of Xiaomi's culture. They are advocates for Xiaomi, while Xiaomi's values and vision are spread far through their words.

What role do Chinese design concepts play in your product design?

Instead of involving prominent traditional Chinese aesthetic elements, such as auspicious patterns, forms, or colors, we put more effort into responding to Chinese users' consumer behavior and designing miscellaneous products that fit into the modern Chinese lifestyle.

Xiaomi www.mi.com

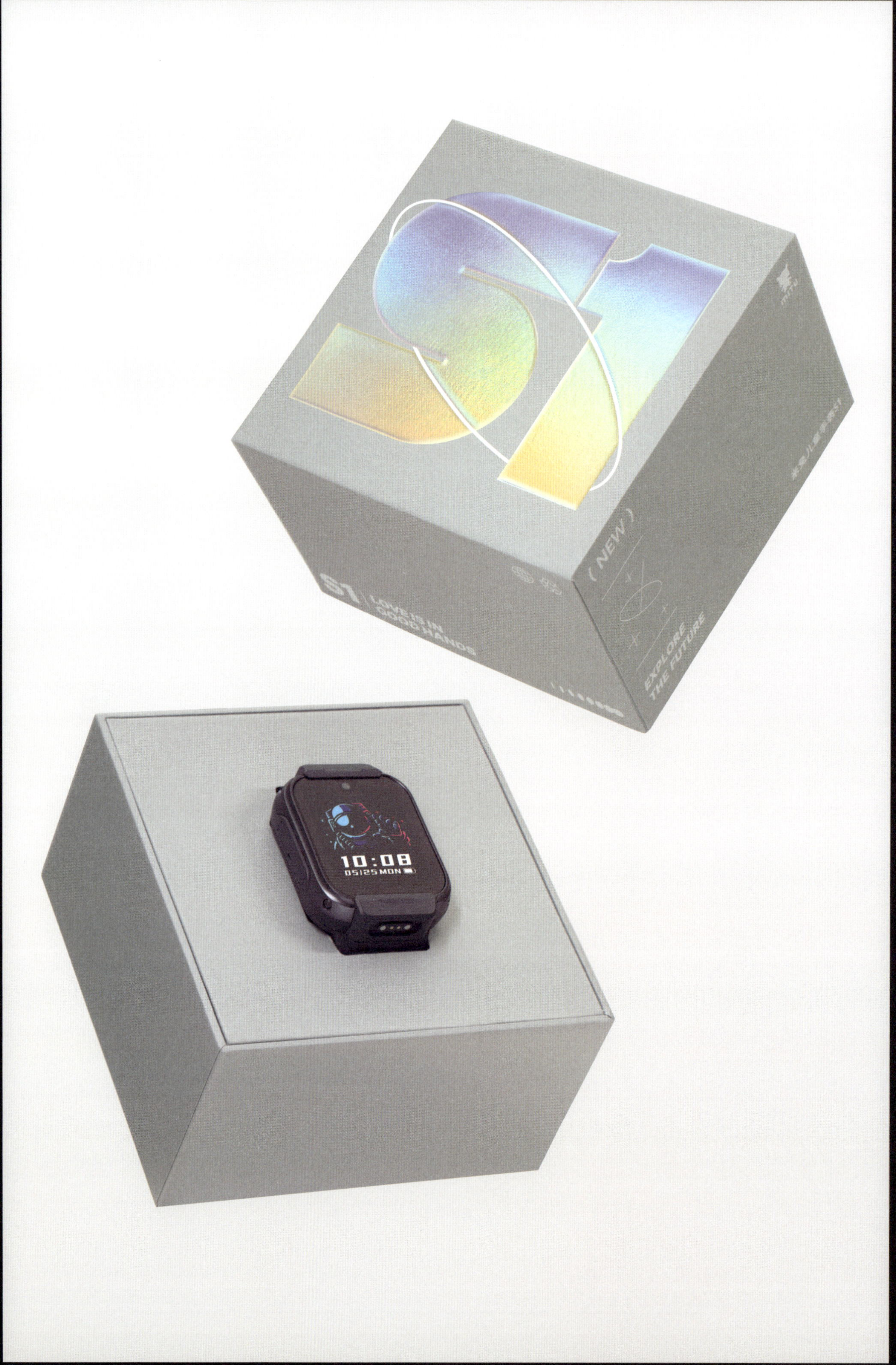

Mitu Kids Smart Watch

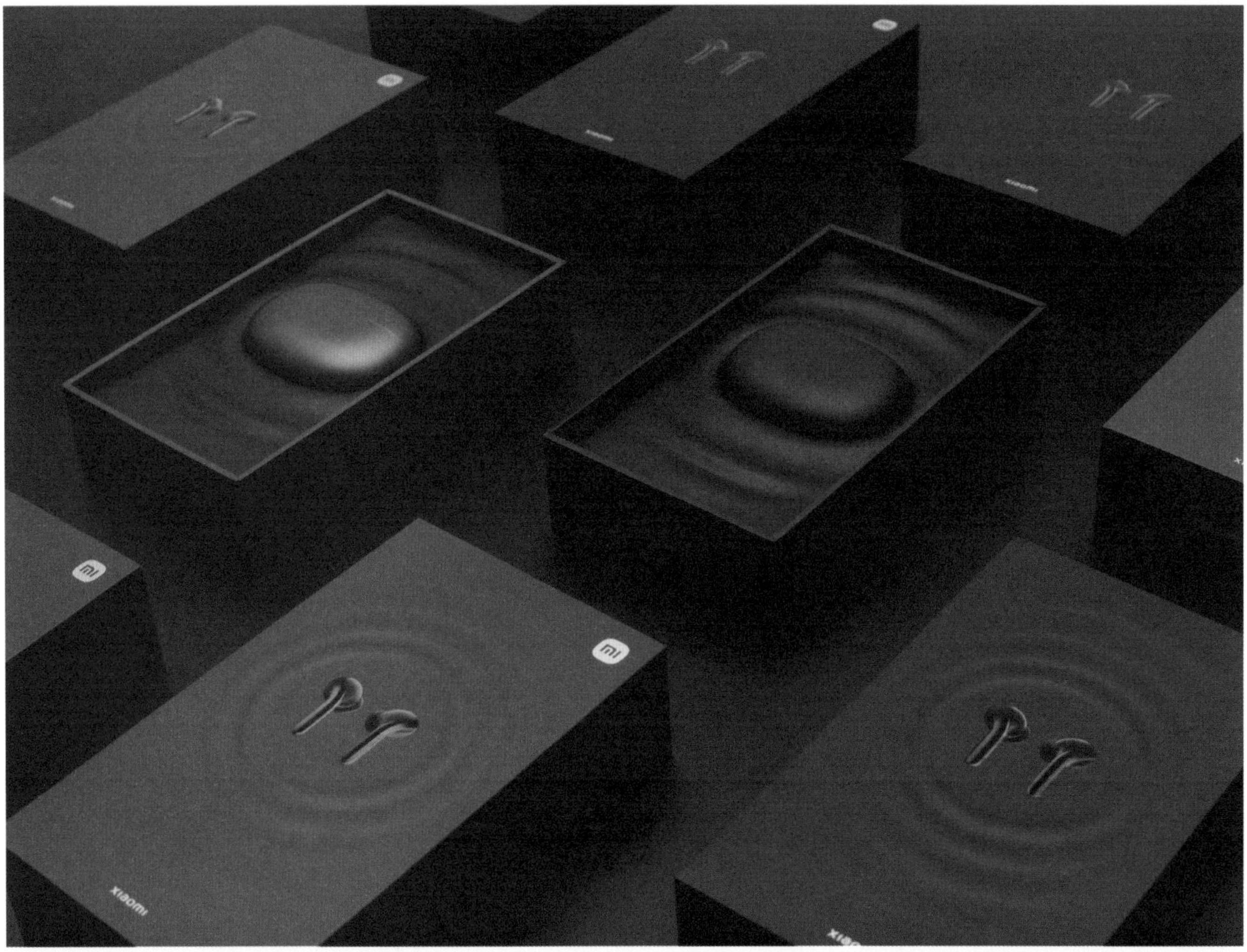

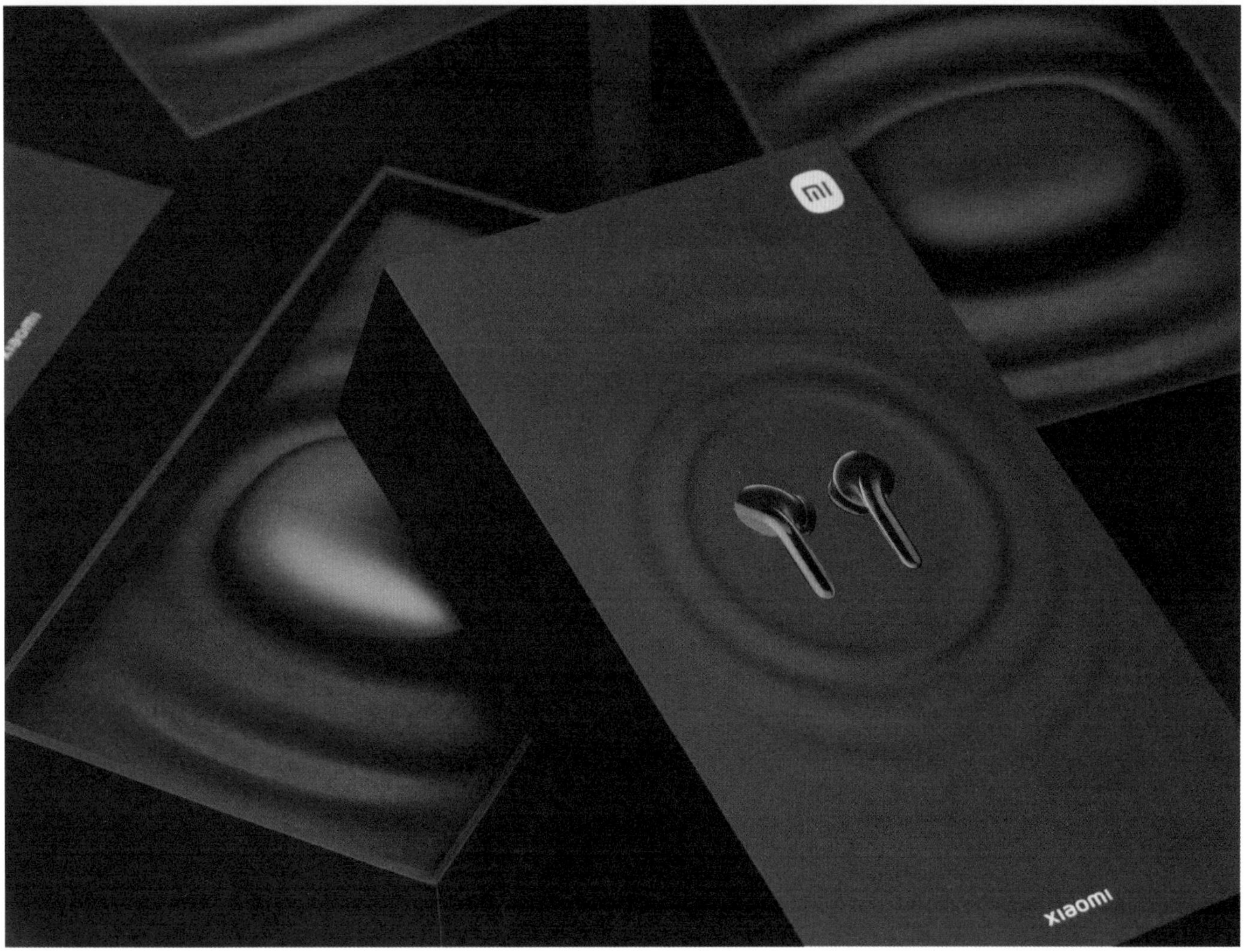

Mi Buds 3T Pro

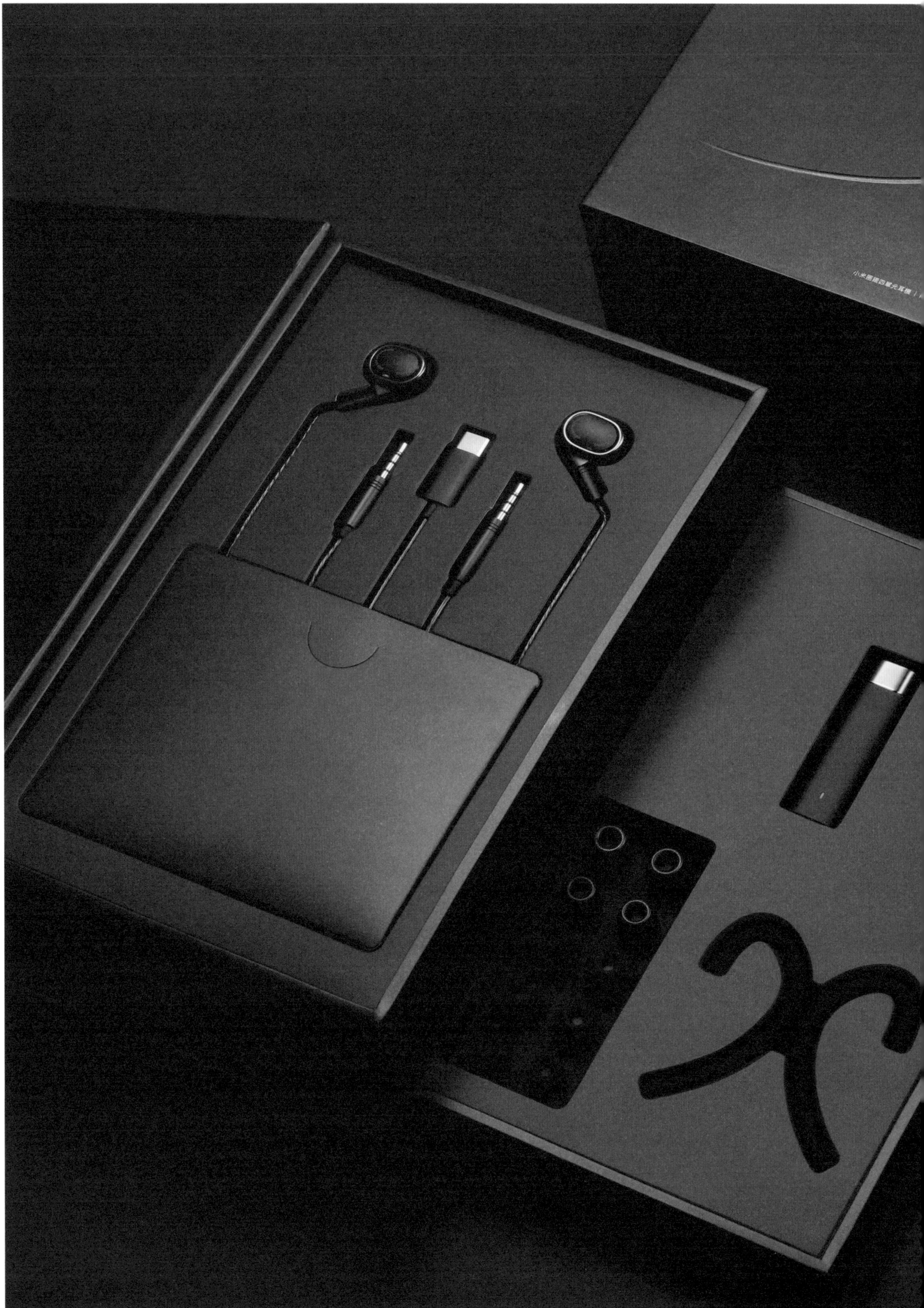
小米圈鐵四單元耳機

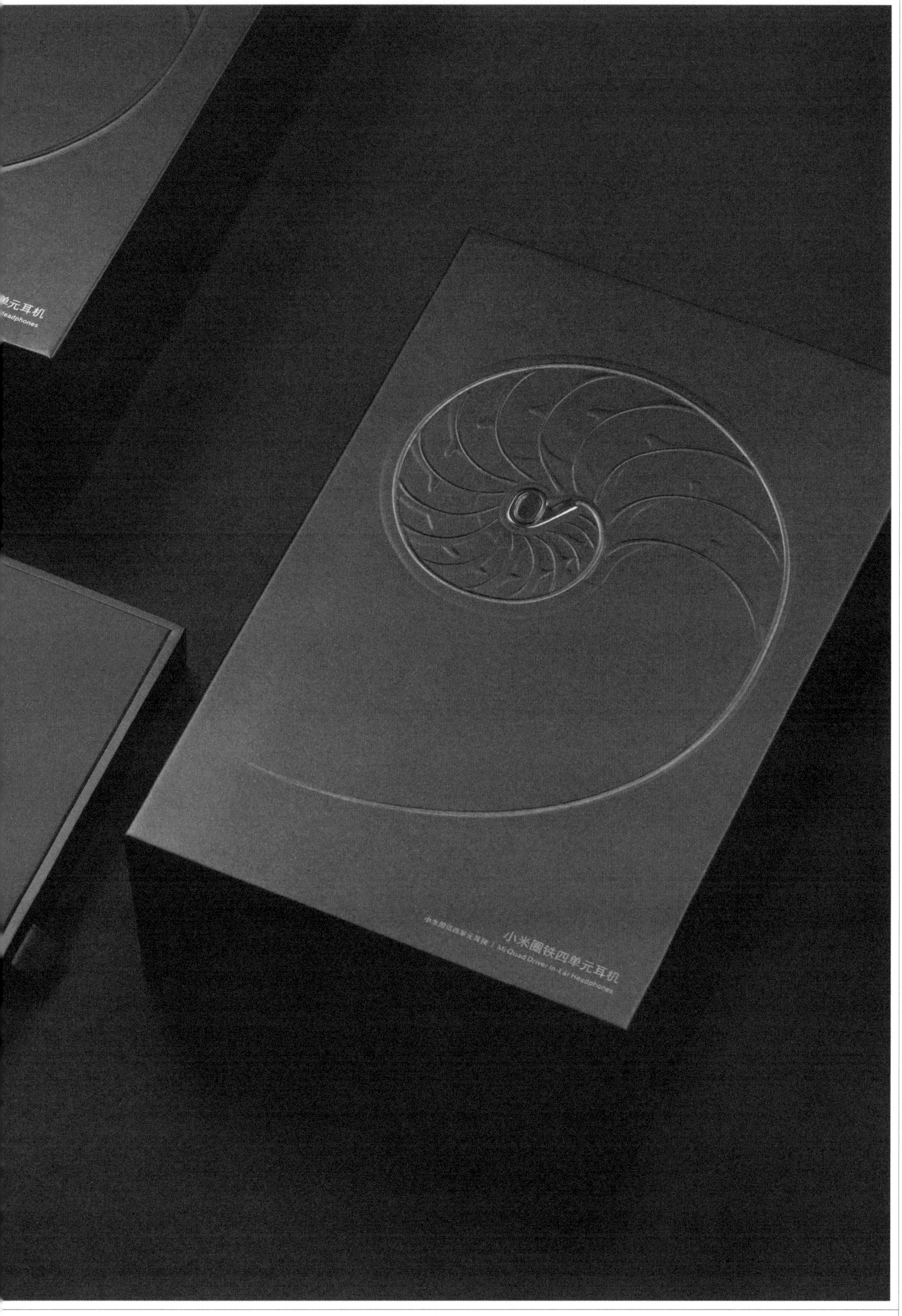

Mi Quad Driver In-Ear Headphone

A

ADVERTISING

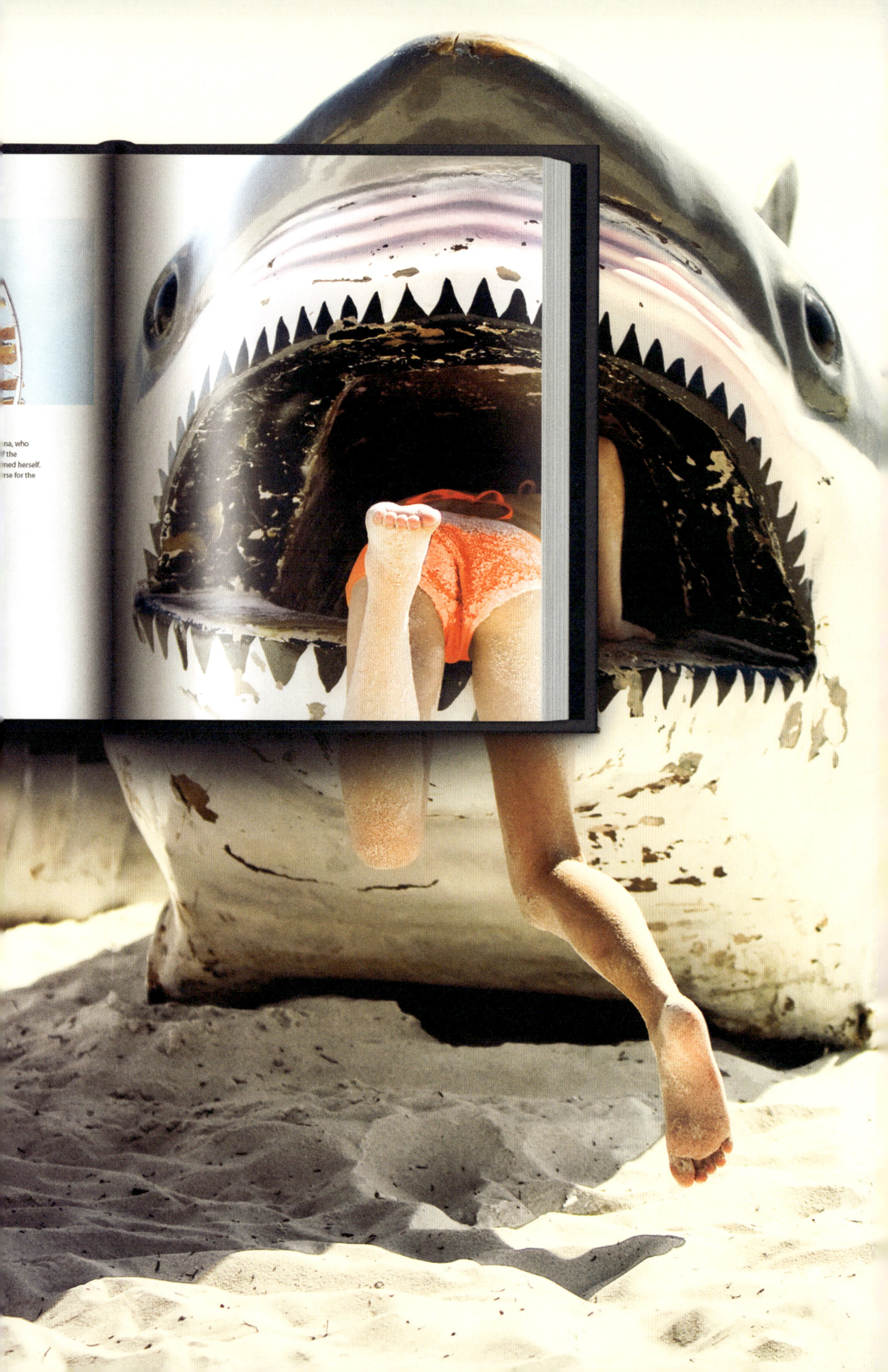
na, who
f the
med herself.
rse for the

DUNCAN CHANNON HAS ALL THE BENEFITS OF A SMALL SHOP WITH BIG-TIME STRATEGY AND BIG-TIME CREATIVITY.

Ken Kunze, *Former CMO, Craft Brew Alliance*

JESSICA CAN DO IT ALL. CONCEPTUALLY, SHE ALWAYS KNOCKS YOUR SOCKS OFF WITH UNIQUE IDEAS. HER TASTE IS IMPECCABLE. SHE'S THE REAL DEAL; YOU'LL COUNT YOUR LUCKY STARS IF YOU WORK WITH HER.

John Kovacevich, *Founder & Creative Director, Agency SOS*

DUNCAN CHANNON'S INCLUSIVE, COLLABORATIVE APPROACH LED TO A CREATIVE CAMPAIGN THAT OUTPERFORMED THE INDUSTRY BY A VAST MARGIN FOR THREE YEARS RUNNING.

Scott Worthington, *Former VP of Marketing & Strategy, DriveTime*

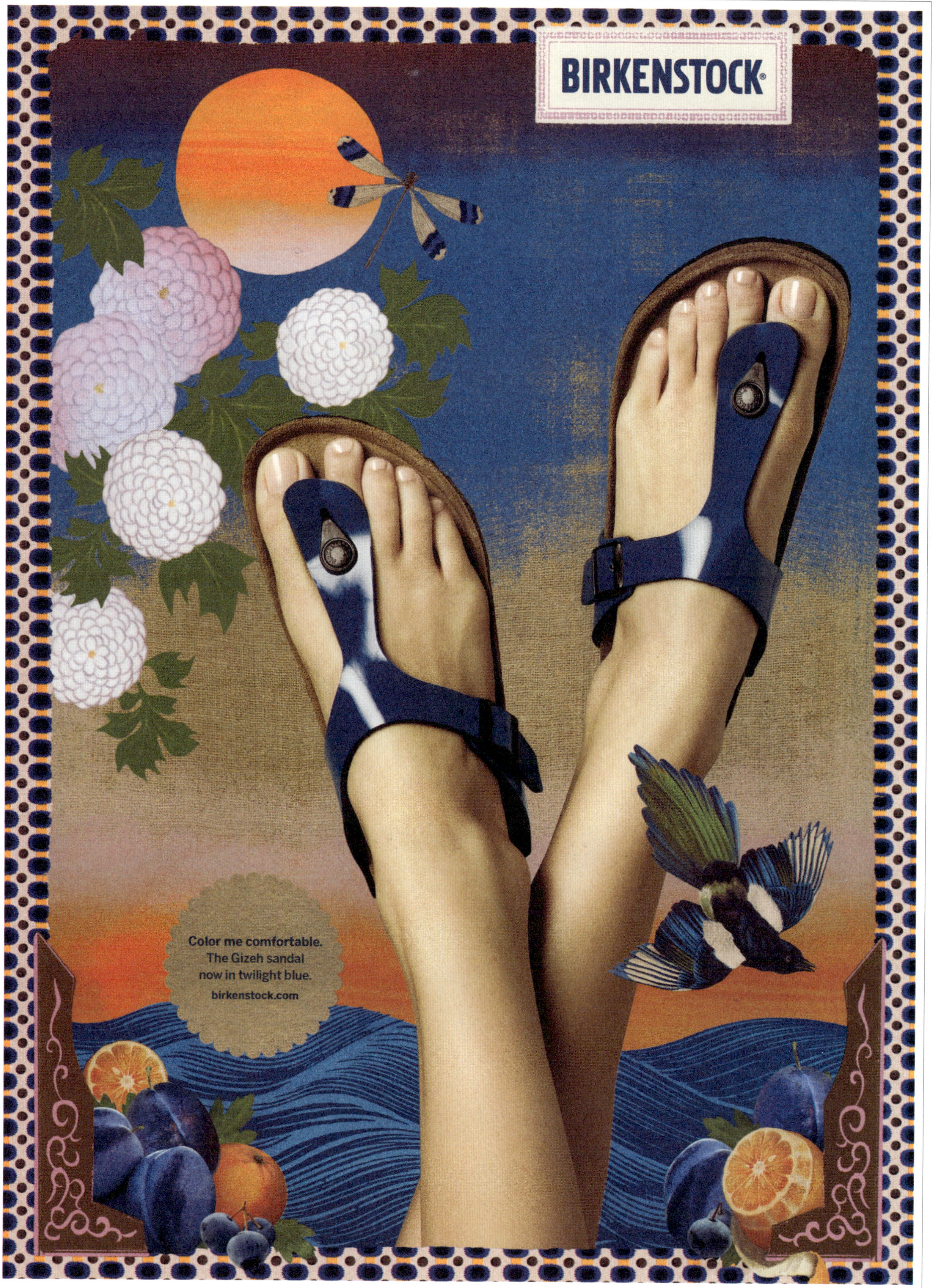

(Page 49) Blurb, "Find Your Book" campaign. Photo by Sean Murphy
(Above) Birkenstock, "Color Me Comfortable." Illustrations by Amy Guip

Introduction by Sean Dee *Executive Vice President & Chief Commercial Officer, Outrigger Hospitality Group*

On paper, Duncan Channon does too much, especially for a smaller independent shop. The modern marketing landscape is populated mainly by specialist agencies and niche players. Branding agencies. Social media agencies. Design shops. Media buying companies. The list goes on. But DC does all of the above and more. And they do it to deliver the exact, correct answer for a brand, even if it wasn't the brand's ask. Over the years, they've consistently delivered that unexpected solution for me—the very thing I needed before I knew I needed it. So, yeah, maybe they do too much. But they do it all very well.

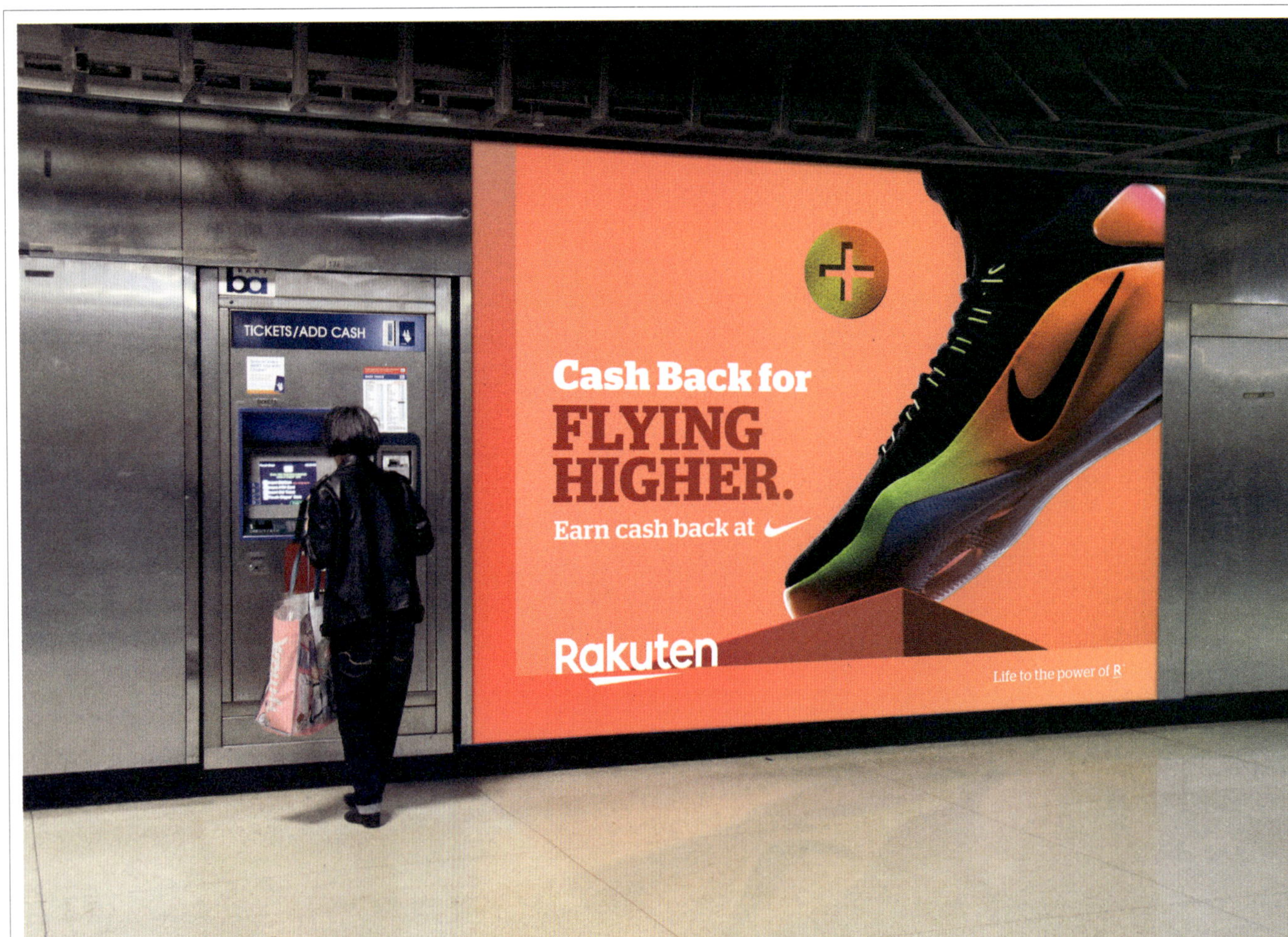

Rakuten, "Life to the Power of R" billboard

SHARE THE GOOD AND DUMB IDEAS YOU'RE
MOST INTRIGUED BY WITH OTHERS,
AND LISTEN TO YOUR GUT WHEN YOU DO.

Michael Lemme, *Chief Creative Officer, Duncan Channon*

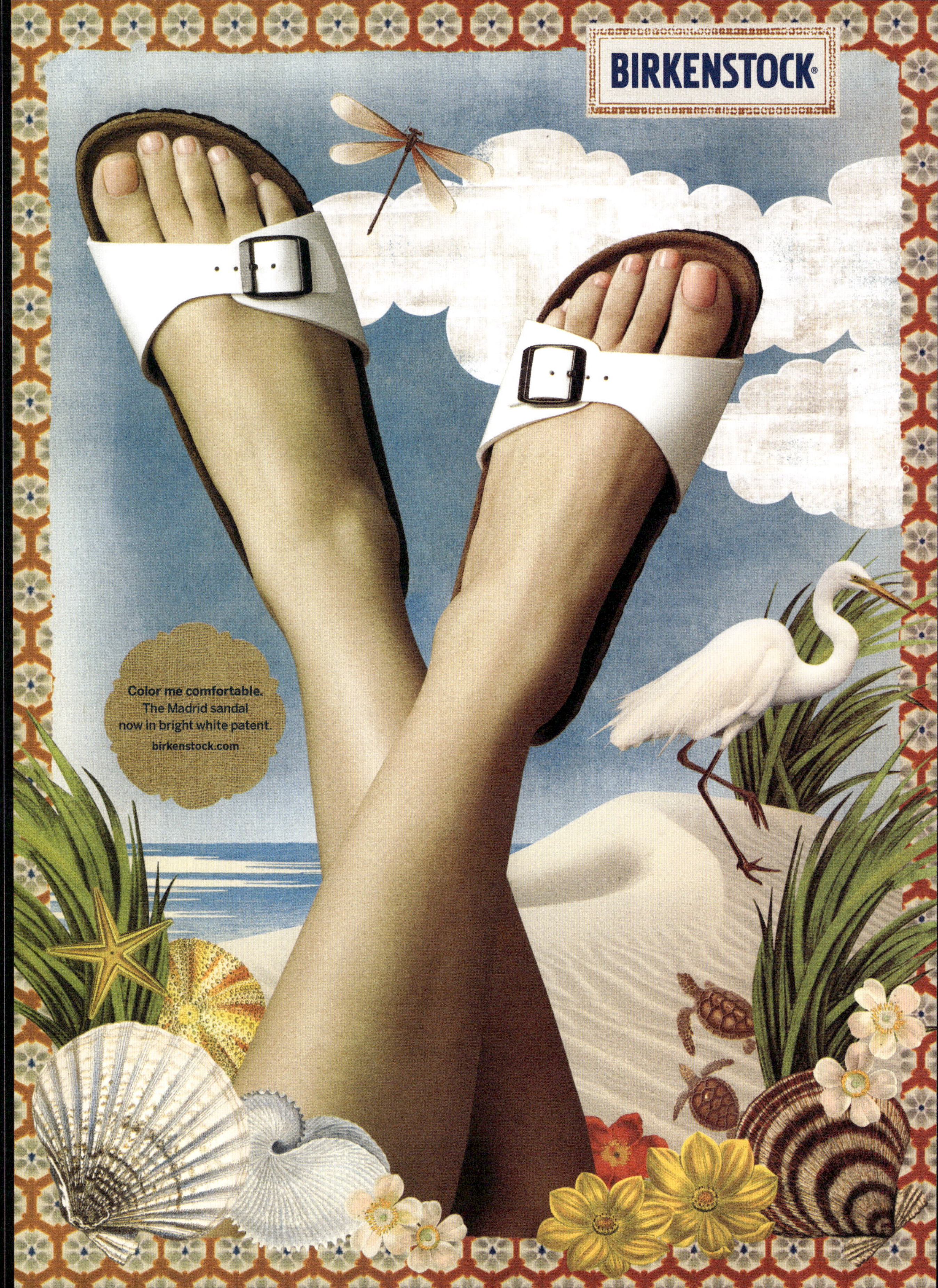
BIRKENSTOCK
Color me comfortable.
The Madrid sandal
now in bright white patent.
birkenstock.com

Duncan Channon focuses on five key disciplines: advertising, branding, social, experiential, and media + analytics. How does each discipline influence the others, and what are some similarities and differences between them that might not be noticeable?

Michael Lemme, Chief Creative Officer: For better or worse, we were never interested in specializing in any one industry or any one kind of output. We wouldn't know how. We focus on understanding the lives of the people we're trying to reach and what we hope to make them feel—and then evaluate where and how we can best do that. Our mantra is "feeling first." People make decisions based on instinct and emotion and then unconsciously use some logic to make it make sense rationally. Reaching people at the gut level comes first and bonds people to brands in more profound, more durable ways. People will tell you they want the facts, but what they really want is the feeling.

What inspired or motivated you to start a design/AD career?

Anne Elisco-Lemme, Executive Creative Director: I think I've always been wired to express a point of view. Even when I work for a client, my perspective is baked into the work. There is something really rewarding about that.

Kalee Abella, ACD Art Director: I had no idea what advertising was until I left college. I studied graphic design and was able to play in the film world a little for my thesis, and that left me hungry to do more in the film and motion world. I still had a love for packaging and branding, but I knew I wanted to be able to touch multiple mediums and found advertising was the place to do that.

Shannon Burns, Design Director: For as long as I can remember, I wanted to be an artist, so I think I fulfilled my childhood career fantasy pretty well. I owe it to my parents for always being supportive and encouraging me to pursue a degree and career in design. There was never a question that art was my passion, and they really nurtured that.

Xavier Rivera, Senior Art Director: I've always had a ton of visual curiosity and wanted to make something. As a kid, I grew up around a unique cultural explosion of creativity in music and gaming, and I take great pride in that. It's a big part of my identity.

What is your personal work philosophy?

M.L.: Soak in every input you can find initially, then set it aside and follow your curiosity. Explore for as long as possible and play around without thinking too hard about the solution. Share the good and dumb ideas you're most intrigued by with others, and listen to your gut when you do. Your gut knows—well, it learns—when you don't believe in something. And the best work is a surprise to everybody.

A.E.L.: Collaborate with people you trust. This is never a one-person show.

K.A.: Your hobbies and interests deserve your time so that you can bring fresh perspectives to ideas and storytelling.

X.R.: We must constantly believe in ourselves and that there's always a better, fresher way to do things.

What is it about advertising that you are most passionate about?

Jessica Wyatt, Creative Director: Without question, the opportunities to collaborate with other creative people.

X.R.: Our work has the potential to do so many things. Change minds and hearts. Make you laugh. Make you cry. Most importantly to me, to help others.

What is the most difficult challenge you've overcome to reach your current position?

X.R.: Balancing your humility with your confidence. In my mind, the worst thing is to appear ungrateful or egotistical. There are always thanks to go around when completing a brief and getting work to go live.

Who is or was your greatest mentor?

A.E.L.: My greatest mentor was Cathy Bowen, a CD I worked with early in my career. She was a phenomenal writer, and her work was always simple but brilliant. She was a great observer of people and brought those observations into her work. I learned to really pay attention to human emotion from her.

J.W.: I've been lucky to have many! When I first found myself in advertising, Brian L. Perkins was significant in encouraging me to make the jump from the design department to art direction and the concept side. Today, I'm grateful for Anne Elisco-Lemme and her unwavering support. She could host a TED Talk on how to build trust with clients.

K.A.: I was fortunate to enter my first advertising job collecting a few creative life mentors. I'll never forget working with two powerful and talented copy/AD teams: Sara Worthington, Aryan Aminzadeh, Megan Penman, and Margie Chidley. One can easily get lost in stressful timelines or unnecessary politics, and those four taught me to focus on having fun when conceiving and doing the work. I valued that they made clients uncomfortable with ideas in the best of ways. They encouraged everyone who worked with them to be themselves. Creative director Kelly McCullough has also been a great mentor. She has given advice about salary and the creative process and helpful insights into navigating my personal growth. Anyone in the ad world is lucky to receive any mentorship from Kelly. I am so grateful to have had influence and inspiration from this group of women that I can still reach out to at any time.

S.B.: I've been fortunate to work with some really talented people over the years, but when I think of who has been an inspiration and guide for me the most, it has to be Duncan Channon's own Michael Lemme. I was a baby straight out of college when I started working at DC, and when I look back on where I was then in my career versus where I am now, I think I owe a lot of that to Michael. He not only has a unique mind that can think creatively, mathematically, strategically, and so on, but he comes from a place without ego. I look forward to collaborating with him and always value his opinion. There is never an idea he can't make more meaningful, never a job too small to push and make better, or a pixel out of place he doesn't see. I know he has made me a better designer and thinker, and I feel lucky to have crossed paths with him.

X.R.: I've been lucky to work with immensely talented people who have profoundly impacted my career trajectory, but I'll pick just one: Trushar Patel. He was the first creative I worked under who helped me understand one thing I value greatly: details matter, even those you don't think anyone will notice.

Who among your contemporaries today do you most admire?

A.E.L.: I would say what Issa Rae is doing with Team Epiphany is exciting. It centers Black women in the work and demands truly diversified production while being rooted in a culture that most agencies dream of. I hope this is where the future of our industry is heading.

S.B.: I seek inspiration from so many different places and people. Some that I find myself going back to over and over again are Paula Scher and her team, as well as Gretel and French agency Les-Graphiquants.

X.R.: Sam Rodriguez's illustrations are striking and fun to look at. Jordan Peele's unique approach to filmmaking has single-handedly renewed my interest in the horror and suspense genres. Jordan Dinwiddie's work on Nike has been incredibly in-

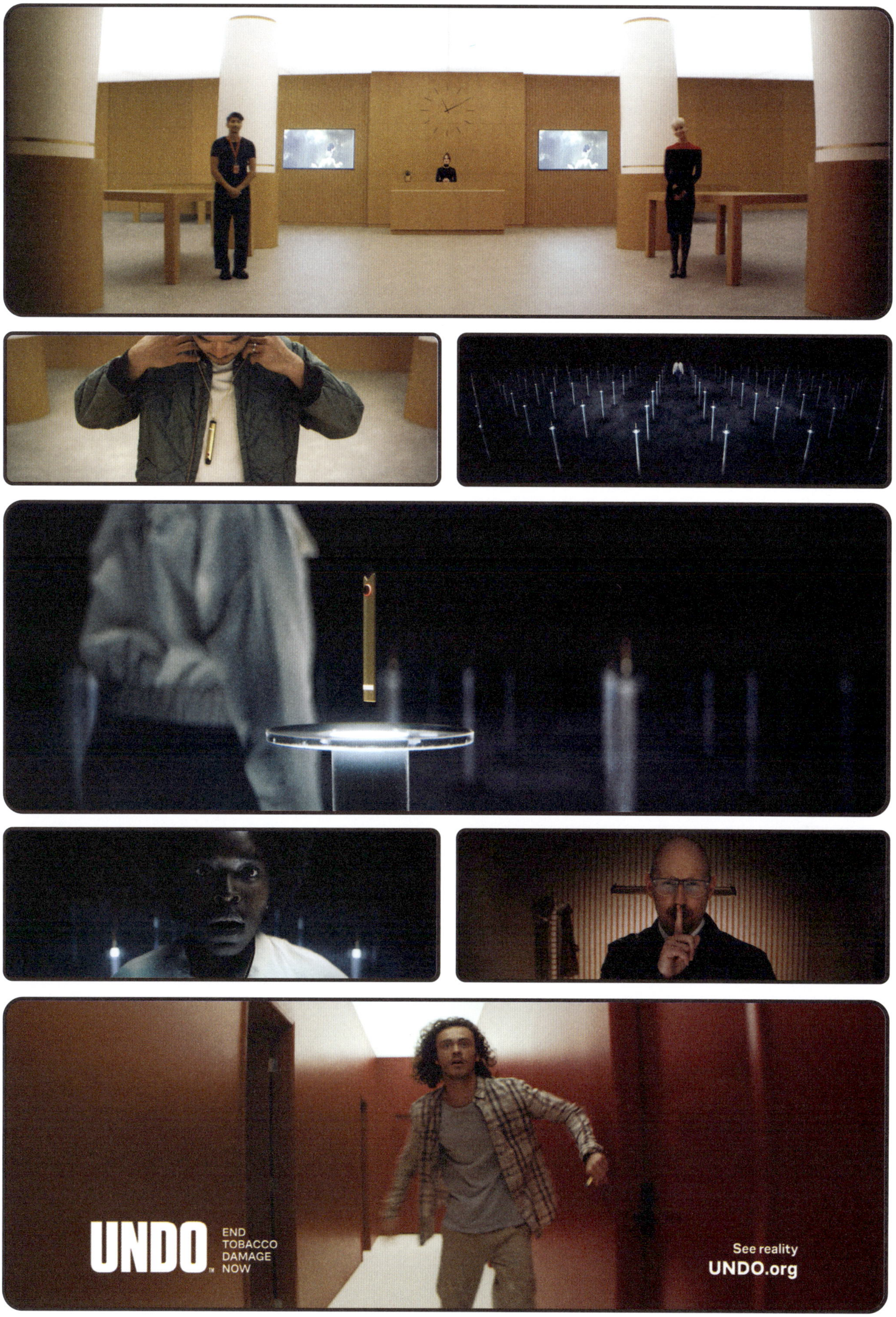

UNDO - End Tobacco Damage Now, "Big Tobacco's Fantasyland"

spiring. And I can't forget Jessica Walsh, the founder of &Walsh. Everything they make is mind-blowingly fun to gaze at.
J.W.: Probably Beyoncé.

Who has been one/some of your favorite colleagues or clients?
A.E.L.: Coming from the art direction side, my favorite colleagues have always been the crazy-talented writers I've worked with. Jessea Hankins and MJ Deery are the most recent. Some people are just born to put words together in a way that makes you stop in your tracks. I'm in awe of that ability. My favorite client has to be UNDO, the California Tobacco Prevention Program. Going after the tobacco industry takes fearlessness, and that mindset is carried into the work. They are a brave group of people. They also understand that creativity is a process, so they allow fluidity all the way through production, which is quite rare.
J.W.: Goodness! Really putting me on the spot here. I'm a boomerang [see below] at Duncan Channon, so obviously, I'm a fan of these people. As for clients, I'm always blown away by the passion and genuine desire to collaborate from UNDO. They're always stoked to see their research come to life in the creative, which is contagious.
K.A.: Some of my favorite clients have been partners who could genuinely trust the agency. Virgin America was one of the first brands I worked on that allowed us to play and create work that was not only fun but boldly stood out in their category. From a playful, surreal, out-of-home launch of their website in Times Square to creating a five-hour and four-minute film, Virgin America was open to showing up in non-traditional ways, owning very memorable work. eBay was another brand that allowed the agency to take the lead in launching its social presence specifically for eBay sneakers and watches. As a creative, it always feels fulfilling when a client can truly understand the work and be just as excited as the agency to make it. We created a campaign for that launch that touched every digital space with eye-catching content, using a fresh look and feel, along with two films and artist collaborations.
S.B.: I've gotten to work on some fun branding and campaign projects at Duncan Channon over the years: Outrigger Resorts & Hotels, SweeTarts, StubHub, and the Golden State Warriors, to name a few. However, some of the most meaningful work that is both wholly challenging and rewarding is the work done for UNDO. Our work for them involves taking very complex information (and a lot of it) and distilling it into elegant campaigns and communications—no easy task. But seeing the work we've done over the years making a difference in fighting Big Tobacco and tobacco use in California is immensely fulfilling.
X.R.: This agency makes it hard to have favorite colleagues in the best way possible. There is a powerful desire to stay away from conventional ideas here, and everyone at Duncan Channon brings something to the table that makes them unique and enjoyable to work with. I greatly appreciate the creative leadership I've experienced working with Anne-Elisco Lemme. She's so precise at getting quickly to the root of what makes an idea great and what needs to be done to execute it beautifully. Anyone out there would be lucky to learn from her. From a larger angle, the women in general at this agency bring it daily across departments. That's something I'm proud to say. I'm grateful for the opportunities to work with great people and brands. In particular, the work we've produced lately with UNDO has been gratifying.

Duncan Channon has won multiple awards, including the Ad Age Agency of the Year title four times. Which award are you most proud of?
M.L.: Beyond the awards… in an industry where people move around a lot, for all kinds of excellent and crummy reasons, we're proud to be a place that people stay at for longer and where more than a few left for a minute but then came back (we call them boomerangs). Having more profound relationships with each other and our clients makes the work more profound and meaningful, too—both in the outputs and the doing. Since its founding, Duncan Channon has had a knack for caring about how we make things as much or more than we care about the things we make. It wasn't a strategy; it's just the nature of the place. And it hasn't been a way to get famous fast (or ever?), but it works for us.

What would be your dream assignment?
J.W.: "Cannibalize our brand." OK, OK, not really. A dream assignment for me would be rooted in a place of no fear and a desire to truly make something memorable, creative testing be damned.
K.A.: To launch a mezcal brand.

What are the top things you need from a client to do successful work for them?
K.A.: Trust, collaboration, and an open mindset.
J.W.: Trust and collaboration.

What do you consider your most outstanding professional achievement so far?
J.W.: As a through-and-through, diehard Beatles fan, probably scoring a Yoko Ono song for a spot.

What advice do you have for students starting out today?
J.W.: Don't be afraid to ask for what you want.
X.R.: Follow your heart as much as possible. Don't get too attached to ideas early in the process. If you believe in something, speak on it. Those words just might change the perspective of everyone in the room for the best.

What do you value most in life?
X.R.: Empathy. It's the most precious resource on the planet.

What would you change if you had to do it all over again?
X.R.: Be more confident in myself from the beginning. Travel more.

Where do you find inspiration?
M.L.: Setting aside friends and family, or maybe including them, almost all of my favorite follows are independent type designers. OH no Type Co. and Klim Type Foundry have been at the top of the list for years, and Contrast Foundry (CoFo) is a more recent favorite. Within the seemingly finite space of 26 letters, there's an infinite space for experimentation, playfulness, meticulous effort, and thinking.
X.R.: It's essential to keep an eye on the work being produced around you. I save things in folders and clip things out that inspire me. As a father of a young teen and an adolescent, I pay lots of attention to what interests them. The imagination is so effortless in a younger person's mind.

In what ways do you see your field changing over the years?
M.L.: Our tools are changing faster than it matters to call them out. So we surrender to the tumble of that—it's part of the fun. Branding and marketing get ever more complex, fussy, and fractured. And yet, we'll always work toward making something simple, beautiful, or compelling that matters to people. Not what any research report or "best practices" listicle says people need, but what is revealed to have been needed.

Duncan Channon www.duncanchannon.com

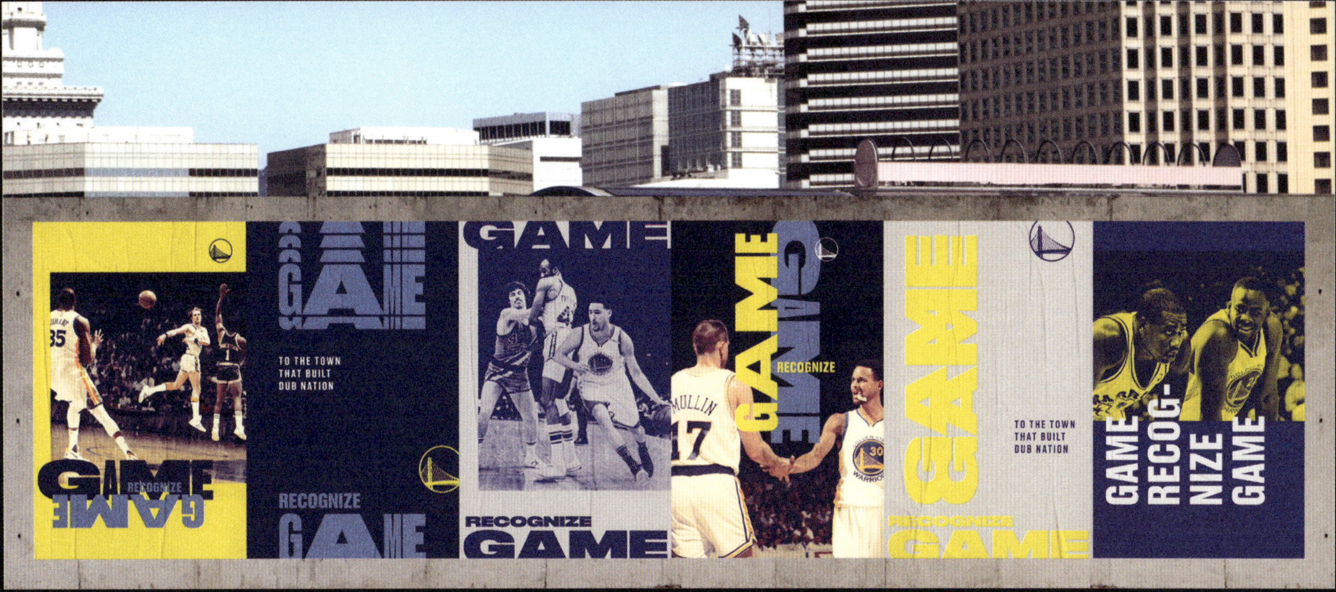
GAME
RECOGNIZE
GAME
TO THE TOWN THAT BUILT DUB NATION
RECOGNIZE
GAME
RECOGNIZE
GAME
RECOGNIZE
GAME
TO THE TOWN THAT BUILT DUB NATION
RECOGNIZE
GAME
GAME RECOG-NIZE GAME

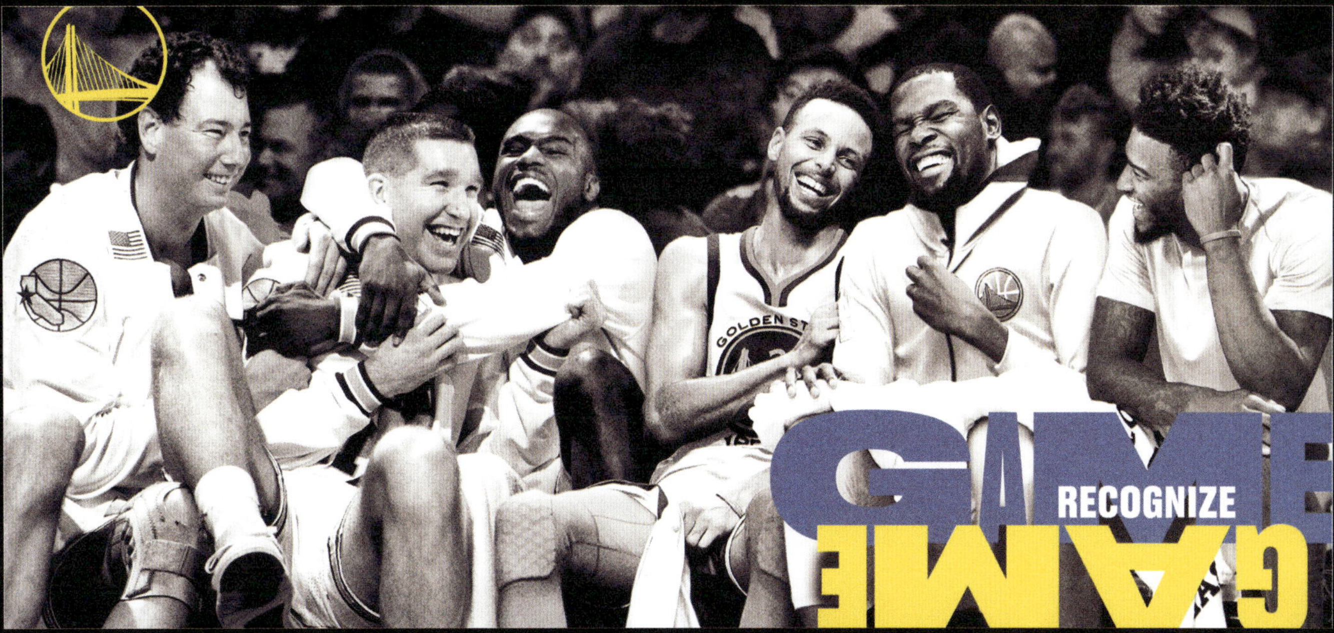
GAME
RECOGNIZE
GAME

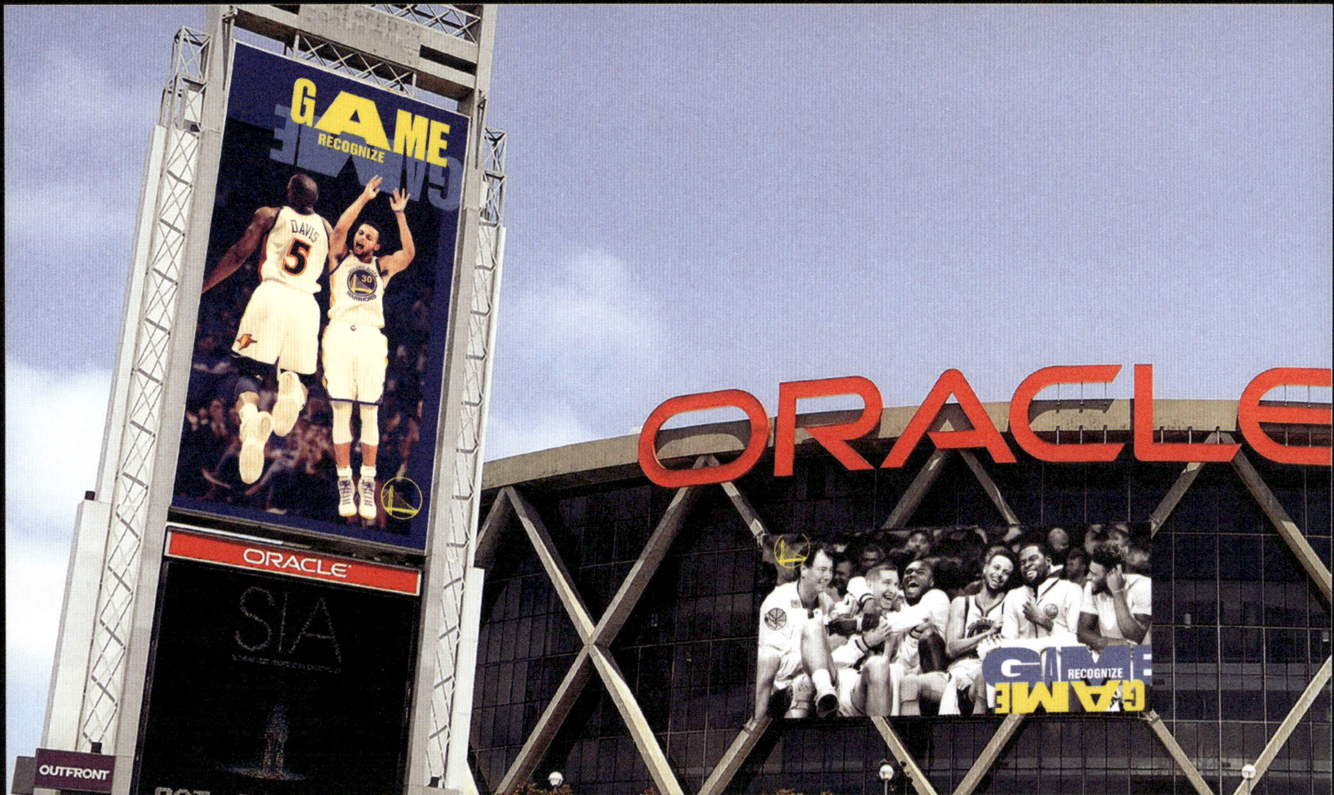
GAME
RECOGNIZE
ORACLE
ORACLE
OUTFRONT

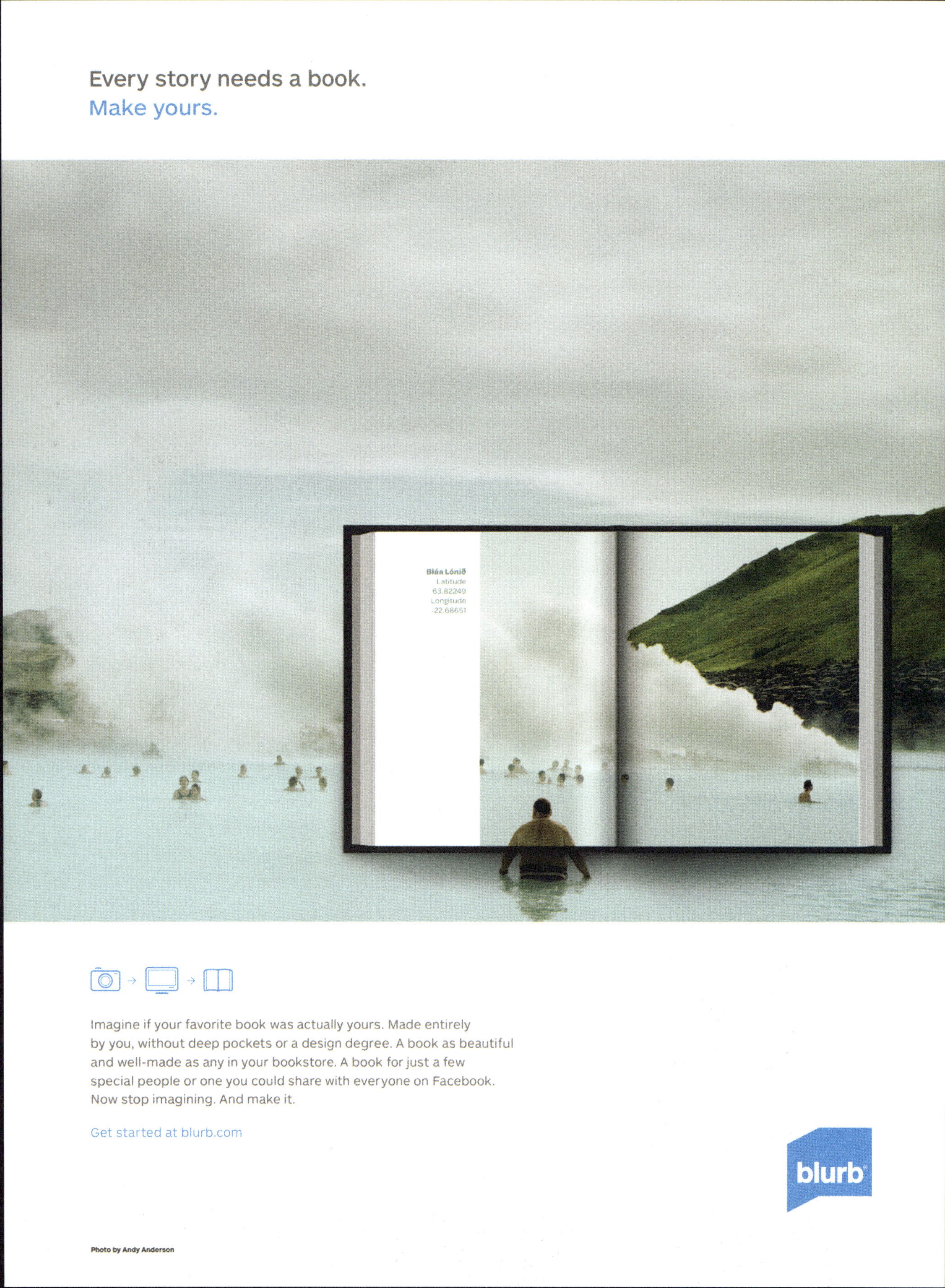

Blurb, "Find Your Book" campaign. Photo by Andy Anderson

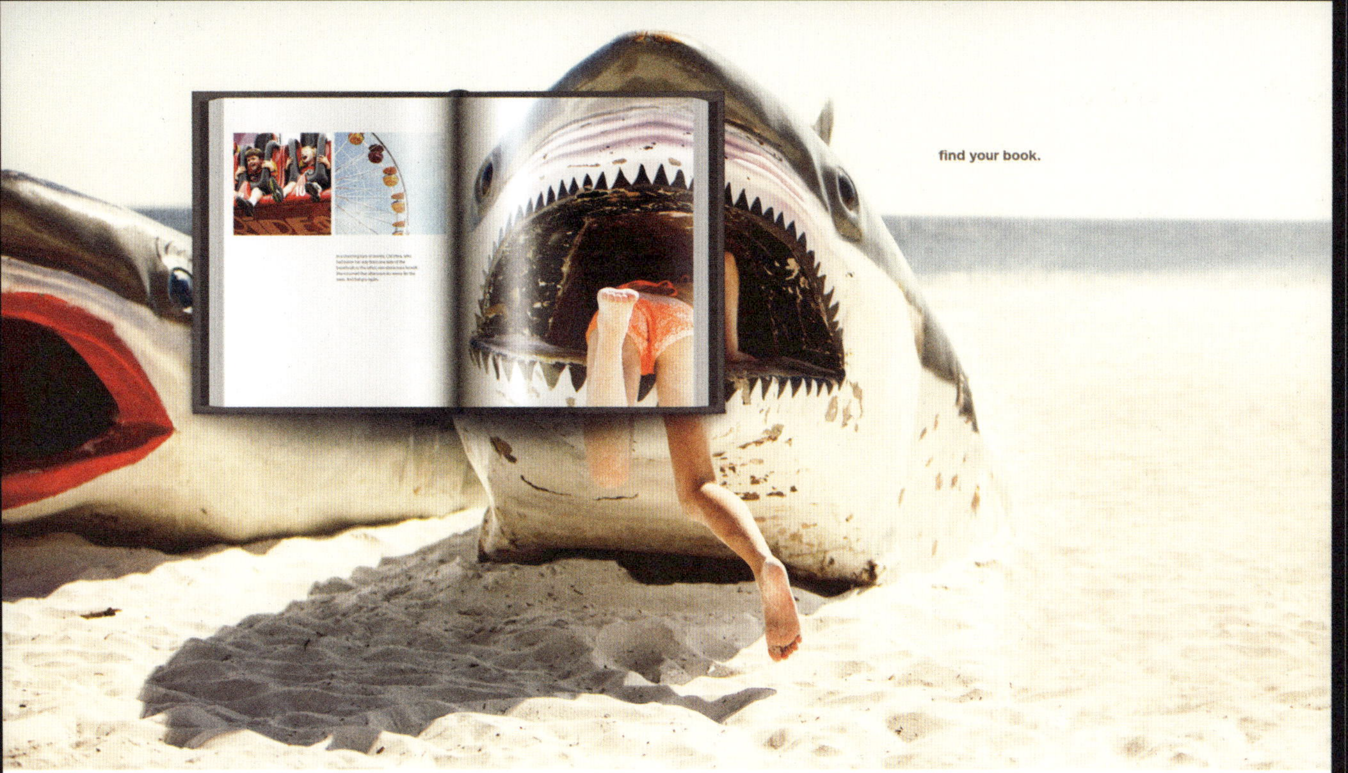

Are we there yet? Are we there yet? Are we there yet? Are we there yet? And then, suddenly, you were there. And the sun shined. And the waves whooshed. And the roller coaster roared. And then all they asked was why do we have to leave?

With a beautiful book, you can always go back.
Make yours at blurb.com

blurb

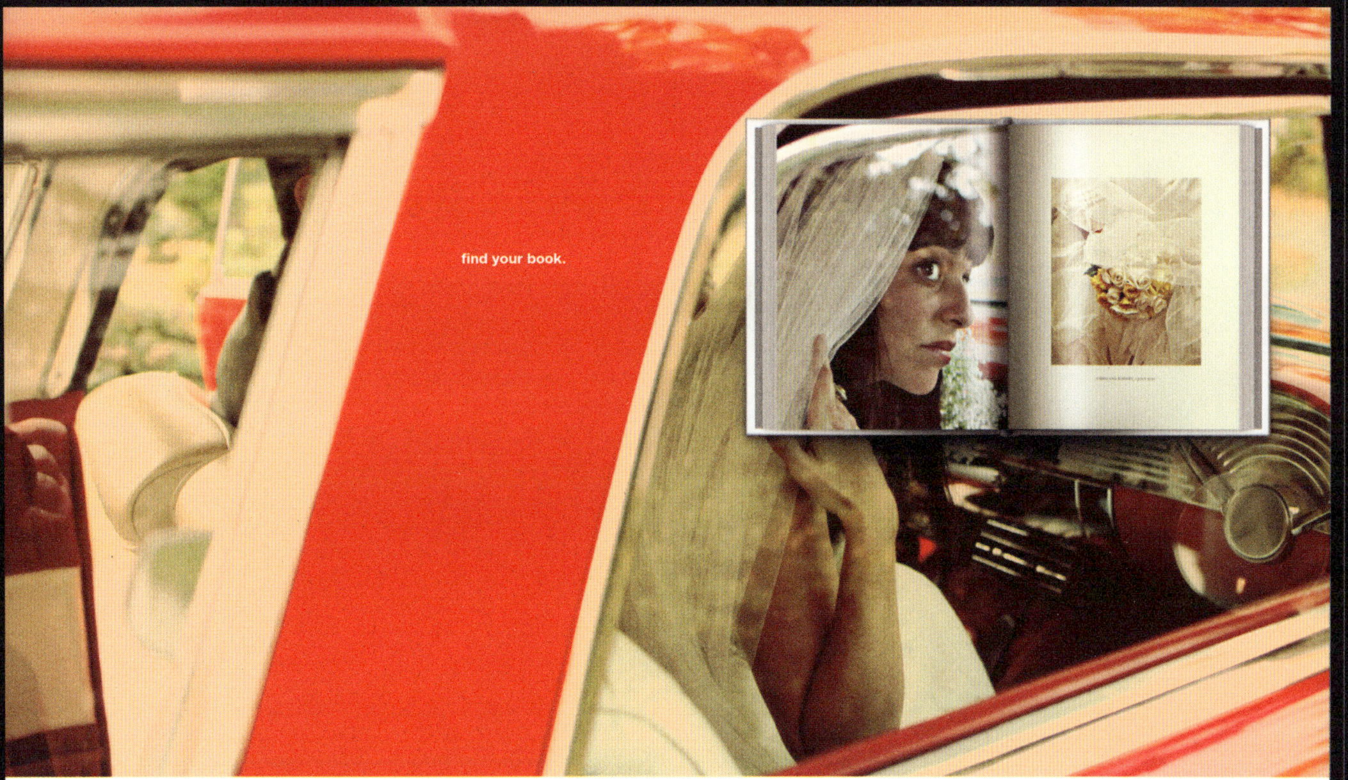

The day you get married is whirlwind. Months of prep and planning are over in an instant. And, before you know it, you're returned to the workaday world. When all you really want is to go back. To take an afternoon that raced by and relive it slowly, frame by frame.

With a beautiful book, you can.
Make yours at blurb.com

blurb

P

PHOTOGRAPHY

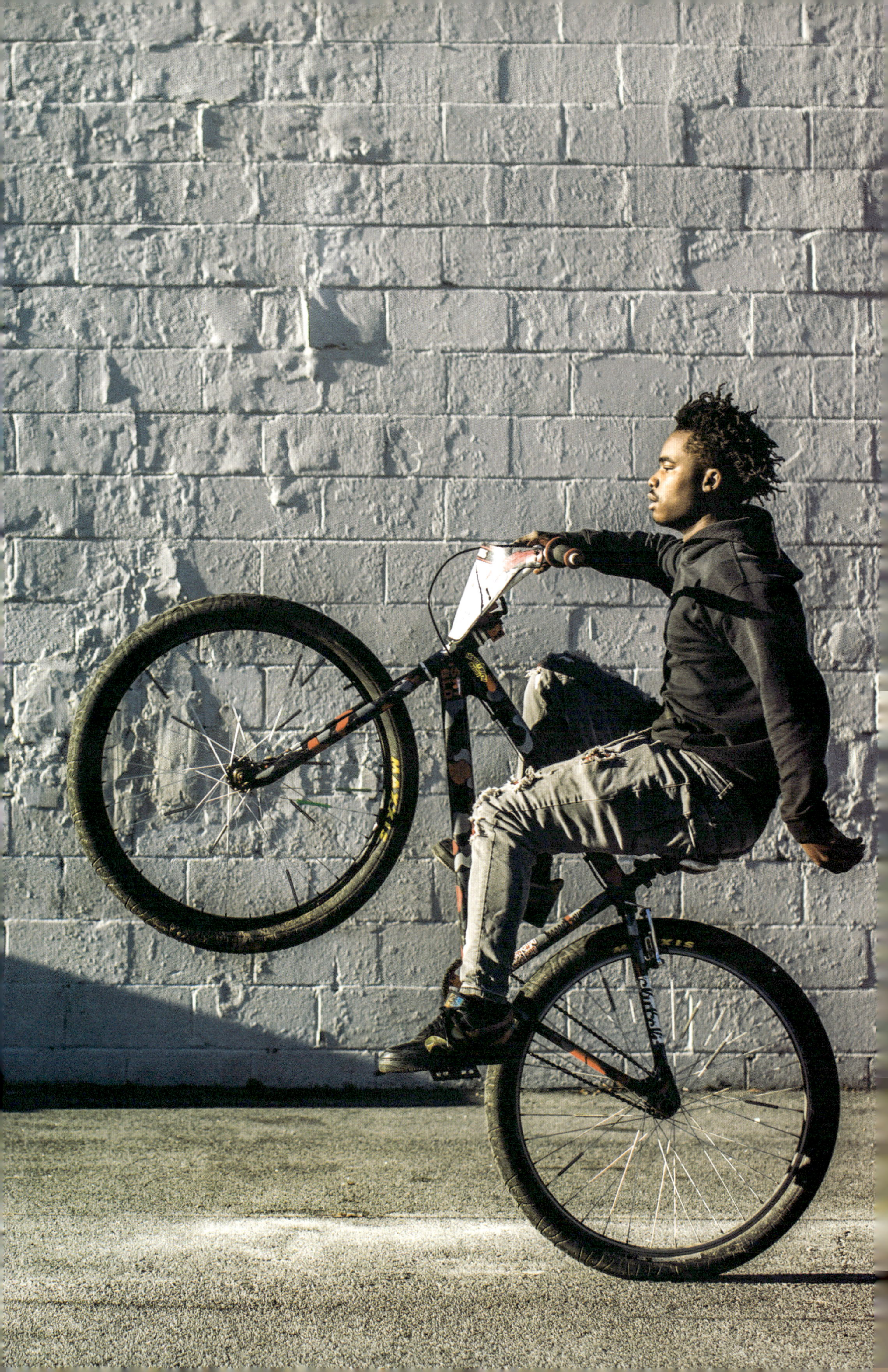
MAXXIS

PAT'S PHOTOGRAPHS ARE LIKE THE MAN HIMSELF: RAW, HUMBLE, HEARTFELT, AND PURE. AS SOON AS YOU SEE ONE OF HIS IMAGES, YOU INSTANTLY KNOW IT'S HIS BEAUTIFUL WORK. PAT IS ONE OF A KIND!

Nick Hall, *Photographer*

PAT MOLNAR HAS THE UNIQUE ABILITY TO AUTHENTICALLY PHOTOGRAPH MOMENTS IN LIFE, TRANSFORMING EACH SCENE INTO AN INTIMATE AND COMPELLING EXPERIENCE.

Darcie Adler, *Founder & Creative Director, The Spin Style Agency LLC*

PATRICK'S WORK EVOKES MY ENVY FOR PHOTOGRAPHERS WHO SEAMLESSLY BLEND COMMERCIAL AND DOCUMENTARY STYLES.

HIS KEEN SENSE OF DESIGN AND METICULOUS ATTENTION TO DETAIL ENTERTAIN MY EYES, WHILE THE CONTENT BROADENS MY AWARENESS.

Hugh Kretschmer, *Photographer*

PATRICK IS TRULY SKILLED AT CAPTURING GENUINE PORTRAITS ACROSS DIVERSE GENRES. WITH HIS GREAT SENSE OF HUMOR, YOU'RE GUARANTEED TO HAVE LOTS OF LAUGHTER ON SET.

Jamie Vance, *Executive Producer, SWEET GENIUS*

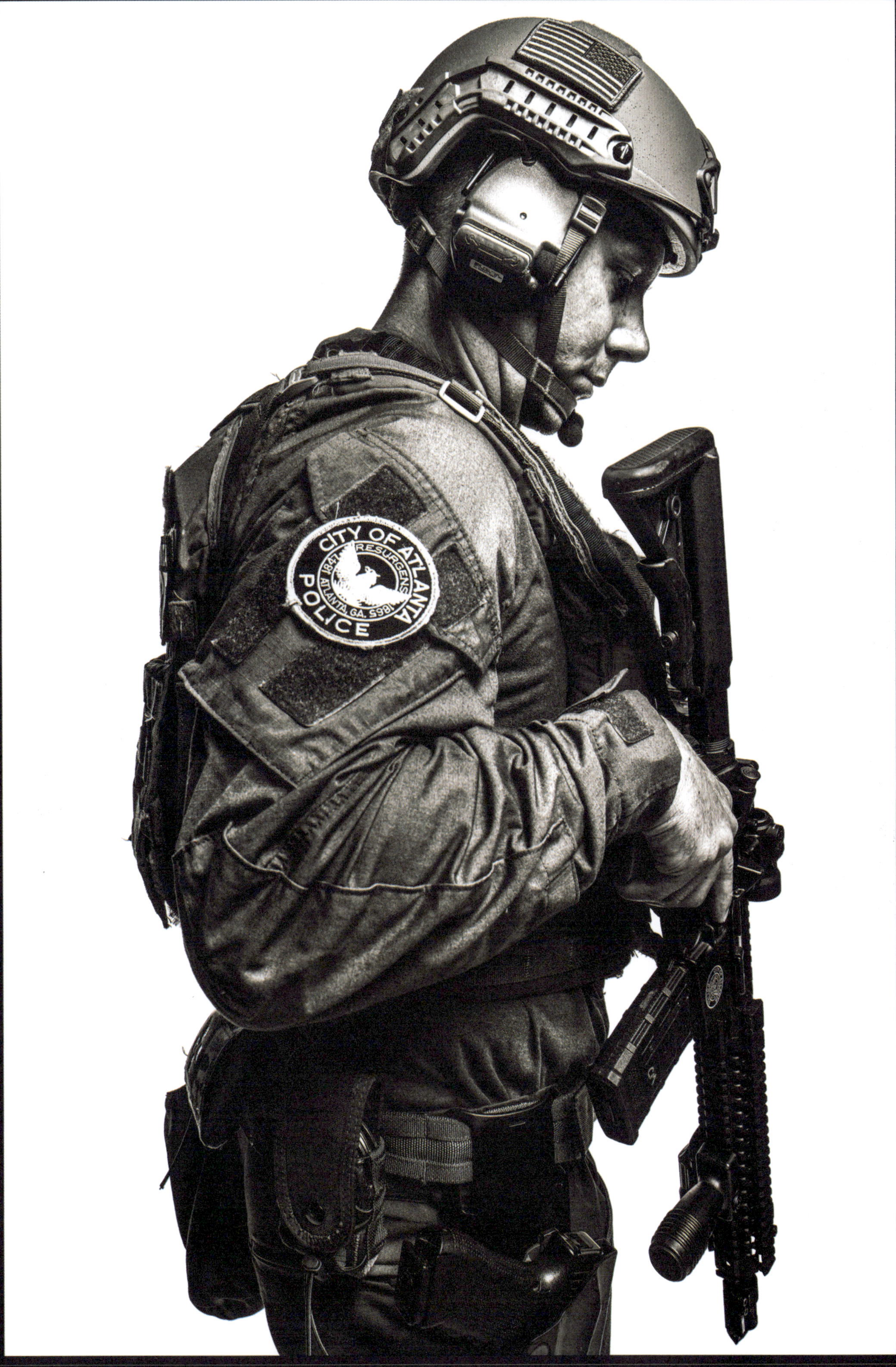

(Page 61) Photographer: Pat Molnar; Client: Personal project; Creative Director: Pat Molnar; Producer: Chilly-O

Introduction by Donna Grossman *Casting Director, Donna Grossman Casting, Inc.*

Patrick Molnar is an extraordinary documentarian and storyteller. With his camera, Patrick captures poignant moments that might otherwise go unnoticed. He allows the viewer to think about what preceded his photos and what followed after the camera's shutter closed. He finds the true heroes in our complicated world. Patrick shows us who they are: heroes in the sky, on the ground, in uniform, holding a gun or carrying a dog on their shoulders, in street clothes on roller skates, seated at a table feeding a baby, or simply playing a guitar. Patrick finds the hero in everyone. As casting directors, it is a privilege to participate in any of Patrick's projects. His trust in our casting process inspires us to help Patrick bring his visions and stories to life.

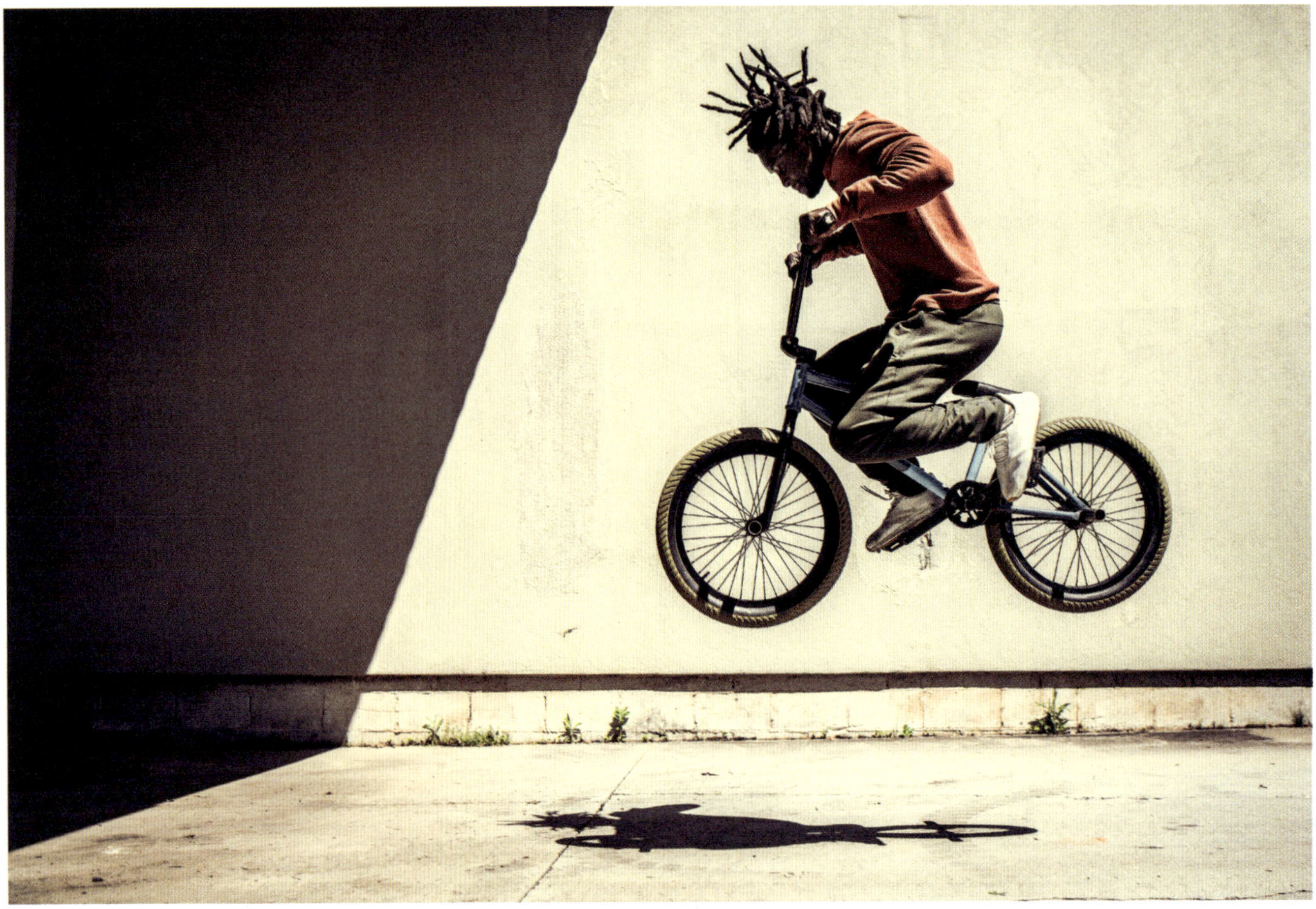

Photographer: Pat Molnar; Client: Personal project; Creative Director: Pat Molnar; Producer: Chilly-O

SHOOT, ASSIST, LISTEN, AND SOAK UP AS MUCH AS POSSIBLE. SHOOT WHAT YOU LOVE, NOT WHAT YOU THINK YOU SHOULD SHOOT.

Patrick Molnar, *Photographer, Patrick Molnar Photography Inc.*

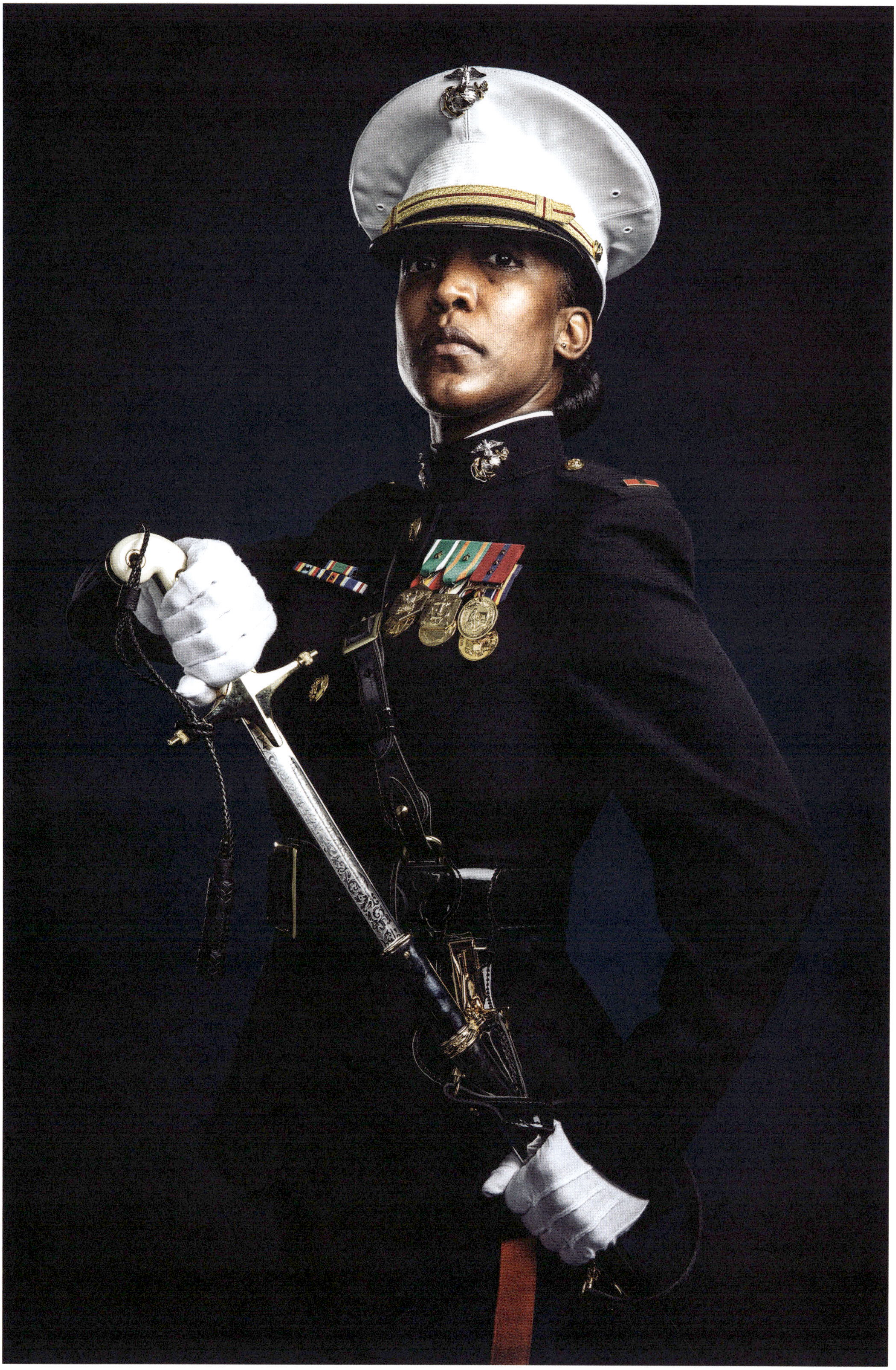

Photographer: Pat Molnar; Client: USMC; Agency: Wunderman Thompson/VML; Creative Director: Alan Whitley; Art Producer: Kaila Hairston; Producer: John Cogan/Goodnoise

What inspired or motivated you in your career?
My aunt Betsy is a photographer. I saw what she did when I was a kid and thought it was the coolest thing ever.

What is your work philosophy?
Don't get too comfortable.

Who is or was your greatest mentor?
My grandmother, Mary Ratcliffe. She was a badass.

What is it about photography that you are most passionate about?
It is recording a beat of time that will never happen the same way again, ever.

What is your favorite type of photograph to take?
The best shoots have the longest safety briefs.

Much of your work is portraiture or has people in it. What draws you to photographing others?
Human beings are unique, weird, and wonderful.

What is a recent photographic project of yours that you're proud of?
I am currently working on a personal series here in Atlanta with some of the people who make the city what it is. It has been a lot of fun, and I have made some great friends.

What is the most difficult challenge you've overcome to reach your current position?
Being my own worst critic.

Who were some of your most significant past influences?
Albert Watson, Richard Avedon, Irving Penn, and Aretha Franklin.

Who among your contemporaries today do you most admire?
Albert Watson, although I definitely would not qualify as a contemporary.

What would be your dream assignment?
I have always wanted to photograph Chuck D from Public Enemy.

Who have been some of your favorite people or clients you have worked with?
I have been lucky enough to work with some of the most brilliant folks out there—creative directors, copywriters, producers, cinematographers, editors, etc. It is incredible just to be in the same room with them. There are way too many to name.

What are the most important ingredients you require from a client to work successfully?
Collaboration, trust, a little creative freedom... and a nice budget never hurt anyone.

You've done much work with the military, like the USMC and the Army. How did you get to take photos of them?
Over the years, we have shot recruiting campaigns for the USMC, the Army, and Homeland Security. It has been a blast and some of my favorite work. It is really hard to have a bad day when you are hanging out of a helicopter or blowing things up.

How do you receive commissions, and what steps do you take to fulfill them?
The ad agency working on the project usually contacts my agents. We then bring in the appropriate production company and start executing the concepts.

You've done a lot of work for companies like Toyota and Mastercard. What is it like shooting for advertising?
You get to go to work with the coolest people in the world, and you get to take pictures all day in great locations. It doesn't suck.

Other than photography, you also do motion work. How did you start doing motion work, and how does your photography influence it?
Honestly... back in 2003, somebody said, "You should do film." So I linked up with a great DP, and we went out and shot a few projects on 35mm. I see it the same as stills, just with more ways to tell a story.

What is your greatest professional achievement?
Working while raising two kids.

What is the greatest satisfaction you get from your work?
Wrapping up a long day at work and seeing clients, the agency, and crew happy.

What part of your work is the most demanding, considering your position?
Sprinting in body armor in the middle of August.

What professional goals do you still have for yourself?
To keep going, learning, and getting better.

What advice do you have for students starting out today?
Shoot, assist, listen, and soak up as much as possible. Shoot what you love, not what you think you should shoot.

What interests do you have outside of your work?
I spend time with my kids, my brilliant architect fiance, and her son, fishing, running, and trying to make better BBQ than my dad.

What do you value most?
My family and friends.

What would you change if you had to do it all over again?
Absolutely nothing.

Where do you seek inspiration?
Everywhere and anywhere I can.

How do you define success?
Being happy with who you are and what you do.

Where do you see yourself in the future?
Fishing and a nap.

Patrick Molnar www.patmolnar.com
See his Graphis Master Portfolio at graphis.com.

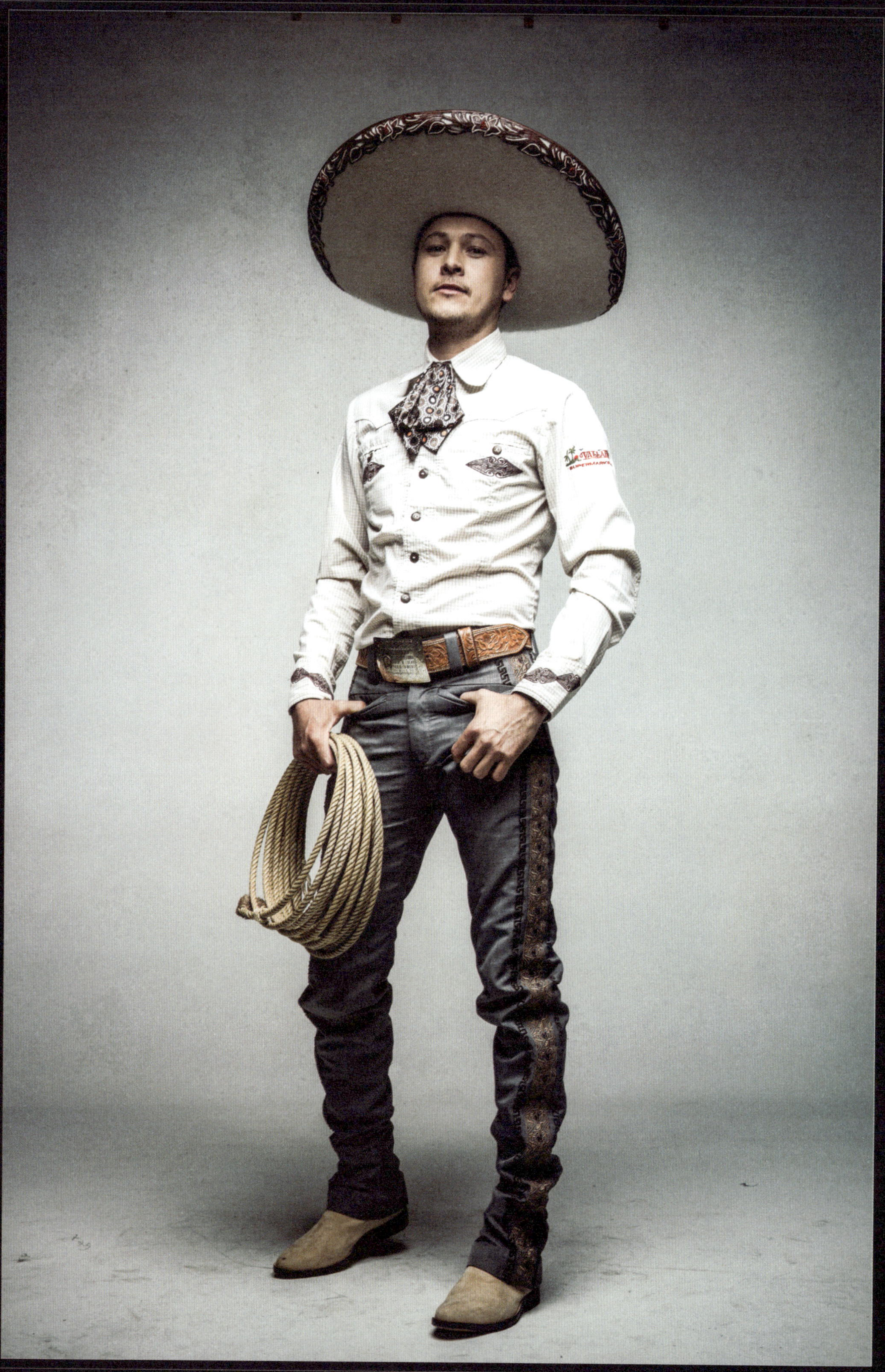

Photographer: Pat Molnar; Client: Covered California; Agency: Weber Shandwick; Creative Directors: John Avery, Peter Sanchez, Kim Beylin, Juan Benitez
Art Producer: Amy Rivera; Producer: John Noonan/Gravy Productions

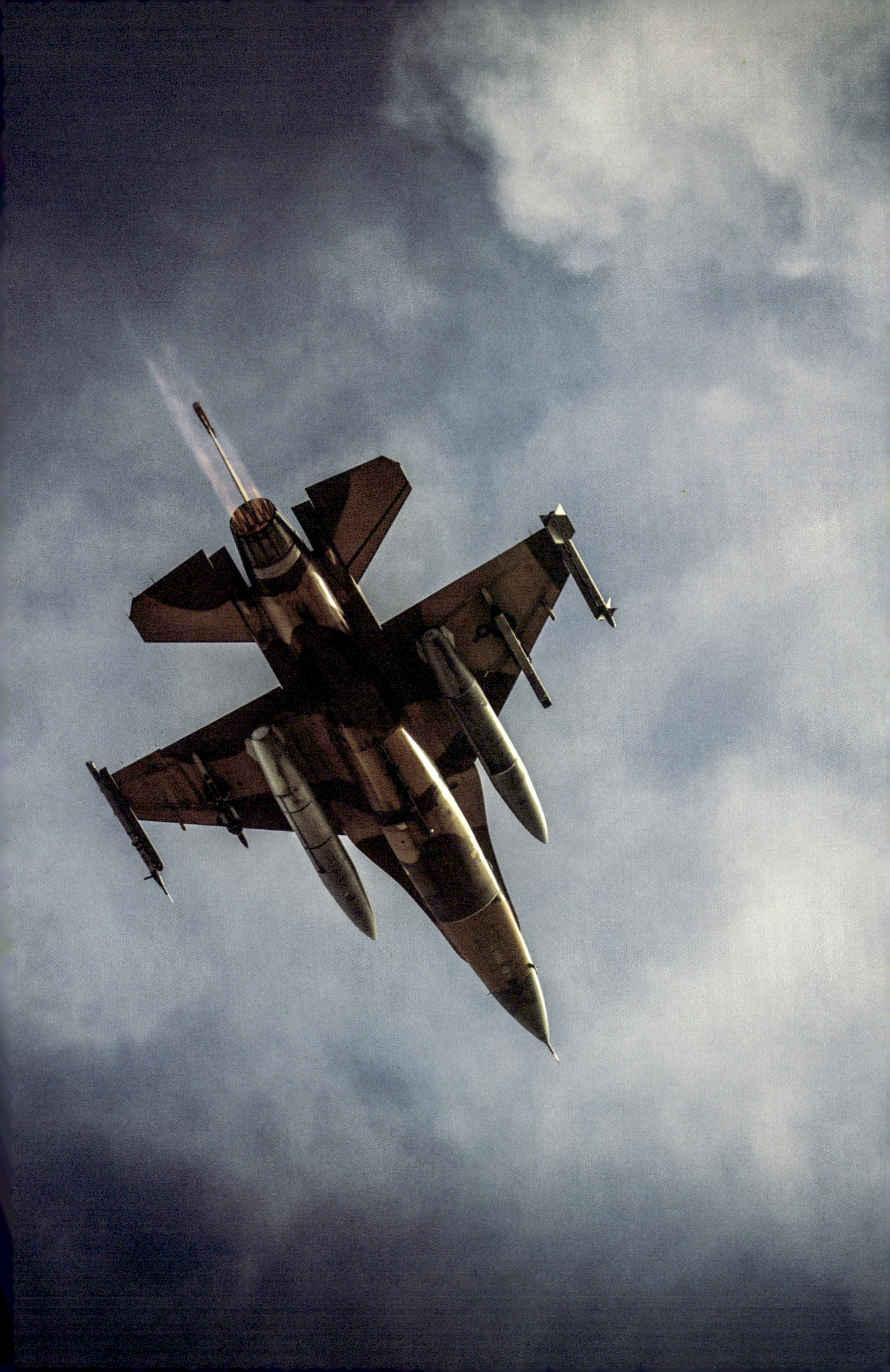

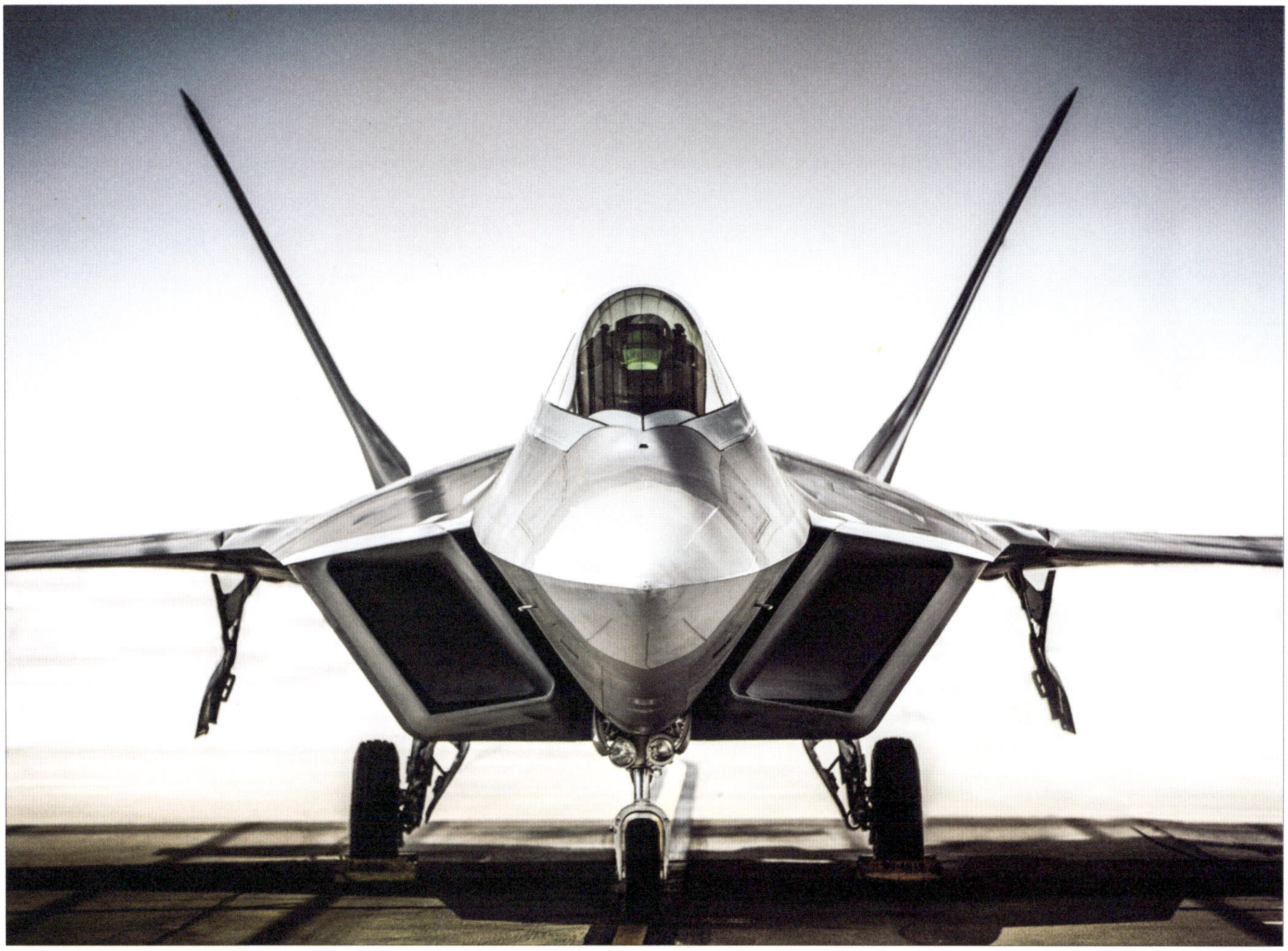

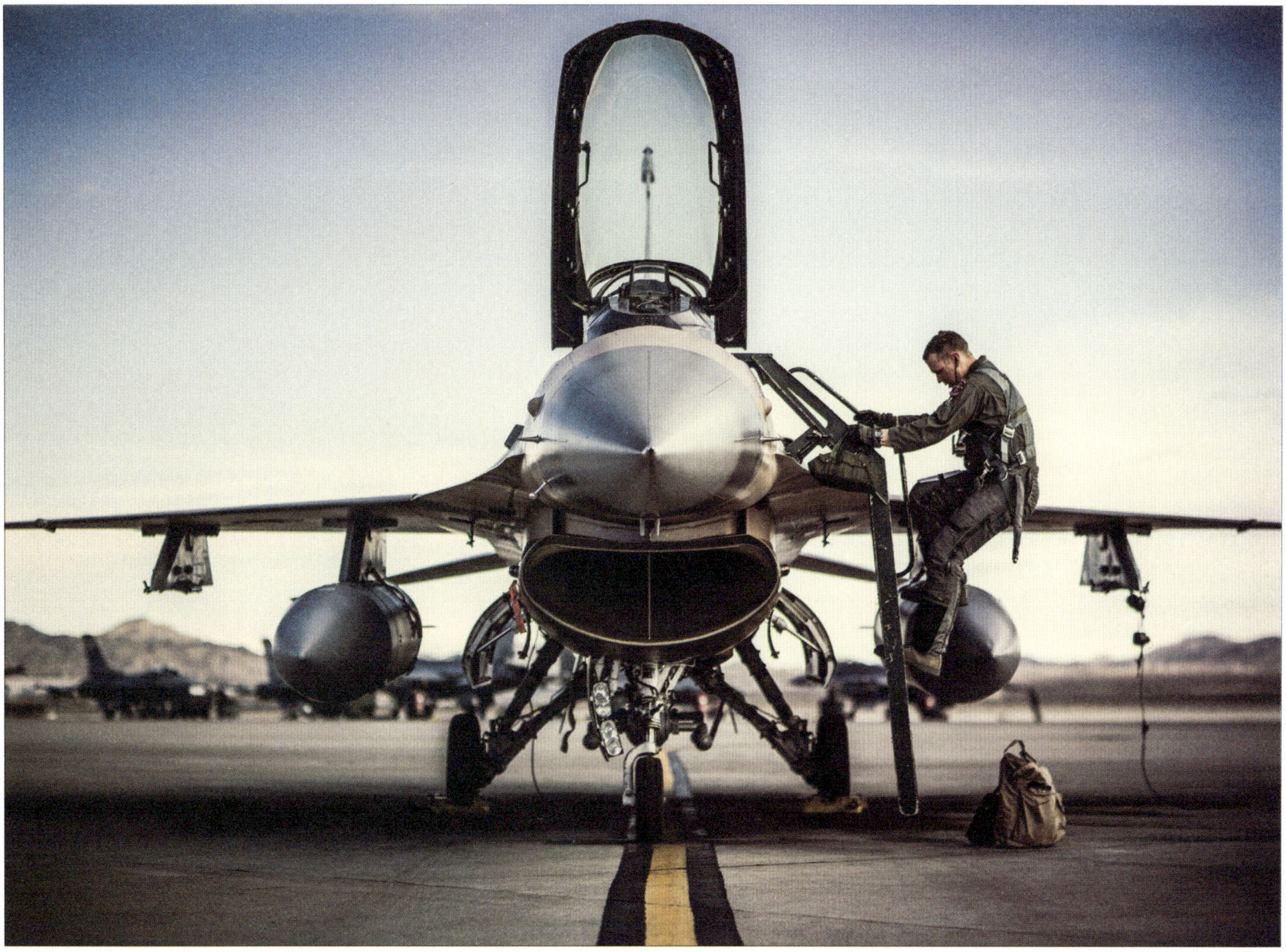

(This spread) Photographer: Pat Molnar; Client: United States Air Force; Creative Director: Chris Vasquez; Producer: John Noonan/Gravy Productions

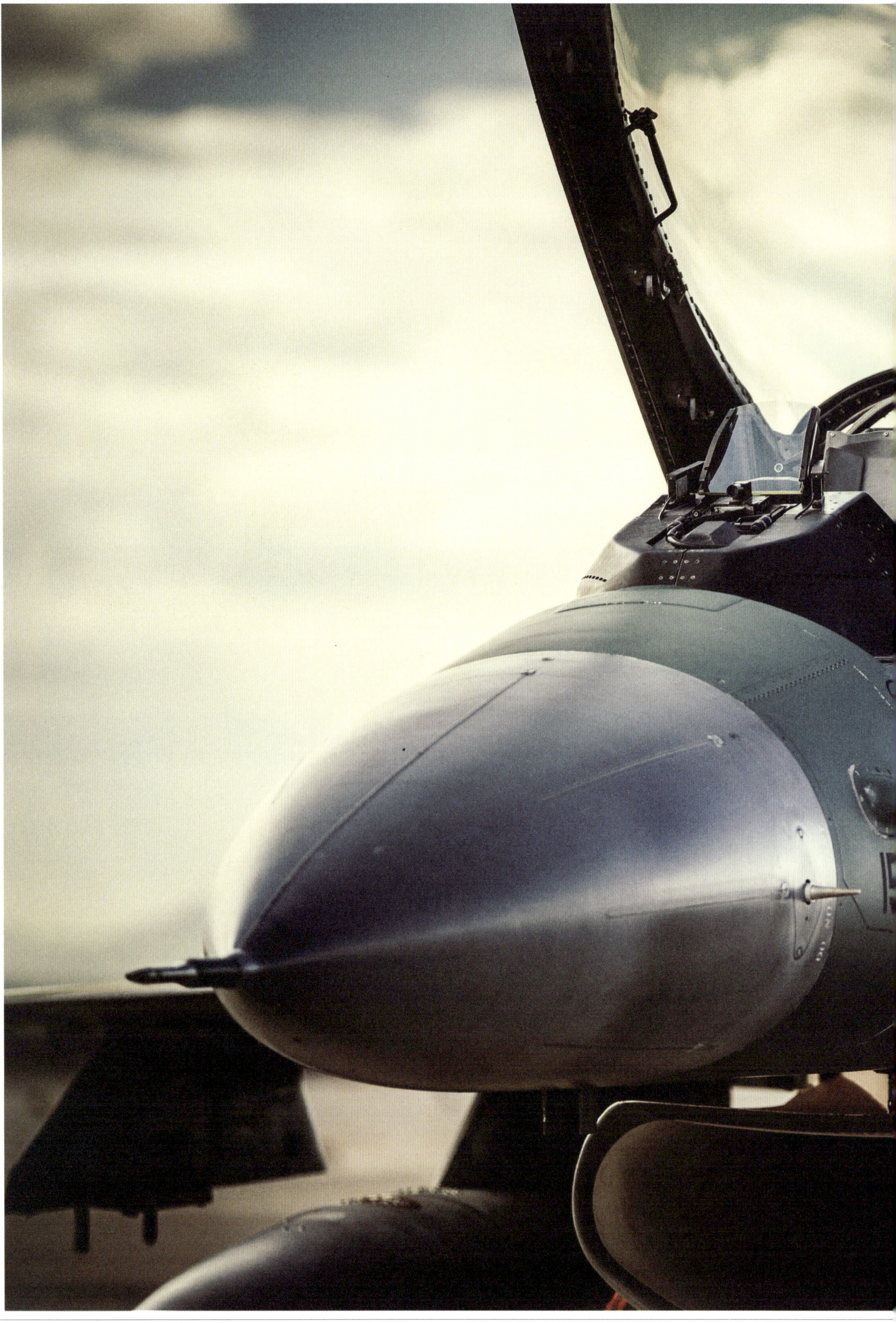

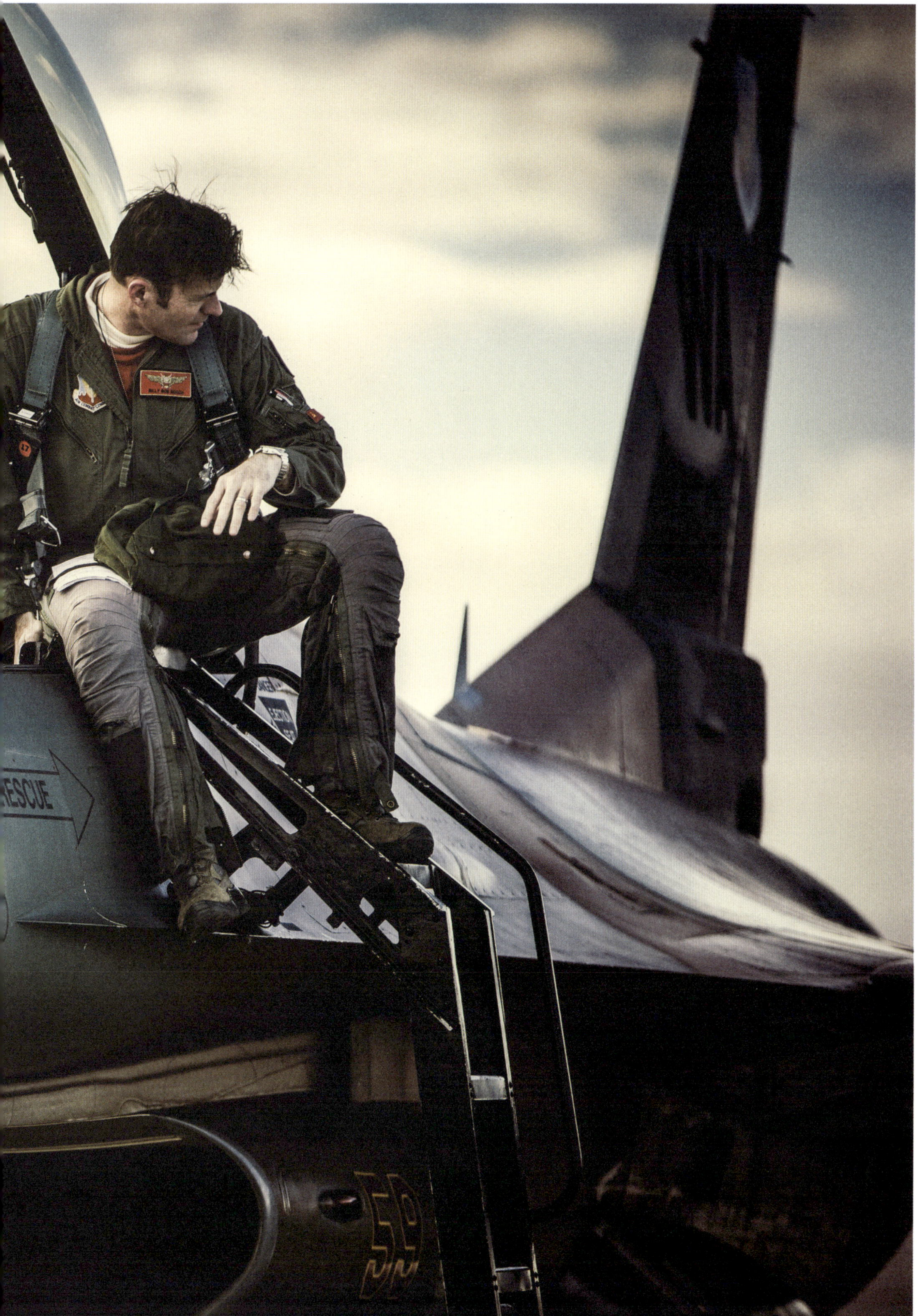

Photographer: Pat Molnar; Client: United States Air Force; Creative Director: Chris Vasquez; Producer: John Noonan/Gravy Productions

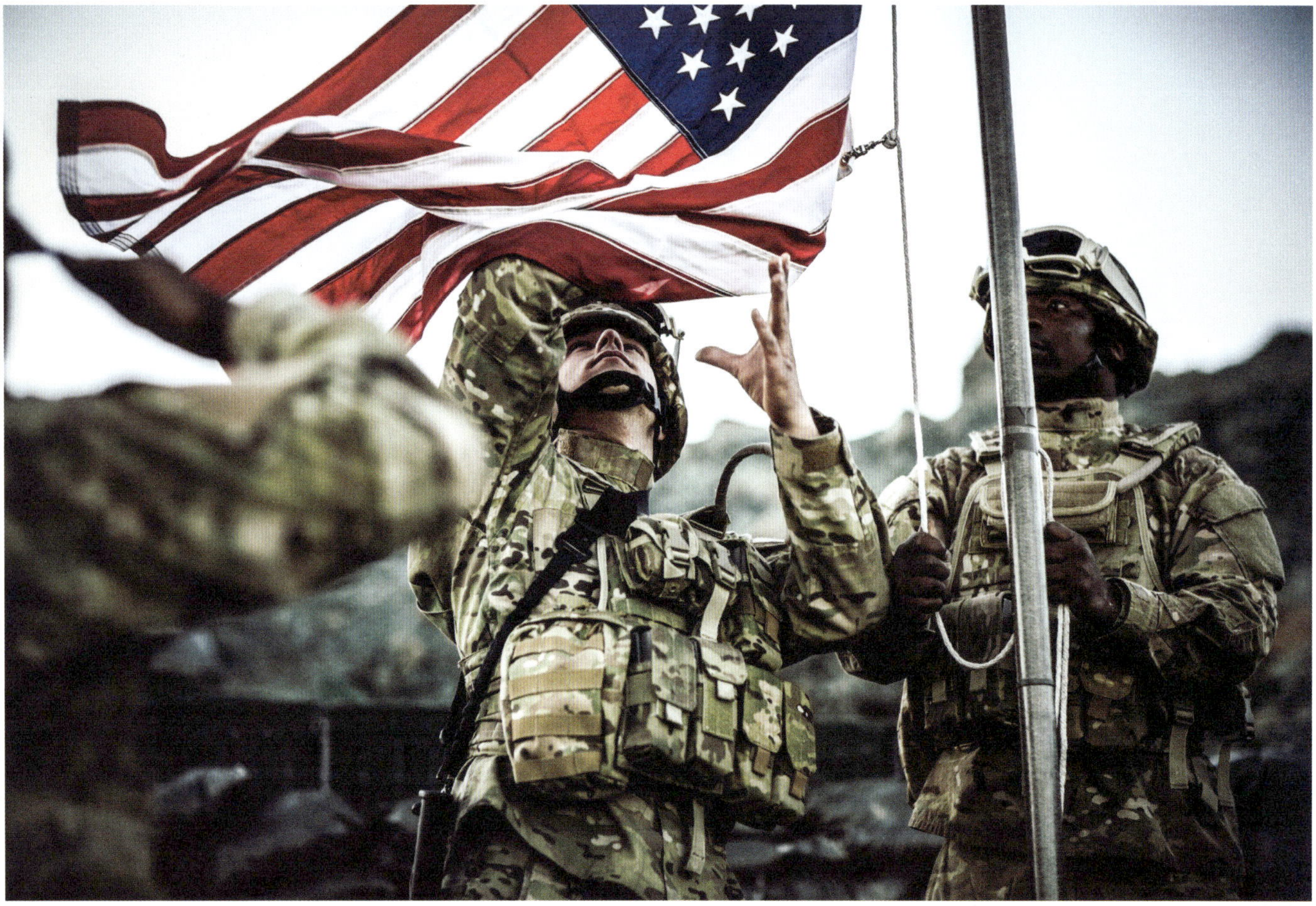

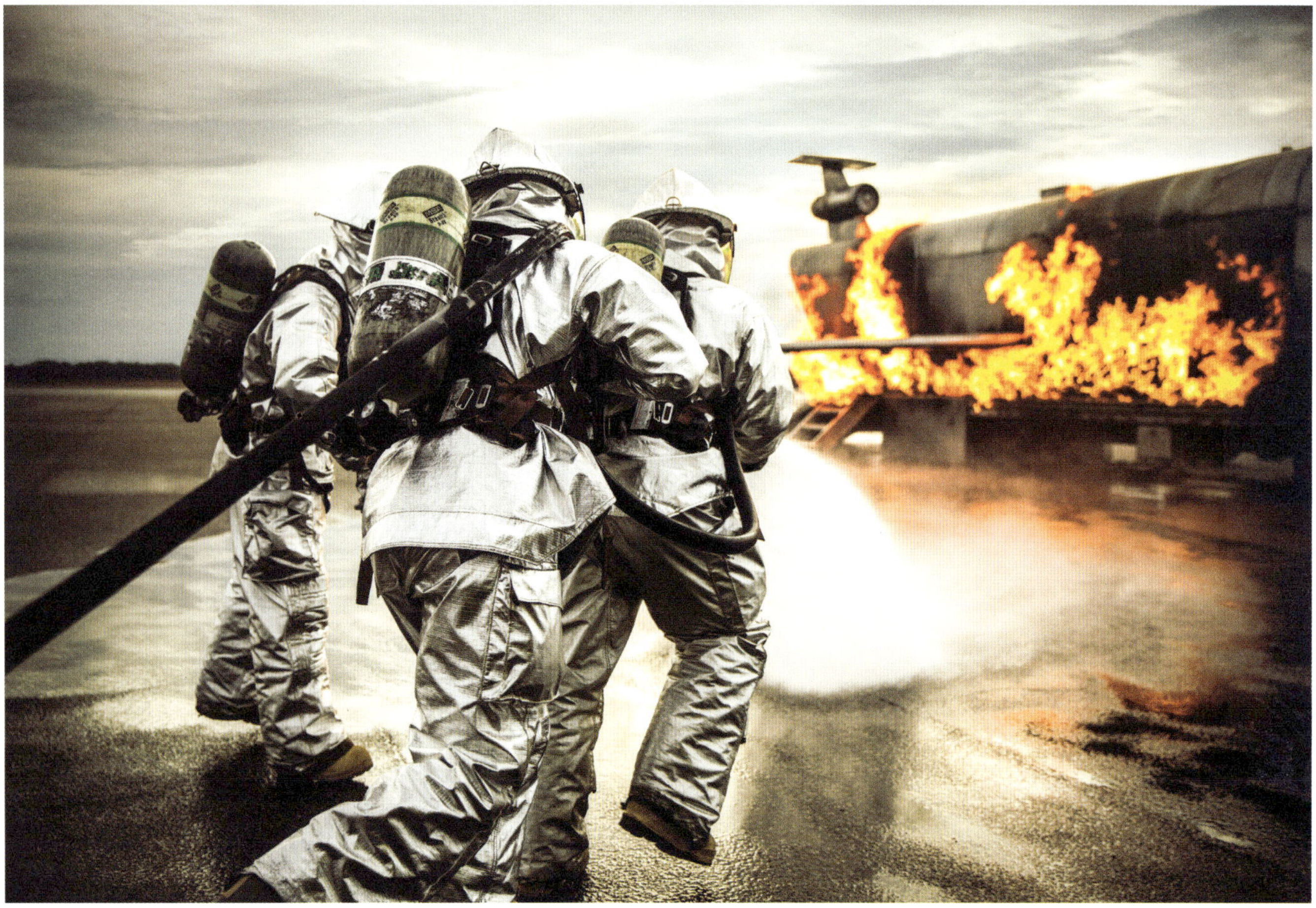

(Top) Photographer: Pat Molnar; Client: USAA; Agency: Campbell Ewald/Detroit; Art Producer: Tat Luneva-Evenchik
Creative Directors: Doug Blanchard, Al Hazen; Producer: John Noonan/Gravy Productions
(Bottom) Photographer: Pat Molnar; Client: USMC; Agency: Wunderman Thompson; Art Producer: Angie Trewhitt; Creative Director: Pedro Gonzalez

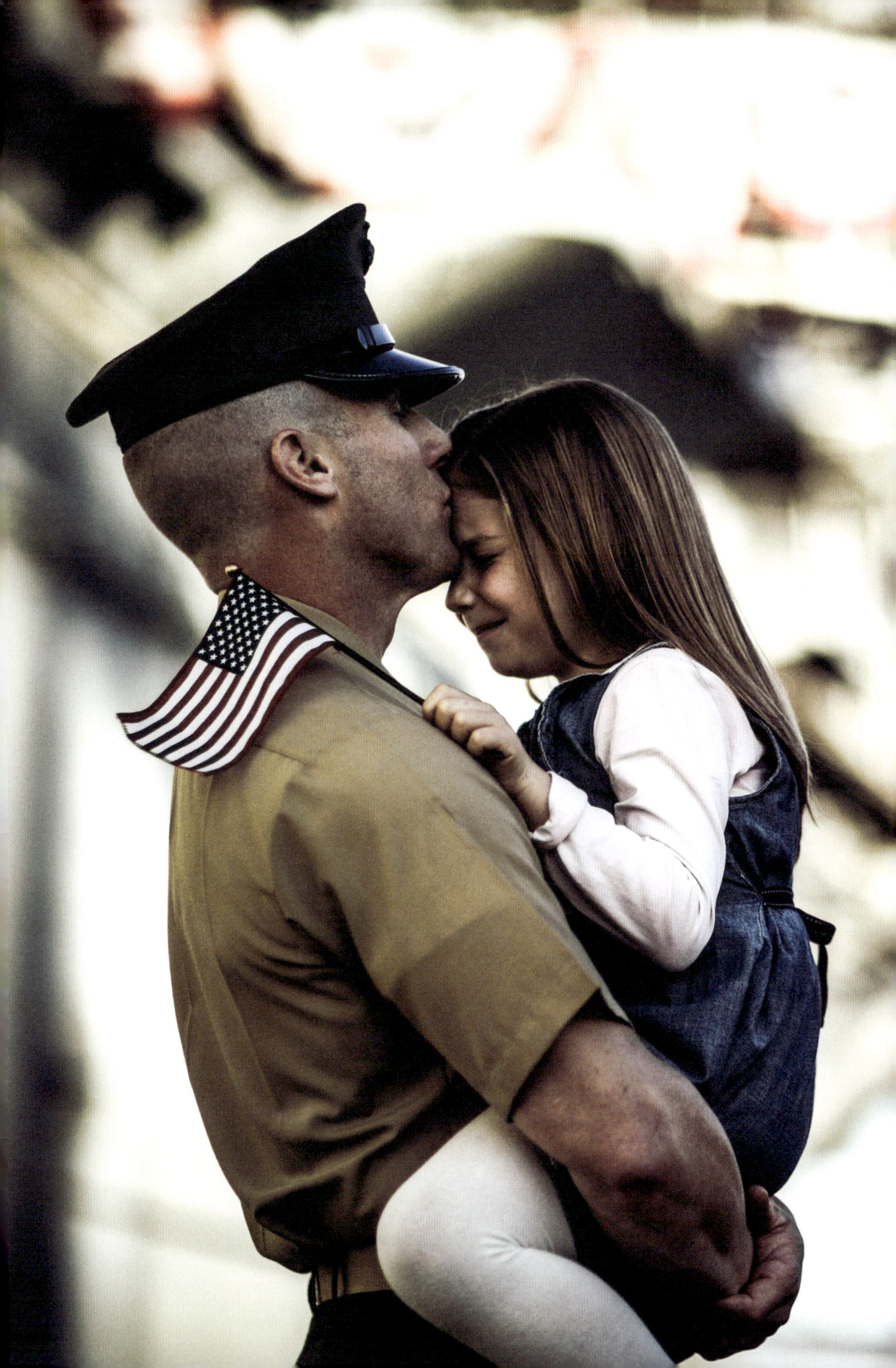

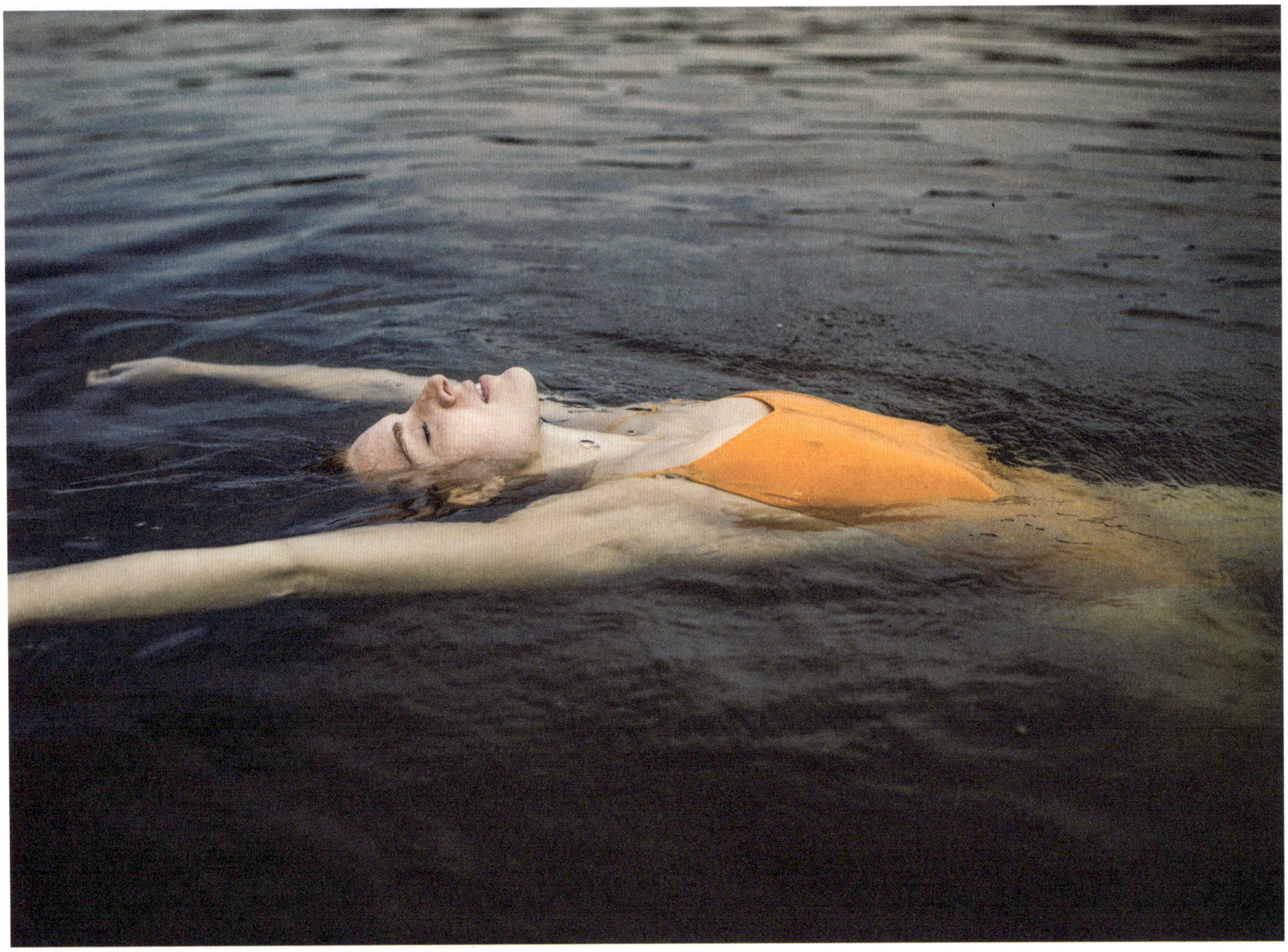

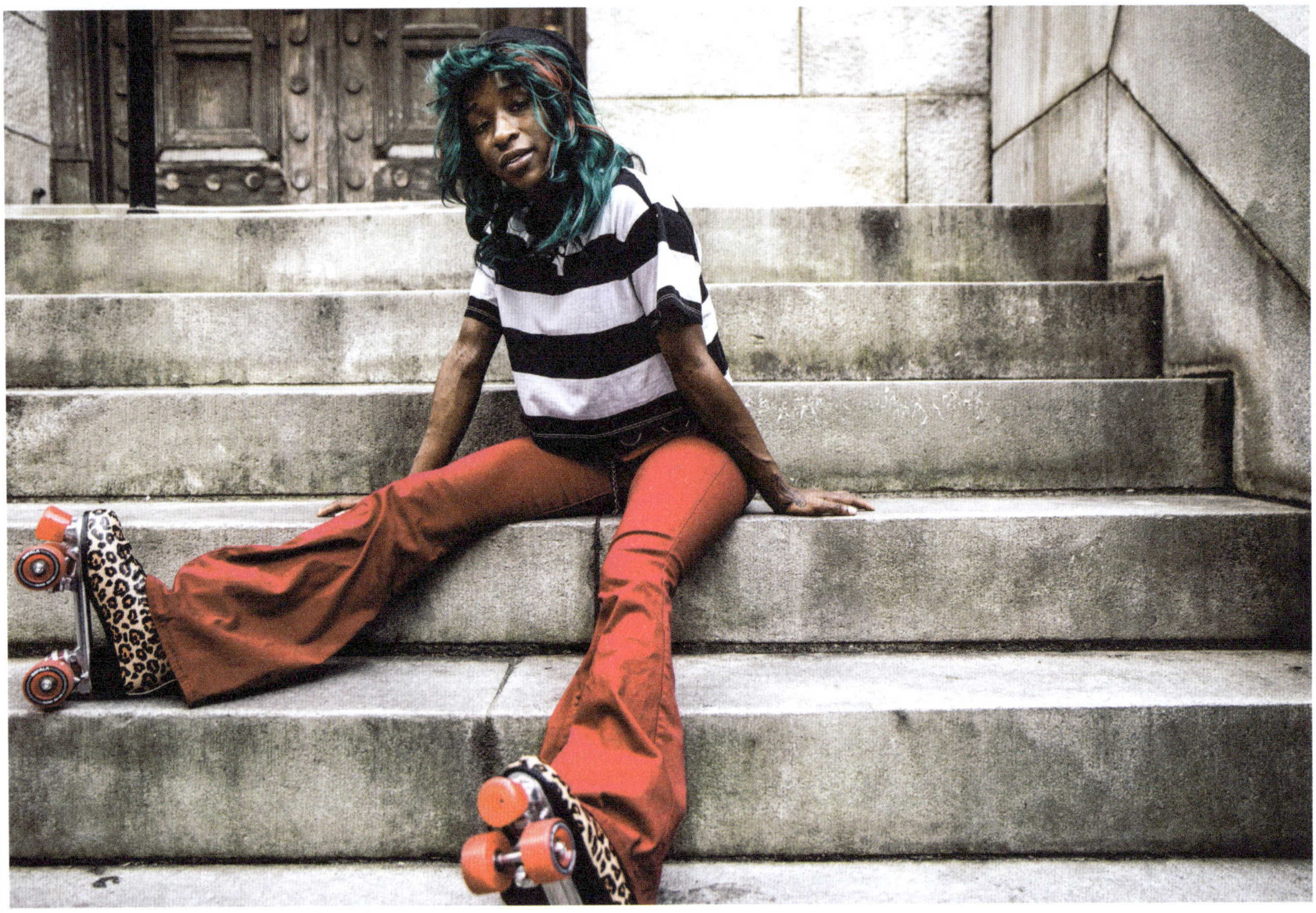

(Top) Photographer: Pat Molnar; Client: Personal project; Creative Director: Pat Molnar
(Bottom) Photographer: Pat Molnar; Client: Personal project; Creative Director: Pat Molnar; Producer: Chilly-O

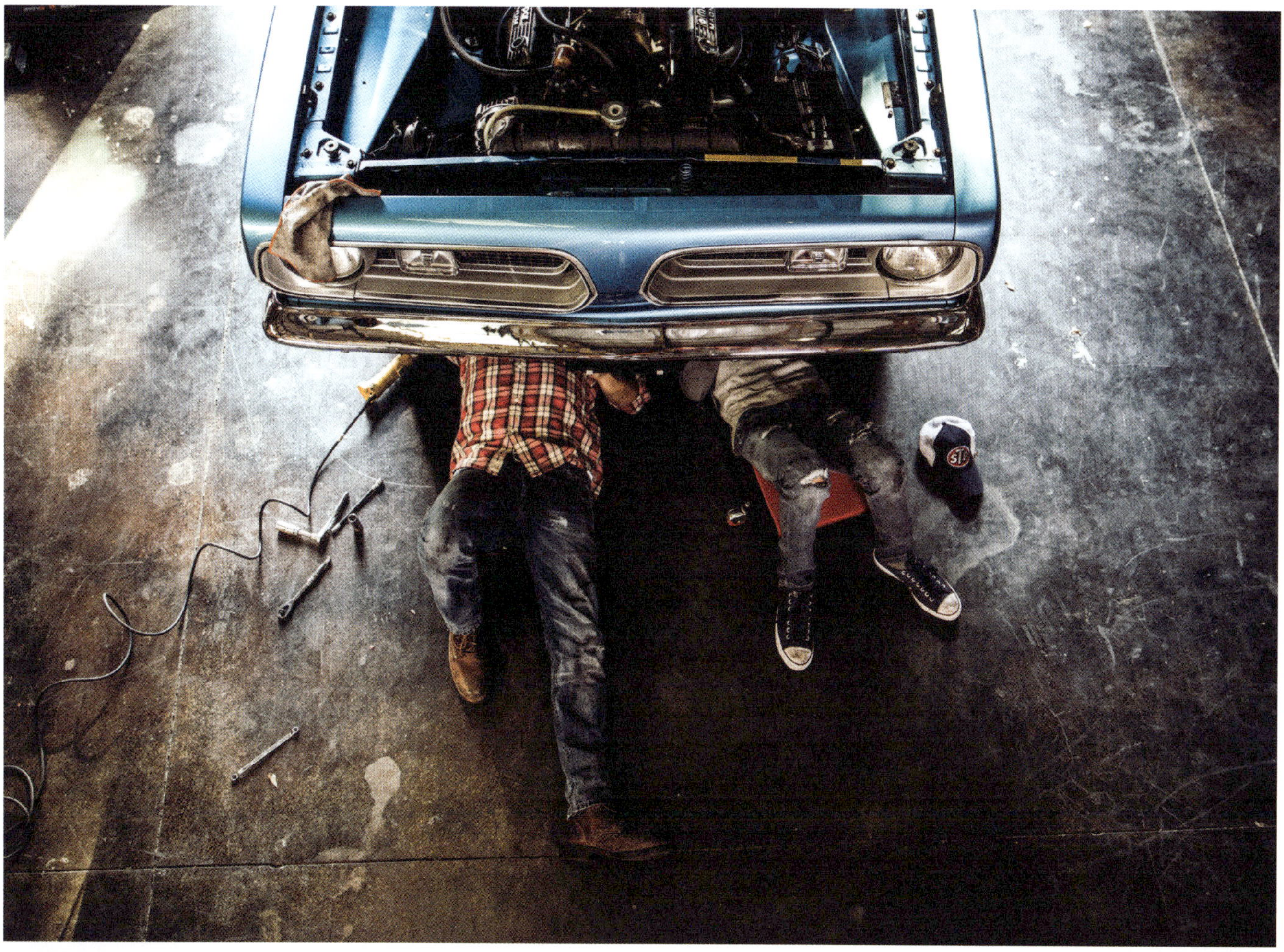

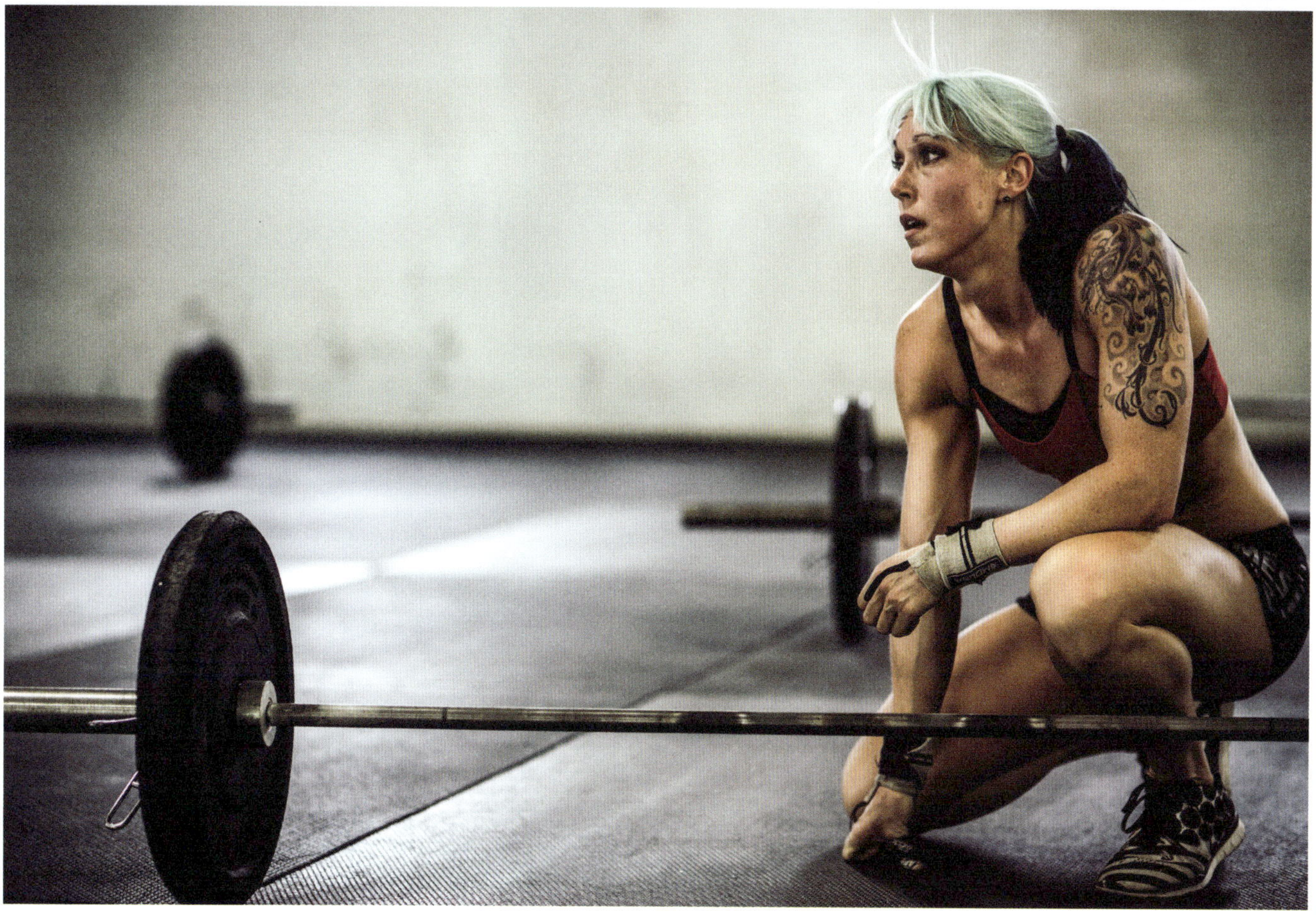

(Top) Photographer: Pat Molnar; Client: STP; Agency: Merkley + Partners; Creative Director: Kirk Mosel; Art Producer: Bev Don; Producer: Amanda Bertany
(Bottom) Photographer: Pat Molnar; Client: Personal project; Creative Director: Pat Molnar

Lindsey Drennan: Creating What Doesn't Exist

LINDSEY IS THAT BEAUTIFUL COMBINATION OF TALENT, CREATIVITY, HARD WORK, AND FUN. FOR THAT REASON, I LOOK FORWARD TO EVERY JOB I WORK WITH HER.

Ryan Francoz, *Photographer*

LINDSEY GOES THE DISTANCE TO SEE HER PEOPLE SUCCEED, BOTH FIGURATIVELY AND LITERALLY. YOU COULDN'T HAVE A BETTER PERSON IN YOUR CORNER.

Danielle Spencer, *Chief Executive Officer & Marketing Strategist, SCA*

WORKING WITH LINDSEY IS A JOY; HER CREATIVITY, PROFESSIONALISM, AND WARMTH ENSURE A STRESS-FREE EXPERIENCE, RESULTING IN STUNNING, STORY-TELLING IMAGES.

Suzanne Campos, *Prop Stylist, P1M*

I'VE NEVER MET A PHOTOGRAPHER WITH SUCH A DEFINED COLOR VISION, AND THE WAY SHE WALKS CLIENTS FLUIDLY THROUGH HER THOUGHT PROCESS AND WORKFLOW IS SECOND TO NONE!

Serge Kerbel, *Creative Director & Stylist, Plutino Group*

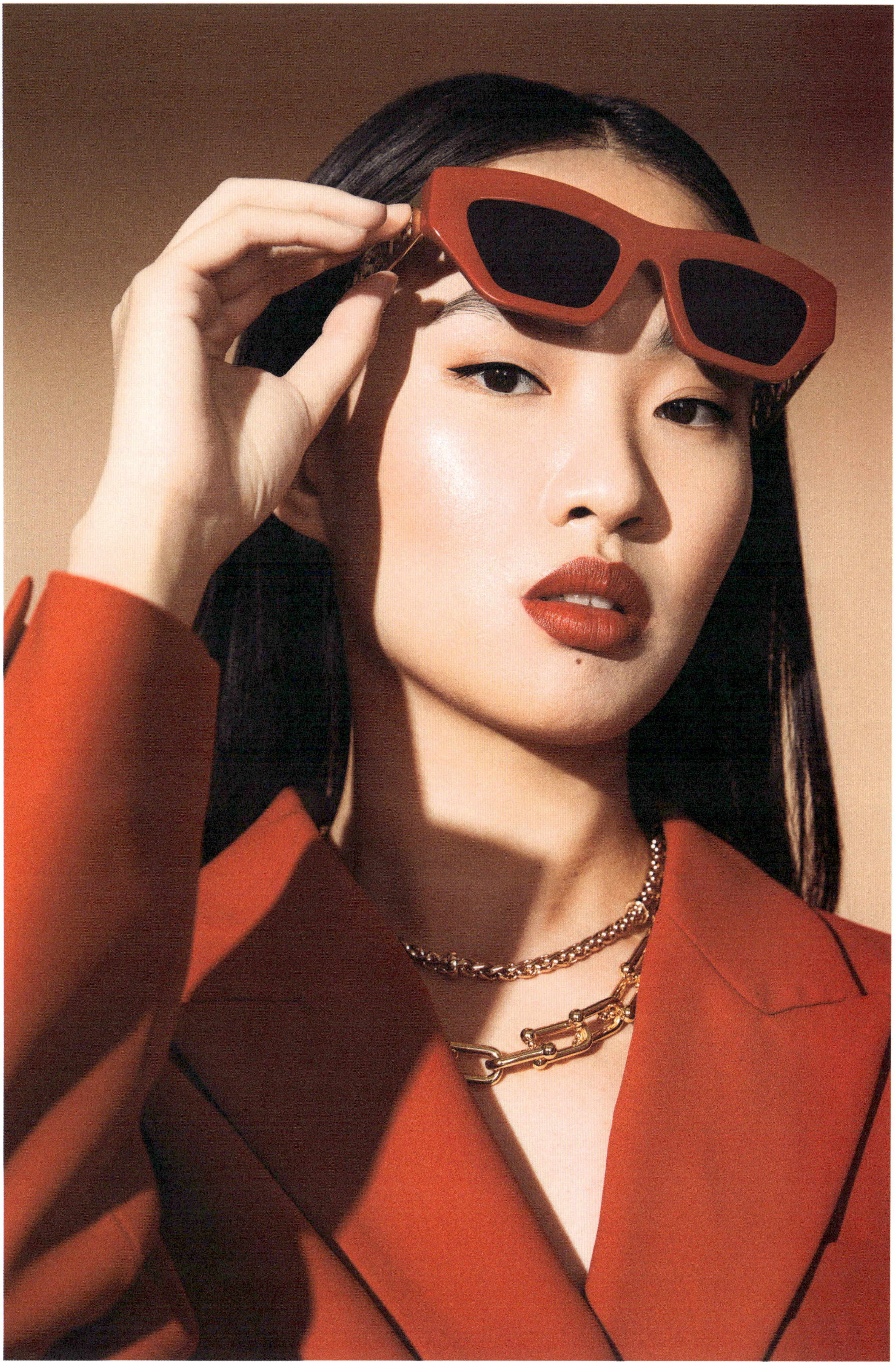

Title & Year: Regal Lips, 2023; Photography: Lindsey Drennan represented by Coup&Co., Self-promotion; Model: Julie F. represented by Spot 6 Management Makeup & Hair: Kim Creton represented by Plutino Group; Wardrobe Styling: Neil Franklyn represented by Judy Inc.; Studio: Sorry Studio

Introduction by **Ashley Barth** *Artist Rep & Producer, Coup&Co.*

Lindsey is a visionary artist with an exceptional eye for what's trending and relevant. Her extensive knowledge of the beauty industry and incredible drive and talent consistently transform creative ideas into realities. She's excellent as a soundboard for new ideas, and stylists love collaborating on her projects because they're always fresh. Lindsey's passion and expertise make her an invaluable asset, while her warm and collaborative nature makes her an absolute pleasure to work with! Having had her with Coup for two years, we believe Lindsey is an asset to our roster, consistently bringing innovation and excellence to every project.

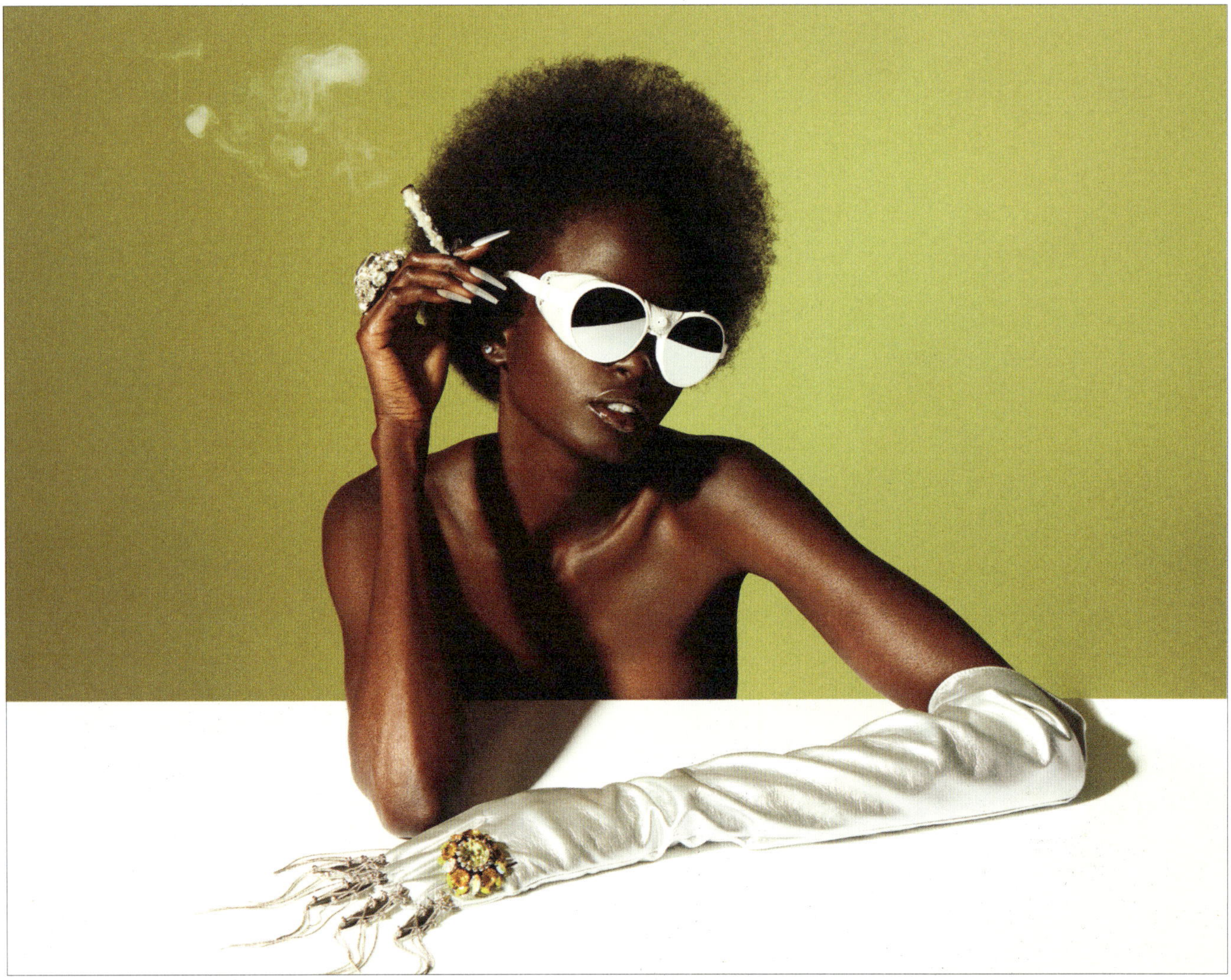

Title & Year: Smoke Show, 2023; Photography: Lindsey Drennan represented by Coup&Co., Self-promotion; Model: Akoy represented by Spot 6 Management Makeup & Hair: Alanna Fennell represented by Plutino Group; Wardrobe Styling: Rodney Smith represented by Plutino Group; Studio: Album Studios

EXPERIENCE HAS TAUGHT ME THAT PUSHING BOUNDARIES IS KEY—NO GOAL IS OUT OF REACH WHEN YOU KEEP MOVING FORWARD.

Lindsey Drennan, *Photographer & Director, Lindsey Drennan Photography*

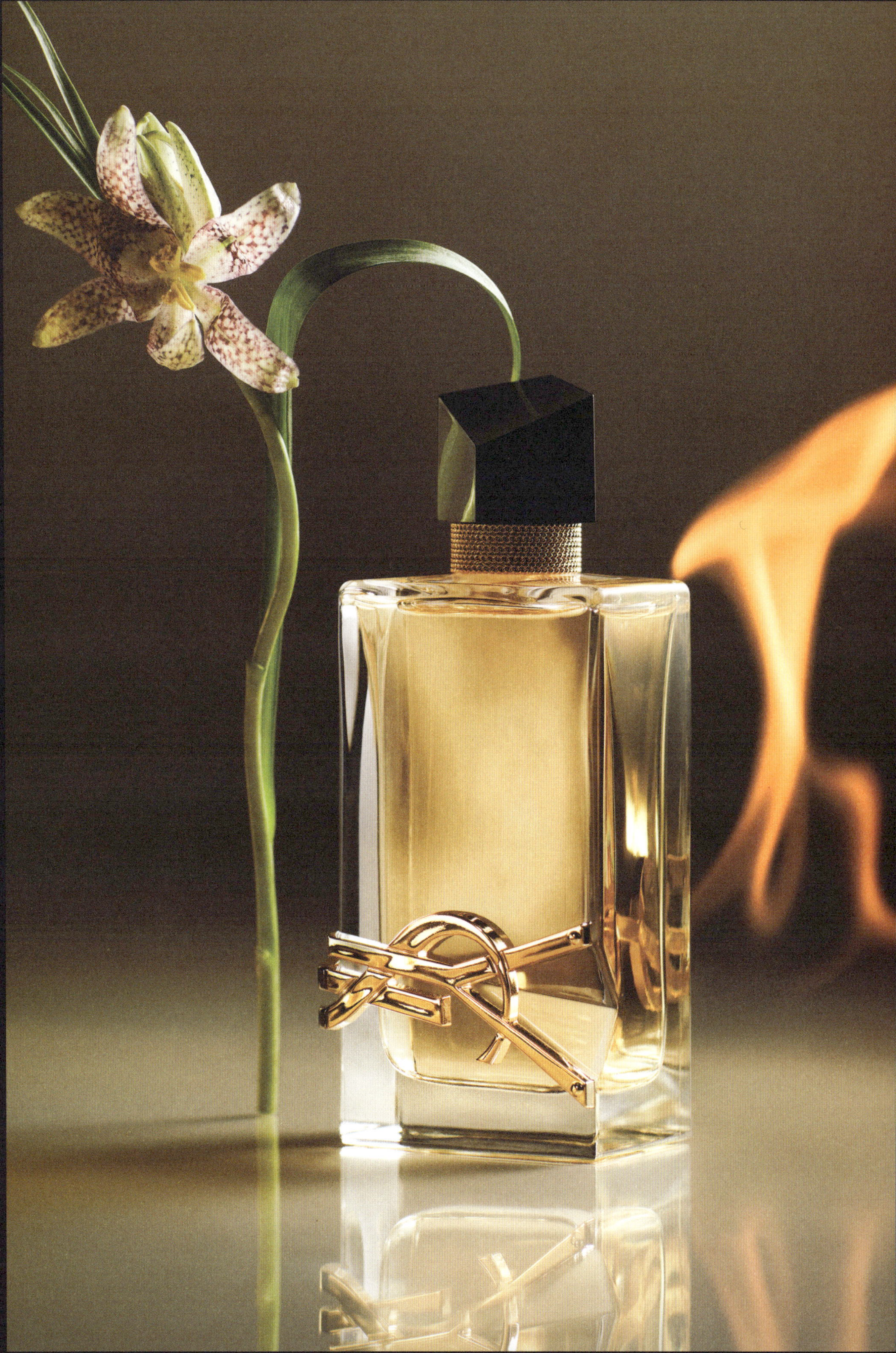

Title & Year: Fragrance On Fire, 2023; Photography: Lindsey Drennan represented by Coup&Co., Self-promotion
Prop Styling: Alanna Davey represented by Cadre Artist Management

What has inspired or motivated you in your career?
Since childhood, I've been driven by a deep passion for fashion and beauty. One of my earliest memories was watching *Fashion Television* hosted by Jeanne Beker with my mom—the show was always on in the background of our home. It showcased the top fashion houses of the '90s, sparking my interest in the industry. The creativity and artistry within the fashion and beauty industry captivated me. Classic fashion and beauty magazines like *Vogue* further fueled my fascination. During my college years, I was fortunate to become the first international student to intern at *Vogue*, an experience that solidified my desire to create within the industry.

What is your work philosophy?
My approach to work has transformed over my nearly 20-year career. Today, it's about relentless perseverance. Experience has taught me that pushing boundaries is key—no goal is out of reach when you keep moving forward. I've also learned that there's enough room for everyone to succeed. By cheering others on and putting positive energy out there, you'll find it comes back to you tenfold.

Who is or was your greatest mentor?
I was fortunate to intern with a thriving local commercial photographer when I was 16, with whom I'm still in touch today. He taught me a lot about the business of photography, which isn't always taught in school. These days, I'm grateful to have an incredible agency, Coup&Co., representing me. The agents and some of the senior photographers serve as amazing mentors from whom I learn daily.

What is it about photography that you are most passionate about?
For me, it's the ability to create something unique that doesn't exist yet. Being an artist and being able to make—nothing beats it.

What is the most difficult challenge you've overcome to reach your current position?
The most difficult challenge I've overcome was the need for security, which isn't always guaranteed in the art world. The fear of stepping out on my own without a stable paycheck held me back for years. However, I firmly believe that everything happens for a reason. Now, I find myself creating my best work without fear. Plus, the skills I've gained from steady jobs, like producing, have only made me a better artist and business owner.

Who have some of your most significant past influences been?
It all started with Steven Meisel. In my eyes, everything he created was the epitome of artistry. From the concept to the creativity and technical execution, it was all breathtaking. Although my focus has shifted from fashion to product and beauty, I still consider him one of the greatest photographers.

Who among your contemporaries today do you most admire?
One artist who stands out to me is Hanna Tveite. Her command of light, color, and texture defines her unique visual style and is evident across all her work, from fashion photography to still life and film direction.

What would be your dream assignment?
I'd have to say it's being published in *Vogue*. It's been a constant source of inspiration throughout my career, and recognition from such a prestigious publication is the pinnacle of career success.

Who have been some of your favorite colleagues or clients?
I've been very fortunate to have had the opportunity to work with such great talent in Toronto. I've recently done some of my favorite work with art director and prop stylist Suzanne Campos from P1M and off-figure stylist Serge Kerbel from Plutino Group. I've also had the opportunity to work with some great models from Spot 6 Management, who represent some of the most current models worldwide.

What about your work gives you the greatest satisfaction?
The greatest satisfaction I get from my work comes from feeling like I'm not working. When I'm in the studio creating, I feel incredibly fortunate to be doing something I would choose to do even on a day off.

What advice do you have for students starting out today?
Always remember that every "no" is a closer step to a "yes."

What would you change if you had to do it all over again?
If I could start over, I would have begun by knocking on the doors of the best studios, offering to sweep floors, fetch coffee—anything to get a foot in the door. Networking would have also been a top priority—building relationships with other creatives in the industry in hopes of working together. Academically, I would have focused on business while refining my photography skills by assisting the photographers whose work I admired most and shooting with as many creatives as possible.

Where do you see yourself in the future?
I see myself achieving the goals I've set for myself. I know what it will require of me, and as I grow, so will my goals—they will evolve with me. The key is to never stop trying: you'll never fail if you never stop trying.

Lindsey Drennan www.lindseydrennan.com
See her Graphis Master Portfolio at graphis.com.

BEING AN ARTIST AND BEING ABLE TO CREATE —NOTHING BEATS IT.

Lindsey Drennan, *Photographer & Director, Lindsey Drennan Photography*

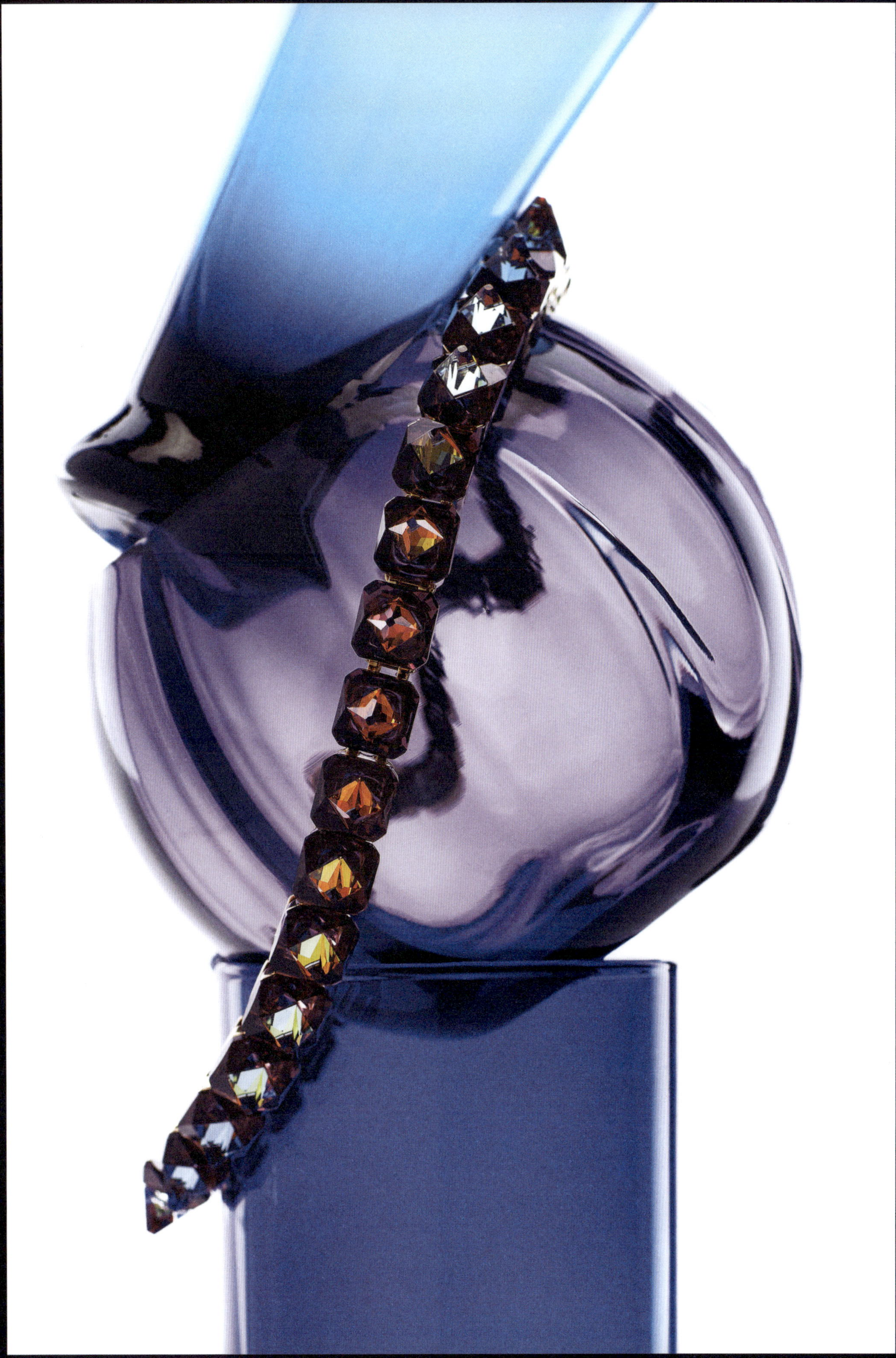

Photography: Lindsey Drennan represented by Coup&Co., Self-promotion, 2023
Prop Styling: Alanna Davey represented by Cadre Artist Management

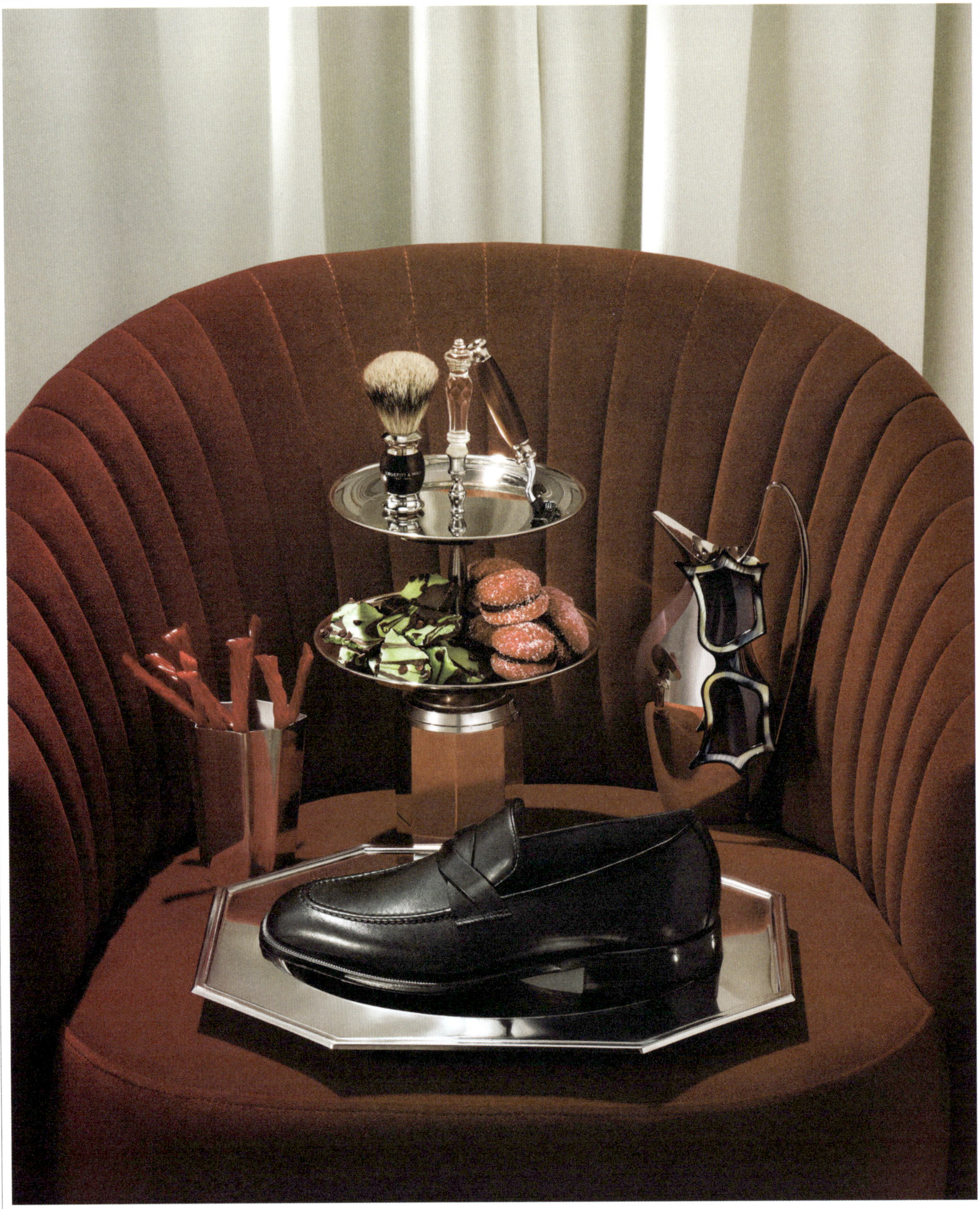

Photography: Lindsey Drennan represented by Coup&Co.; Client: Brookfield Properties
Project: Holiday Gift Guide, 2023; Prop Styling: Suzanne Campos represented by P1M

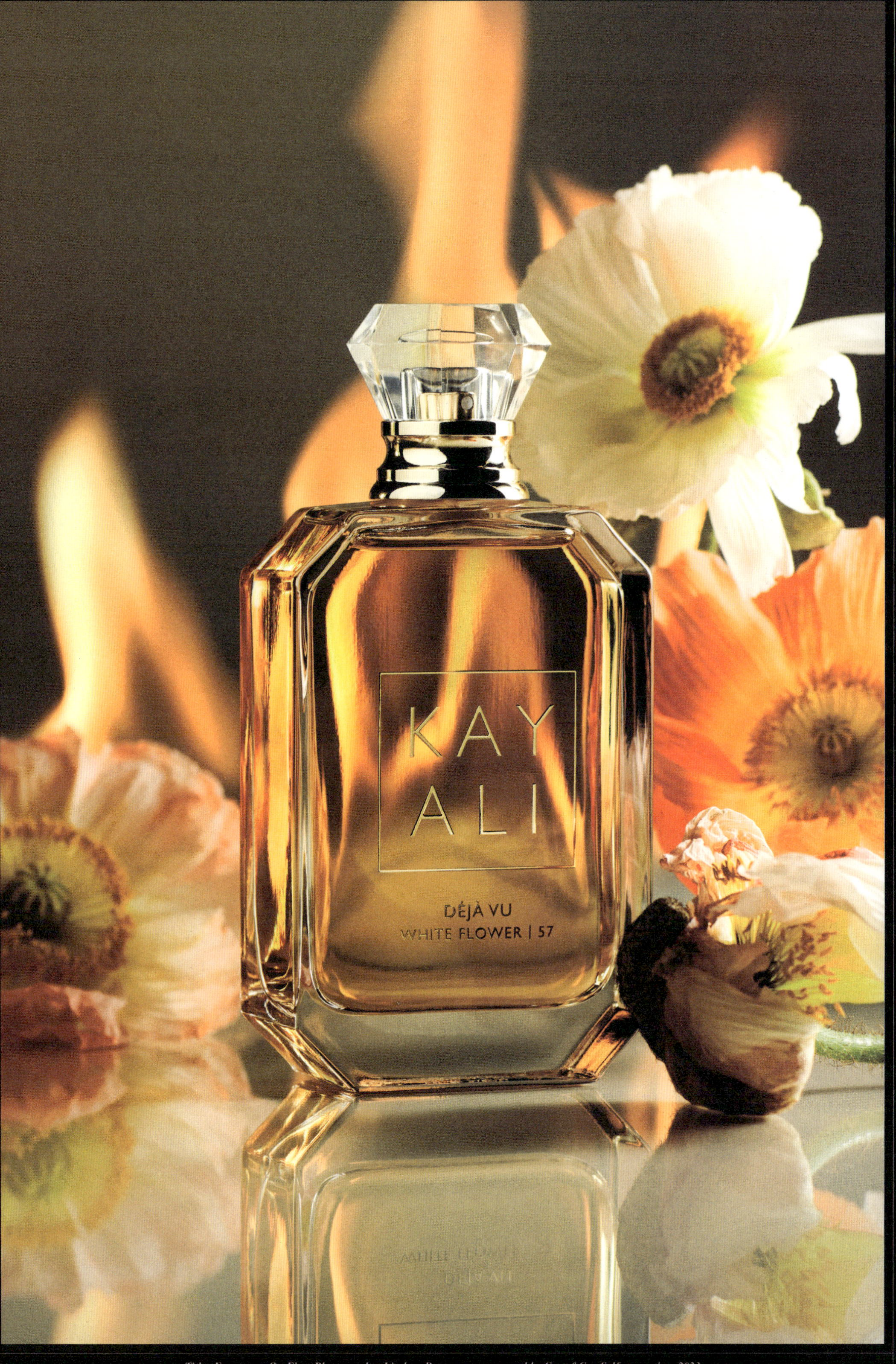

Title: Fragrance On Fire; Photography: Lindsey Drennan represented by Coup&Co., Self-promotion, 2023
Prop Styling: Alanna Davey represented by Cadre Artist Management

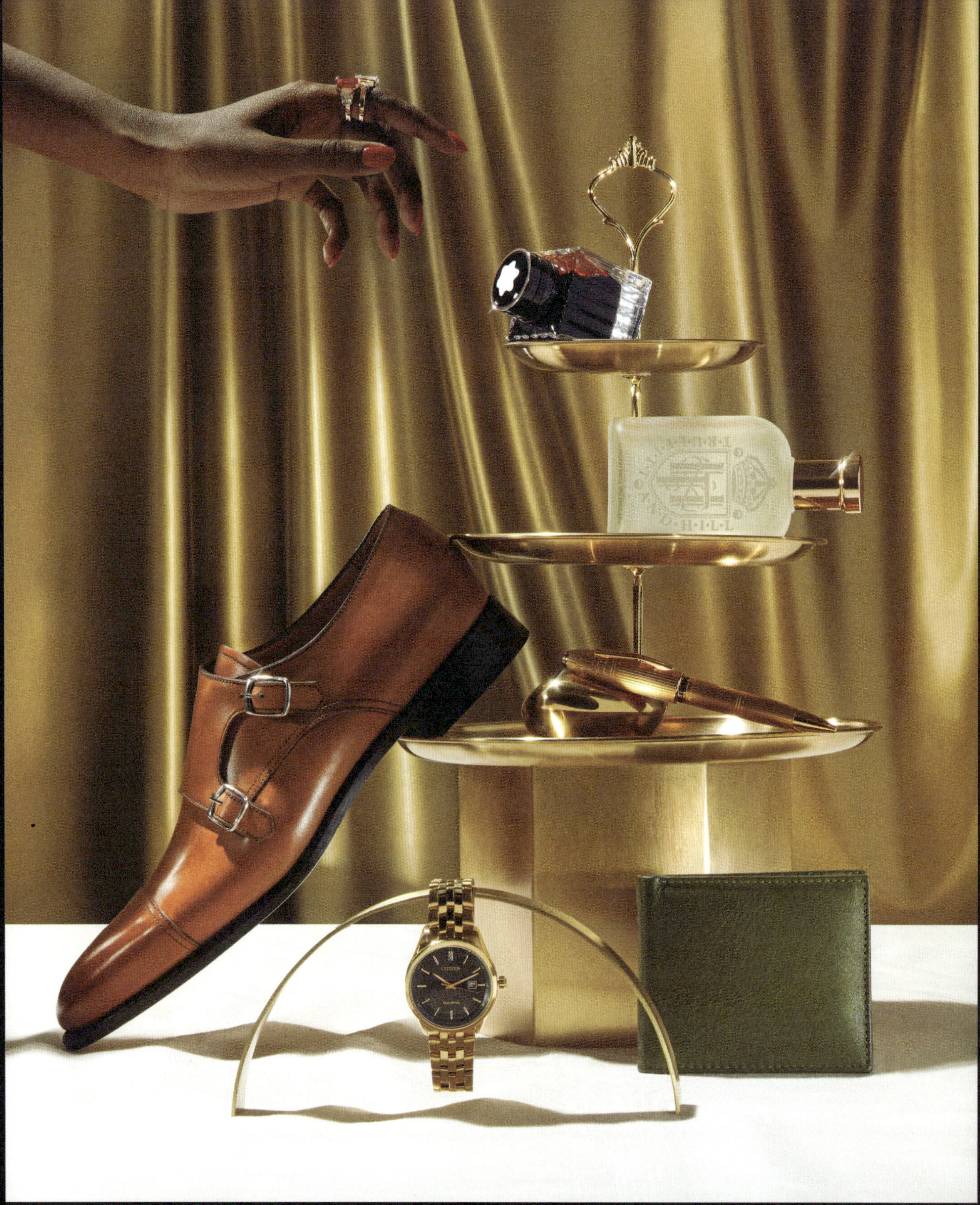

Photography: Lindsey Drennan represented by Coup&Co.; Client: Brookfield Properties
Project: Holiday Gift Guide, 2023; Prop Styling: Suzanne Campos represented by P1M

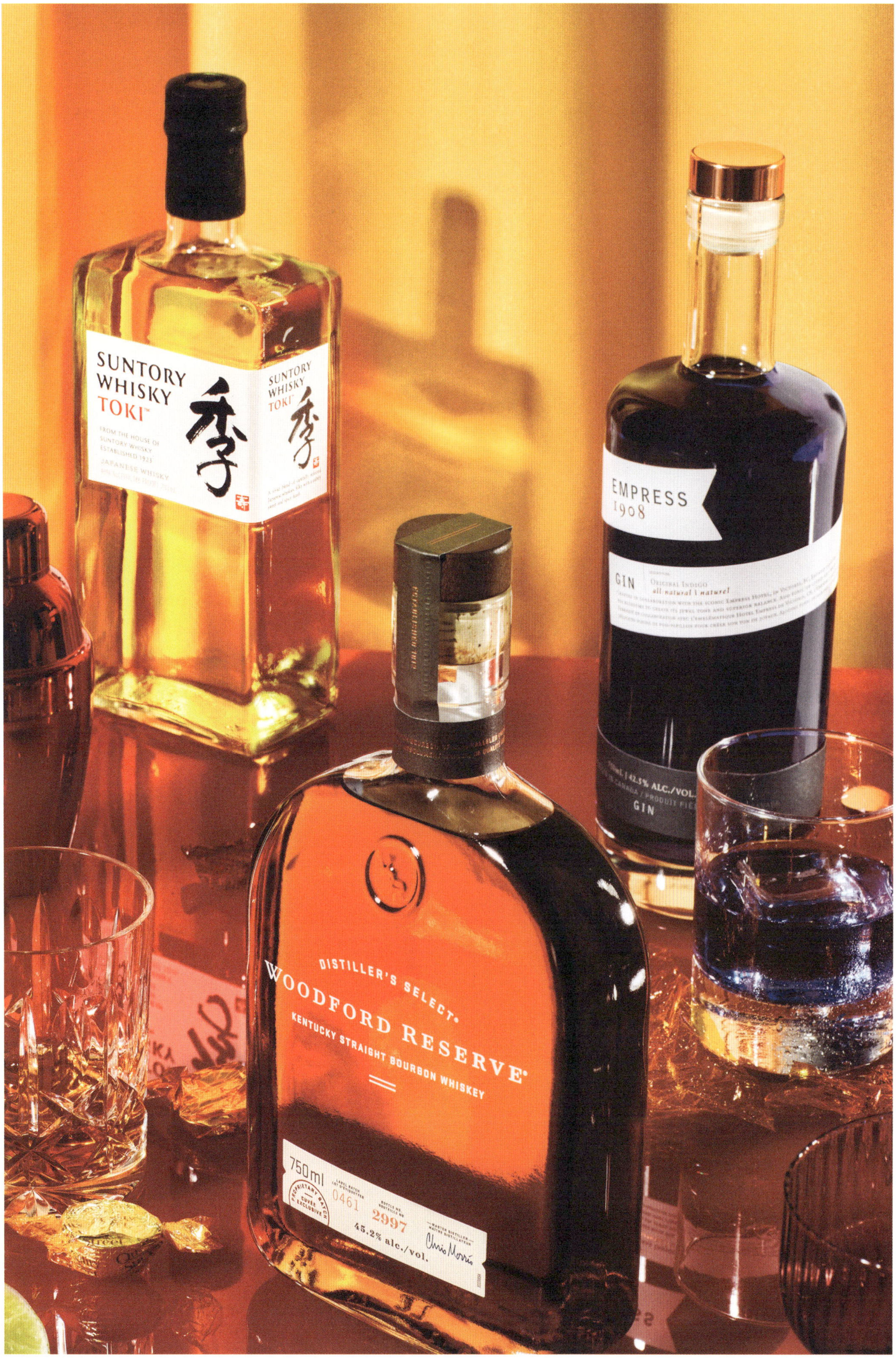

Photography: Lindsey Drennan represented by Coup&Co.; Client: Brookfield Properties; Project: Holiday Gift Guide, 2021
Prop Styling: Dani Reynolds represented by Cadre Artist Management

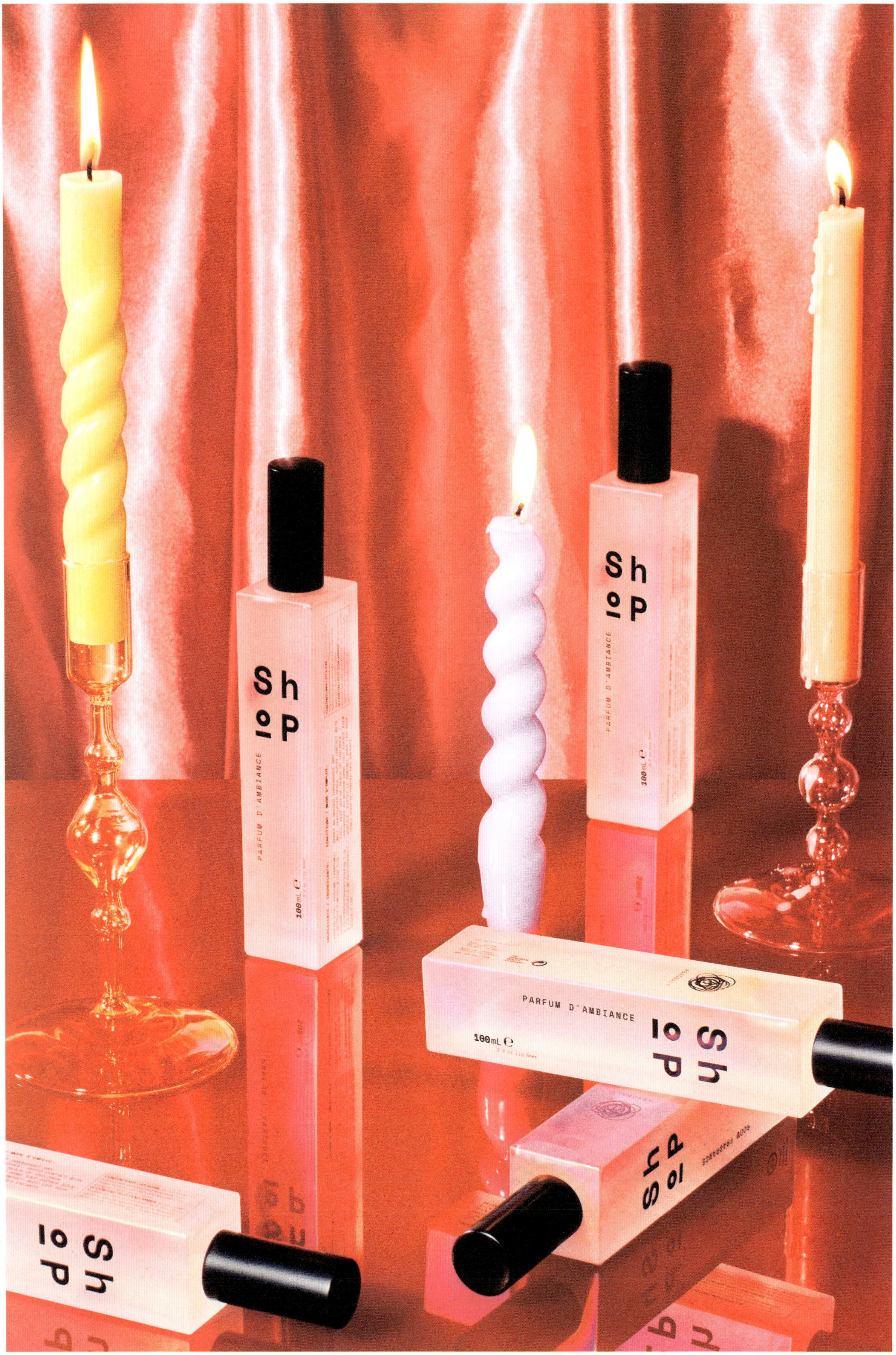

Photography: Lindsey Drennan represented by Coup&Co.; Client: Brookfield Properties
Project: Holiday Gift Guide, 2021; Prop Styling: Dani Reynolds represented by Cadre Artist Management

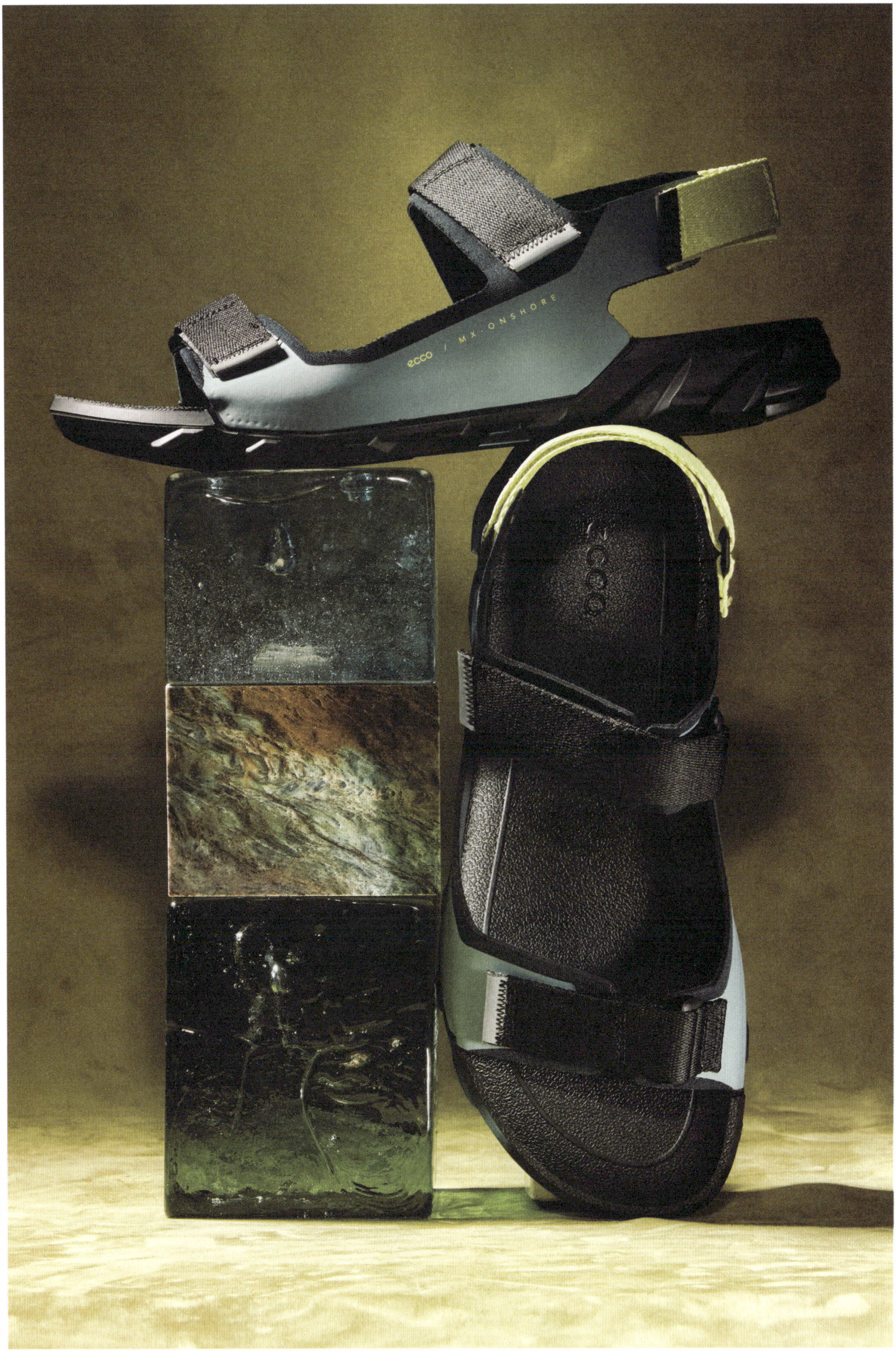

Photography: Lindsey Drennan represented by Coup&Co.; Client: Brookfield Properties
Project: Father's Day Gift Guide, 2022; Set Design & Prop Styling: Jess Anderson

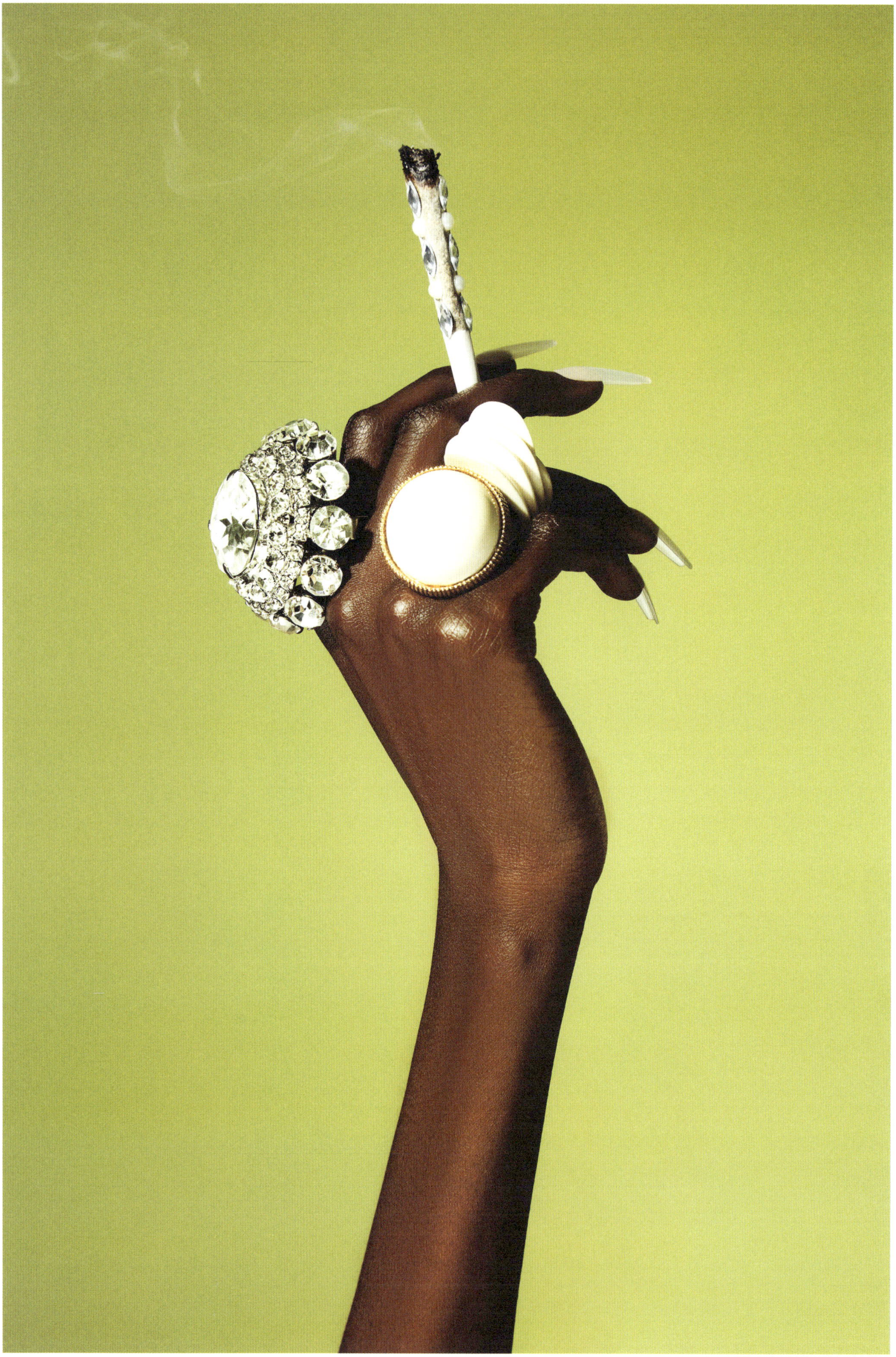

Title & Year: Smoke Show, 2023; Photography: Lindsey Drennan represented by Coup&Co., Self-promotion; Model: Akoy represented by Spot 6 Management
Makeup & Hair: Alanna Fennell represented by Plutino Group; Wardrobe Styling: Rodney Smith represented by Plutino Group; Studio: Album Studios

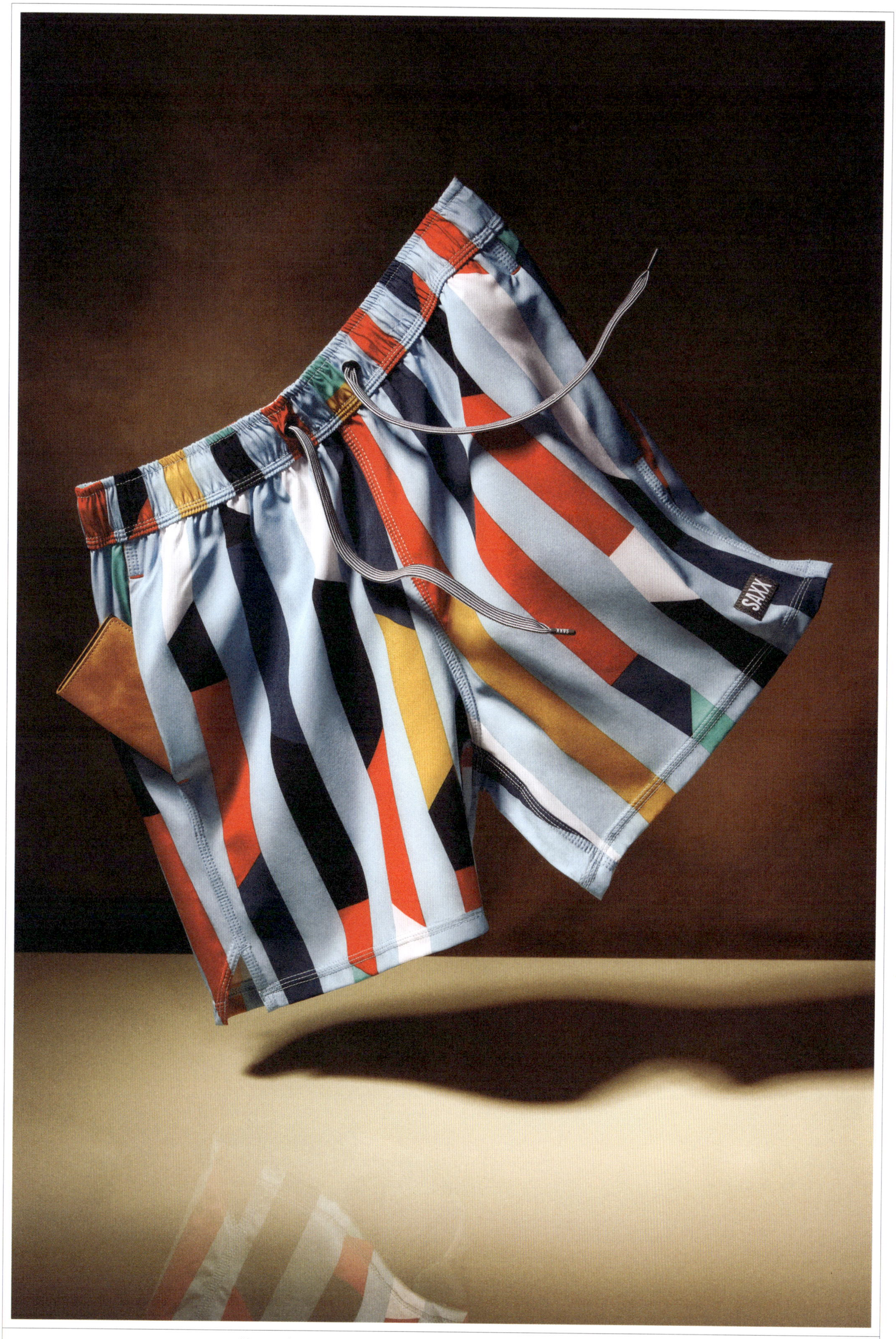

Photography: Lindsey Drennan represented by Coup&Co.; Client: Brookfield Properties
Project: Father's Day Gift Guide, 2022; Set Design & Prop Styling: Jess Anderson

A

ART/ILLUSTRATION

92 CRAIG FRAZIER / USA

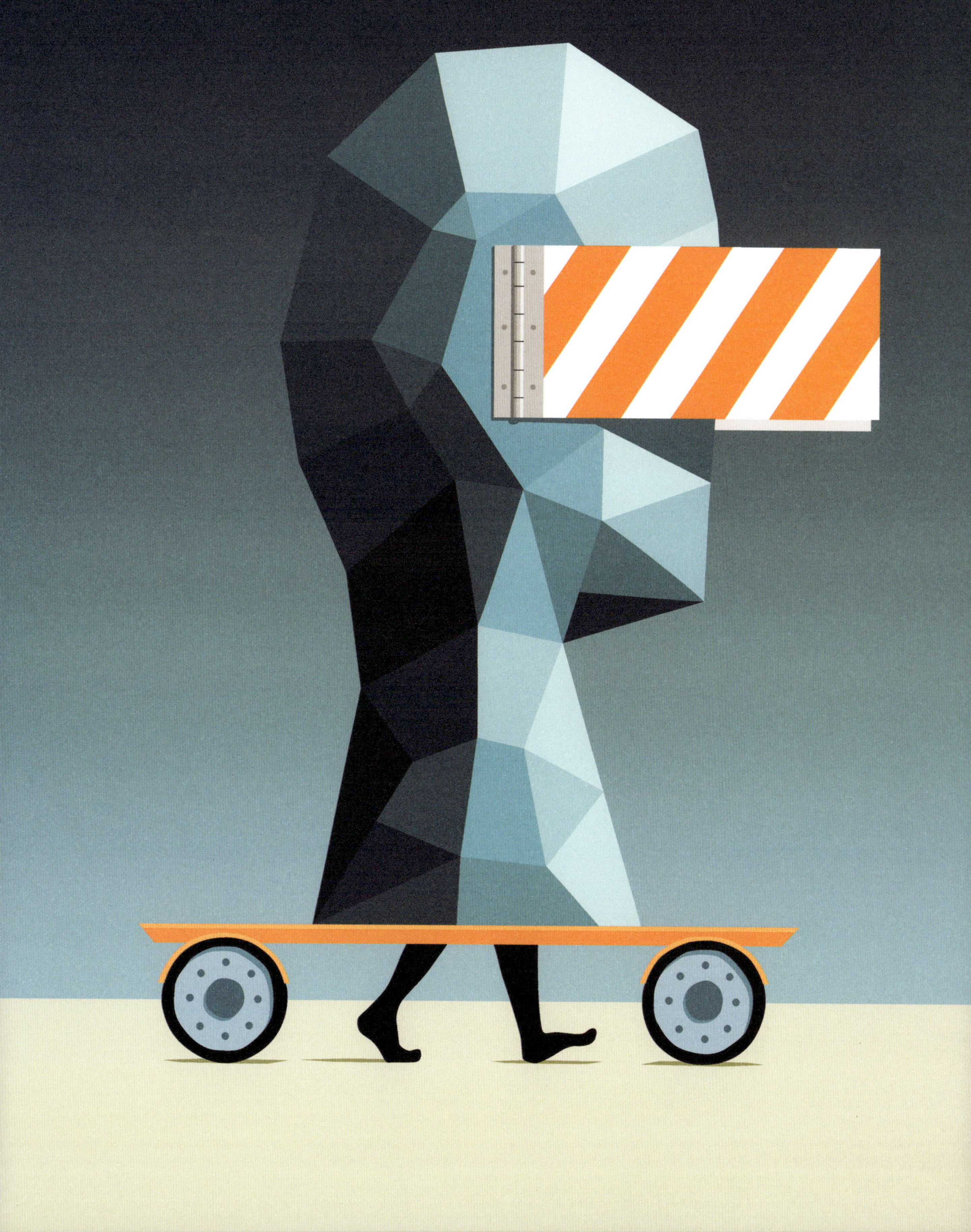

I INSIST THAT MY STUDENTS AIM FOR SMART AND BEAUTIFUL SOLUTIONS. GETTING THERE REQUIRES CURIOSITY, TENACITY, PASSION, AND WORK. THIS IS WHAT *DRAWN* IS ALL ABOUT: SHARING CRAIG'S WORK AND HIS ARDUOUS AND FRUITFUL PROCESS.

Antonio Castro H., *Designer & Professor, University of Texas at El Paso*

AS A YOUNG ITALIAN ILLUSTRATOR, I USED TO LOOK AT AMERICAN MASTERS IN THE ANNUALS. THAT'S WHEN I DISCOVERED CRAIG FRAZIER.

I COULD EASILY RECOGNIZE A CLARITY OF INTENTION THAT IS MORE COMMON IN GRAPHIC DESIGNERS THAN ILLUSTRATORS.

Emiliano Ponzi, *Illustrator, Artist, & Author*

CRAIG'S DESIGN TALENT AND RELENTLESS FOCUS ON EXPRESSING BIG IDEAS THROUGH IMAGERY ALWAYS ADD A PERFECTLY PITCHED NOTE.

Karin Hibma Cronan, *Principal, CRONAN*

CRAIG FRAZIER, MASTER OF CONCEPTUAL STYLE, HAS DEFINED AMERICAN ILLUSTRATION FOR OVER 30 YEARS. *DRAWN* PROVES THAT HIS APPROACH IS AS FRESH TODAY AS WHEN HE BEGAN.

Steven Heller, *Author, Critic, & Co-chair of MFA Design, School of Visual Arts*

I'VE ADMIRED CRAIG'S WORK FOR YEARS. I SHOW HIS WORK TO MY STUDENTS AS AN EXAMPLE OF THE BEST CONCEPTUAL THINKING IN ILLUSTRATION.

Paul Rogers, *Illustrator & Professor, ArtCenter College of Design*

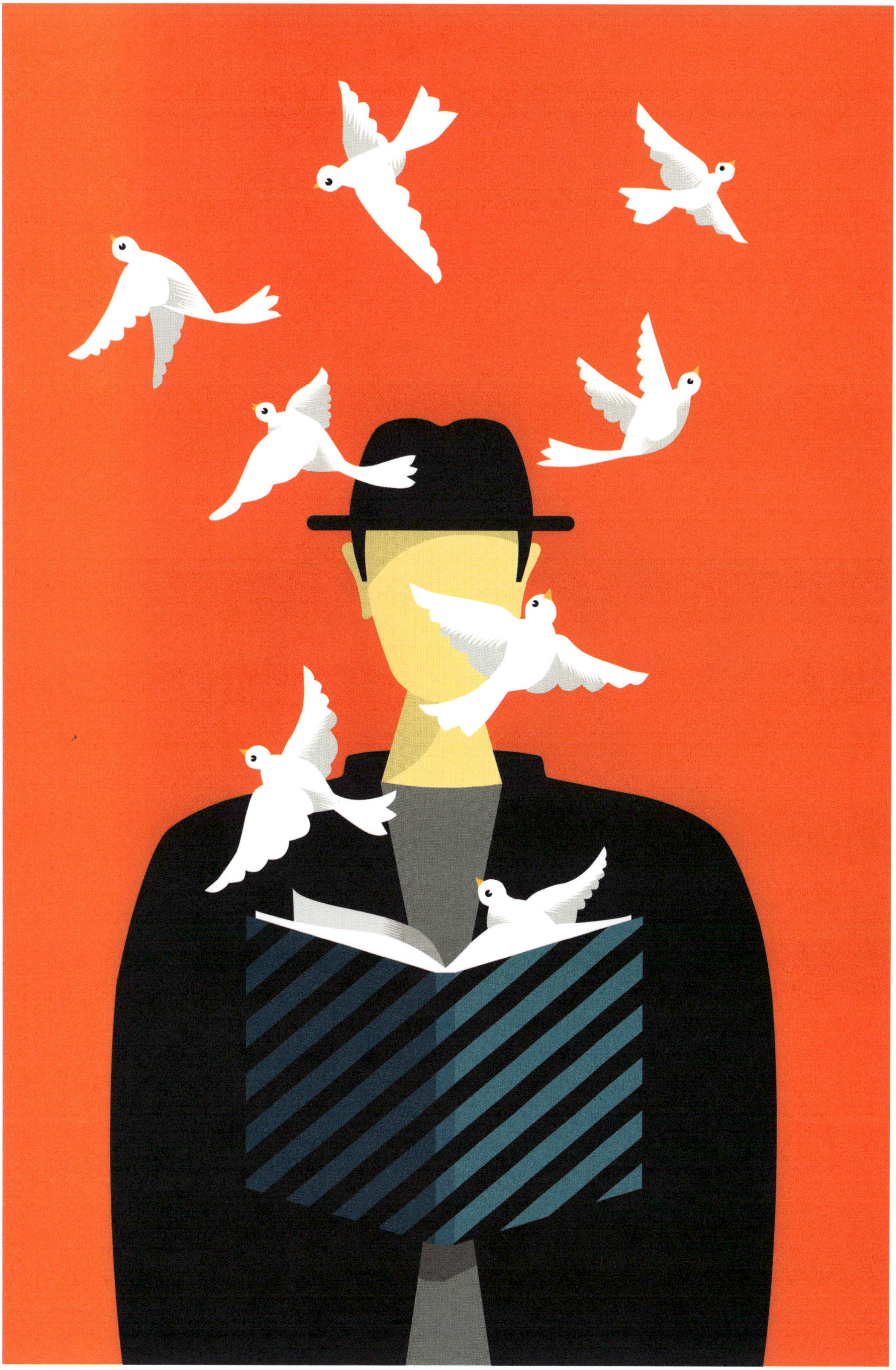

(Page 91) Headcart, 2024 / (Above) Birdbook, 2018, Identity for Sonoma Valley Authors Festival

Introduction by **Ken Segall** *Author & Former Creative Director, Apple*

As agency lead for Apple in LA, I once enthusiastically sent a great candidate for our team north to get Steve Jobs' blessing. He rejected her outright. "She wasn't curious. She didn't ask questions. Smart people are curious," he said. It's brutal but accurate. Steve would have loved Craig. He is the poster boy for curiosity. Craig is like a child in that he picks up an idea, rolls it around like a toy, and pokes at it from every angle, unafraid to break it in the process. And when he's not breaking things, you can talk to him like the wonderfully wise adult he is. I don't know what makes me smile more—Craig's visual wit or his ability to compress so much human and strategic insight into such little space.

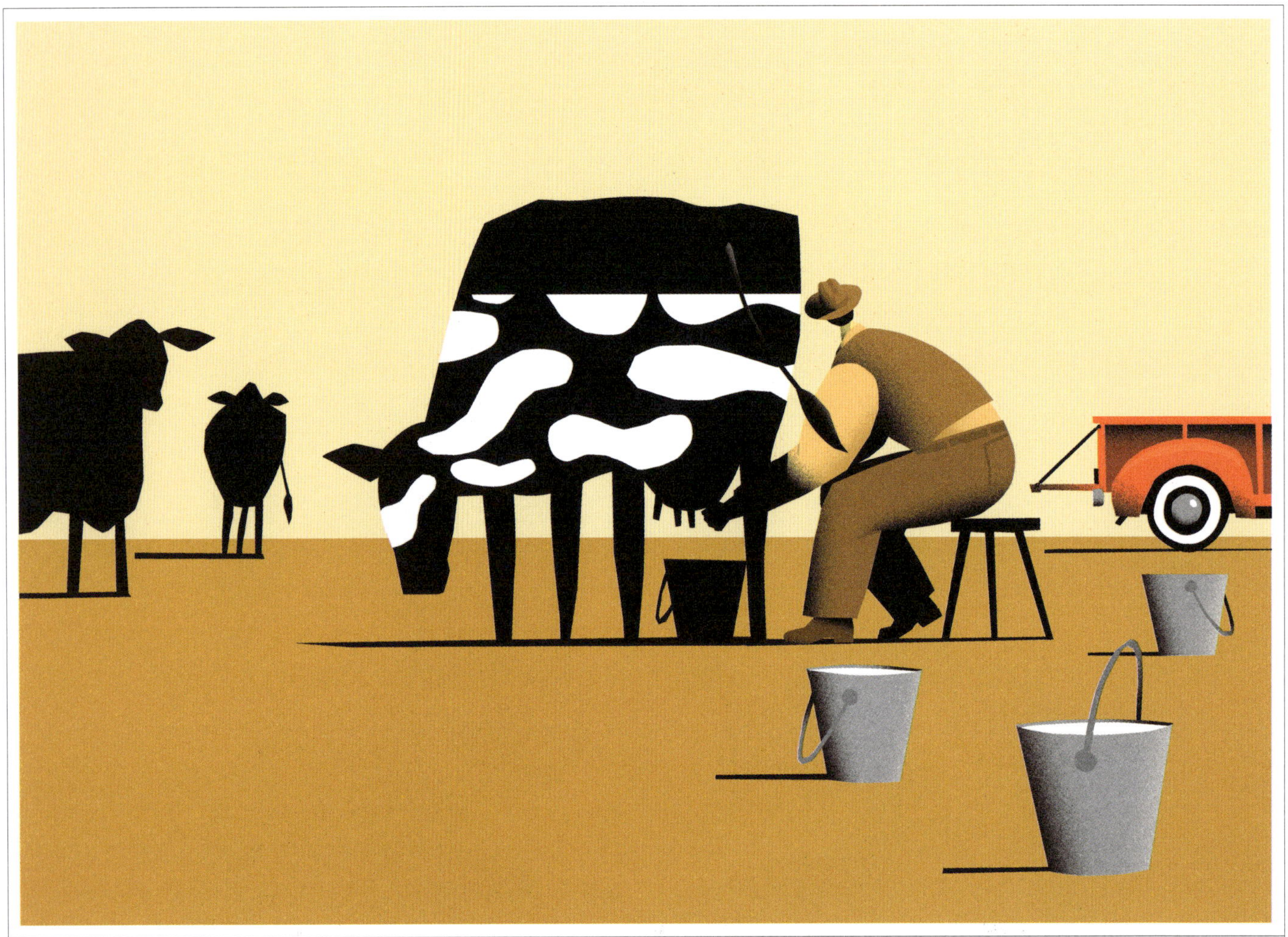

Illustration from Stanley Goes for a Drive, 2004, Chronicle Books

Q&A: Craig Frazier

Congratulations on the release of your new book, Drawn, which we highlighted recently. What inspired you to create it?
At this point in a 45-year career, there's a fair body of work produced and experience to go along with it. I was interested in examining that work and better understanding what connects it and what factors influenced it. The fact that I was a practicing designer for 18 years before committing to illustration had a significant bearing on that work—and is not that common. My design career formed the lens that I look through as an illustrator, shaping my work even today, almost 30 years later. As I watch the design business change, I see the value of sketching and idea-making wane, so I want to leave a testament to my honor of both.

Your illustrations often exhibit a unique blend of simplicity and sophistication. What inspires your artistic style, and could you walk us through your creative process when starting a new project?
My work is always in service of expressing a particular notion or message. I'm most interested in bringing the reader into a conversation with the idiosyncrasies of the drawing. I design from the desired effect backward. I draw scenarios that beg the question, "What's happening here?" Without that, the picture is of something that may not interest or engage the reader—and ultimately, not serve the client. With a riddle to solve, there's a better chance of engagement. I suppose the sophistication is a function of connecting unusual symbols and metaphors. I've

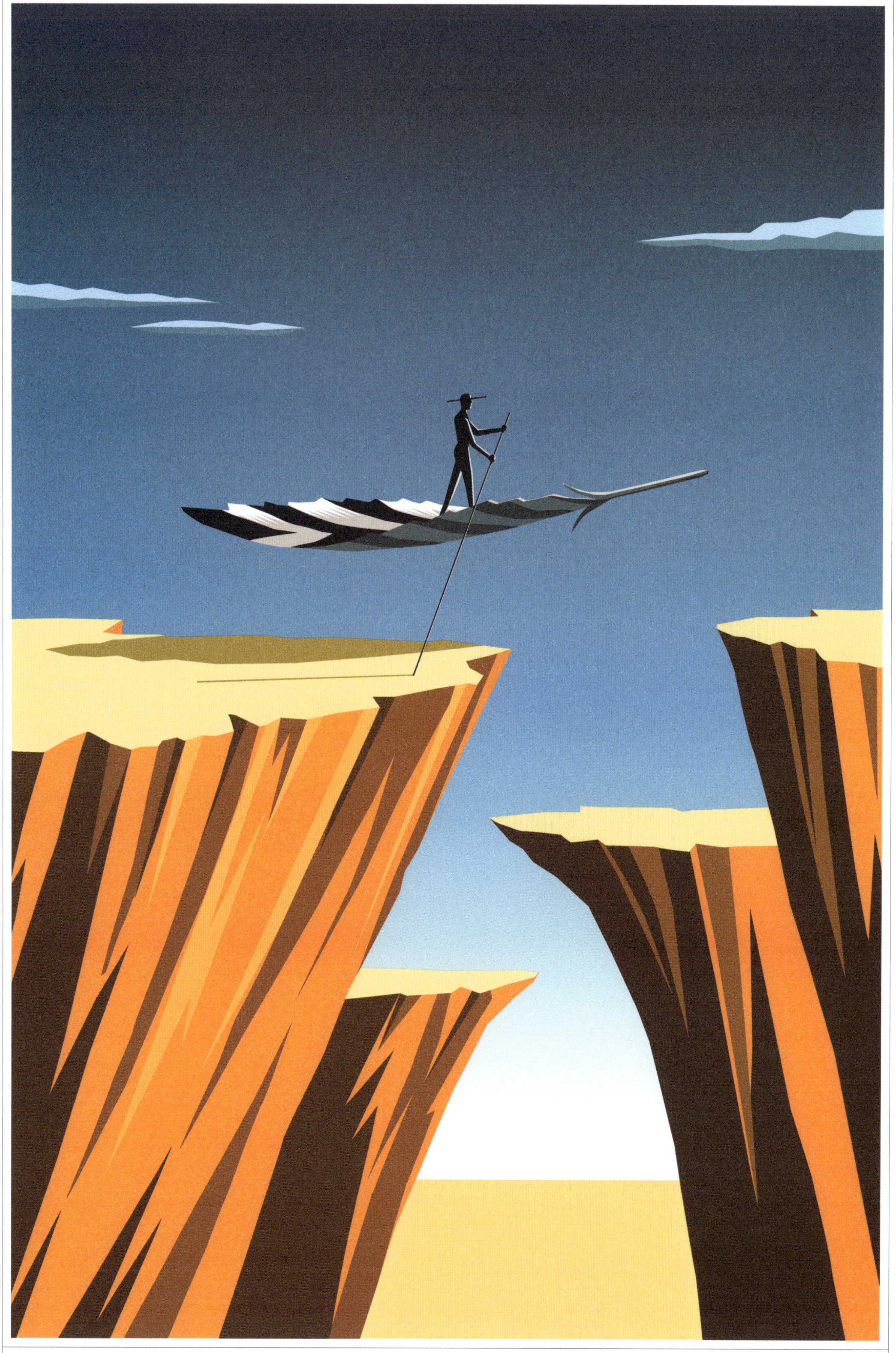

On a Wing, 2023

built a trustworthy visual vocabulary over the years. Simplicity is always a result of removing unnecessary elements or details. Simply, my process requires a lot of sketching to find a story to tell. I know if I give up on an idea too early; it takes persistence. I also rely entirely on my sensibilities, not my client's. I want to be surprised with the possibilities I see.

Over a career spanning more than 40 years, how have your illustration styles and techniques evolved? How do you stay motivated and inspired?
If my style has changed, I'm certainly not aware of it. I've always felt that your style arrives when you become comfortable with your shortcomings and embrace the principles you are drawn to. It's a strange combination of your limitations and your preferences. For me, the only real change is a sharpening of technical and conceptual skills. I'm always trying to make the image simpler, more concise, and more interesting. I'm motivated to stay relevant; it's the only way to stay in the game. Inspiration is a job requirement—you must remain attentive to the world around you and look for the oddities that can show up in a drawing.

Your work spans various mediums, from editorial illustrations to children's books and beyond. How do you adapt your style and approach for different projects and audiences? How do you decide what elements to include or exclude to communicate your message effectively?
The primary difference in the mediums is the messages I'm asked to communicate. Editorial is more far-reaching in content and subject, corporate more expected, yet—in the case of finance and technology—more inviting of metaphor and abstraction. I'm often trying to explain subjects that require abstract ideas to communicate. Keeping things simple is critical to making tough subjects understandable and interesting. I think of my job as portraying subjects "in other words" in service of comprehension. Kid's books require an elemental description of things, like a snake in a car or pouring milk into the sky. Kids can accept the most far-reaching notions. I have full license to be playful and fun. Anything is possible. Ironically, I try to apply that same discipline to adult illustrations.

Your illustrations often incorporate playful and whimsical elements that appeal to readers of all ages. How do you balance creating accessible illustrations for younger audiences while still resonating with older readers?
I never think about the age of my readers. Even when I make a kid's book, I let the publisher decide the age group for my work after I make it. Good symbols and clarity are universal and not age-sensitive. Honestly, playfulness and whimsy are critical to me as they can bring a smile to the mind, and everyone enjoys that. Sometimes, just the slightest visual twist permits a viewer to leave the boredom of reality, even if it's only for a moment.

Color plays a significant role in your illustrations, often conveying mood and emotion. How do you select color palettes for your projects, and what considerations do you take into account?
Color is very intuitive to me by now. I gravitate toward brighter, more saturated color, which serves the boldness and simplicity of my illustrations. I temper the hues occasionally if I want the mood to be more solemn or dark, but I generally use color for emphasis and to direct eye movement. A little well-placed color sometimes speaks louder than a lot of color everywhere. I'm drawn to great poster design and apply that same sensibility to most of my illustrations.

How much of your work is design versus illustration today, or is it co-mingled?
I've done a little more design in the past couple of years simply because opportunities have presented themselves. If I'm designing, I never pass up a chance to illustrate, often trying new mediums or methods. Much of this work is around packaging and the wine industry. It's different than my early years in design. I'm not trying to build a business and a portfolio; I'm just trying to help companies communicate better.

How has the business side of illustration and design changed for you since you started? And how has the advent of digital tools and platforms influenced your work?
This question warrants a lengthy discussion, but in summary, we have become so technology-enabled that production has eclipsed idea-making. It shows in the sameness of so much work, particularly corporate. Since print is virtually non-existent in corporate communication, companies commission—or worse, produce in-house—work that is safe, often derivative, and fundamentally lacking in ideas. The commitment that was once invested in print is replaced with posting digital work that is subject to change by the whims of many cooks in the kitchen. It's fast and relatively inexpensive due to technology. Lastly, when everyone uses the same tools, the products bear an uncanny likeness—the opposite of the goal. I still cut my illustrations out of amberlith and scan them into Photoshop. I could use the second version of Photoshop for everything I do. The internet has made doing business easy and fast—sometimes too fast. With all the technological advancements, the price of illustrations has stayed the same or declined. Stock, AI, and Pinterest have all contributed to the devaluation of illustration and photography. AI may be the final blow to the careers of creators. It is infringement at a global level.

Your essays in Drawn delve into the personal stories behind your work. Is there one story or anecdote that particularly resonates with you?
Well, they all resonate with me! I think the overarching story is that I have always been drawn to a certain kind of work and spent a career learning and perfecting it. I'm drawn to simplicity, wit, and, above all, inviting the viewer to take a second look. These are the principles of good design, and they transcend into illustration. I am truly a designer at the core and work toward function first. The second story is my dedication to keeping my hand in my work. Besides the physiological effect of making marks on paper, sketching and keeping the process as analog as possible slows the pace and—for me—produces meaningful ideas and works with character. That's the goal.

How do you see your work influencing future generations of illustrators and designers?
My goal has always been to figure out what I am drawn to and how to find it and create it. I want to find what I have to offer and what is authentically mine to contribute. If I can help another do the same, I'd be delighted.

What is the value of sketchbooks to you?
I can't imagine approaching a project in design or illustration without the benefit of a habit I formed early on—working in a sketchbook. Drawing in a sketchbook makes me feel like I'm making room in my head, like moving stuff from the dining room table to the garage. It permits a certain aimless visual wandering with no particular destination. No creative brief, no rules, no deadline, no judgment; it's a perfect place for conducting tests and storing pieces of ideas.

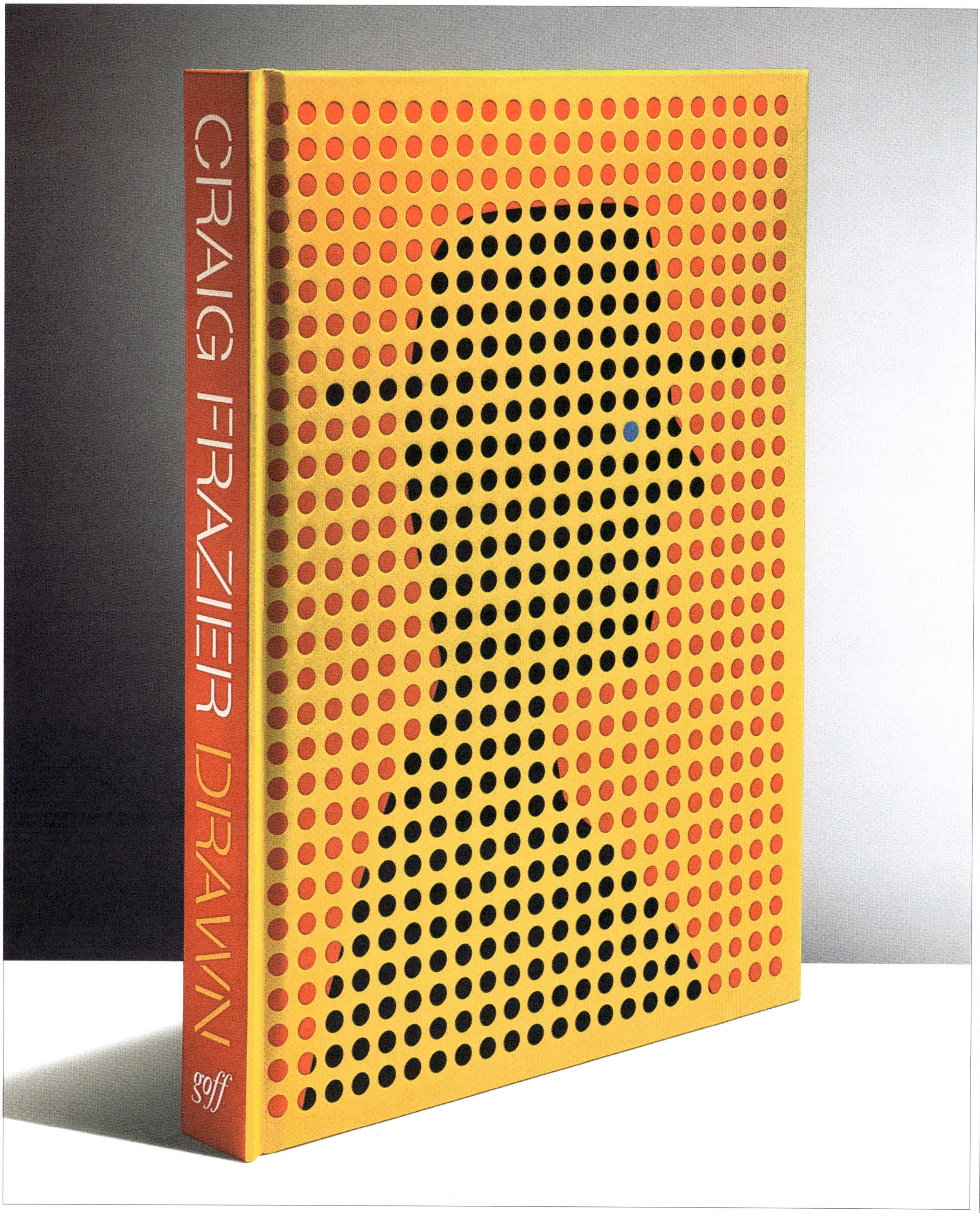

Craig Frazier | Drawn

Do you have any secrets to problem-solving?
I have maintained the "multiple solutions" approach my entire illustration career. With this process, several things can happen. When you abandon the single-solution tact, you are free to "walk around the problem." This leads to expanding the horizon of ideas. It sustains a state of ideation and suspension of judgment for a longer time, which means more ideas. It's the opposite process of going down a single rabbit hole that, in fact, may not lead to the best solution at all. To focus on creating one solution only narrows the funnel. It rushes you to the tail end of the process before there is a lot to choose from. The fact is that multiple solutions reveal myriad vantage points from which a problem can be viewed. Frequently, I will develop a couple of solid solutions, which gives me the liberty to think outside the given definition of the problem. As a result, I may discover something that supports a redefinition of the challenge. Discovery can't be truncated. Some of my most exciting ideas arrive when I'm about to put my pen down.

Craig Frazier www.craigfrazier.com
See his Graphis Master Portfolio at graphis.com.

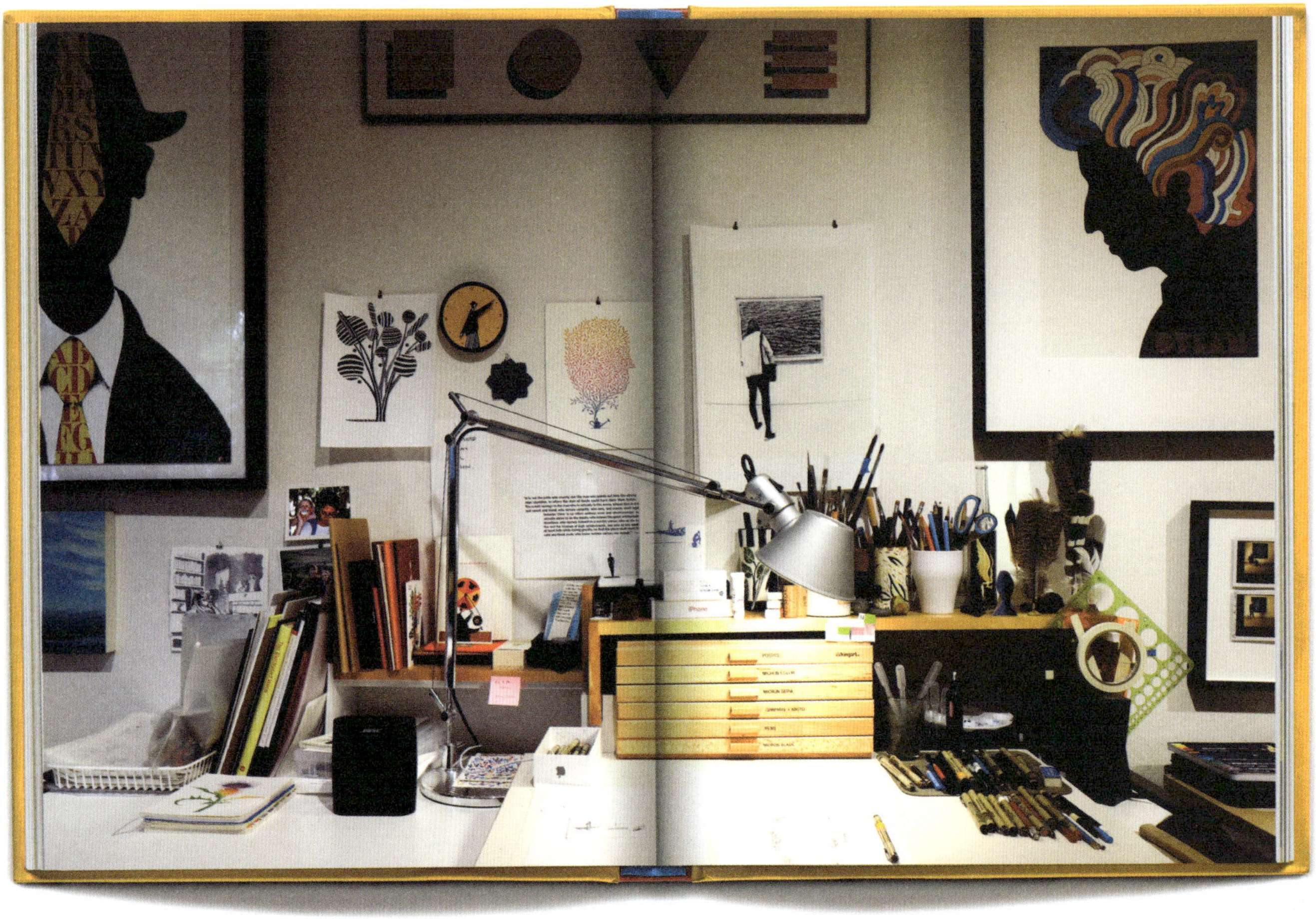

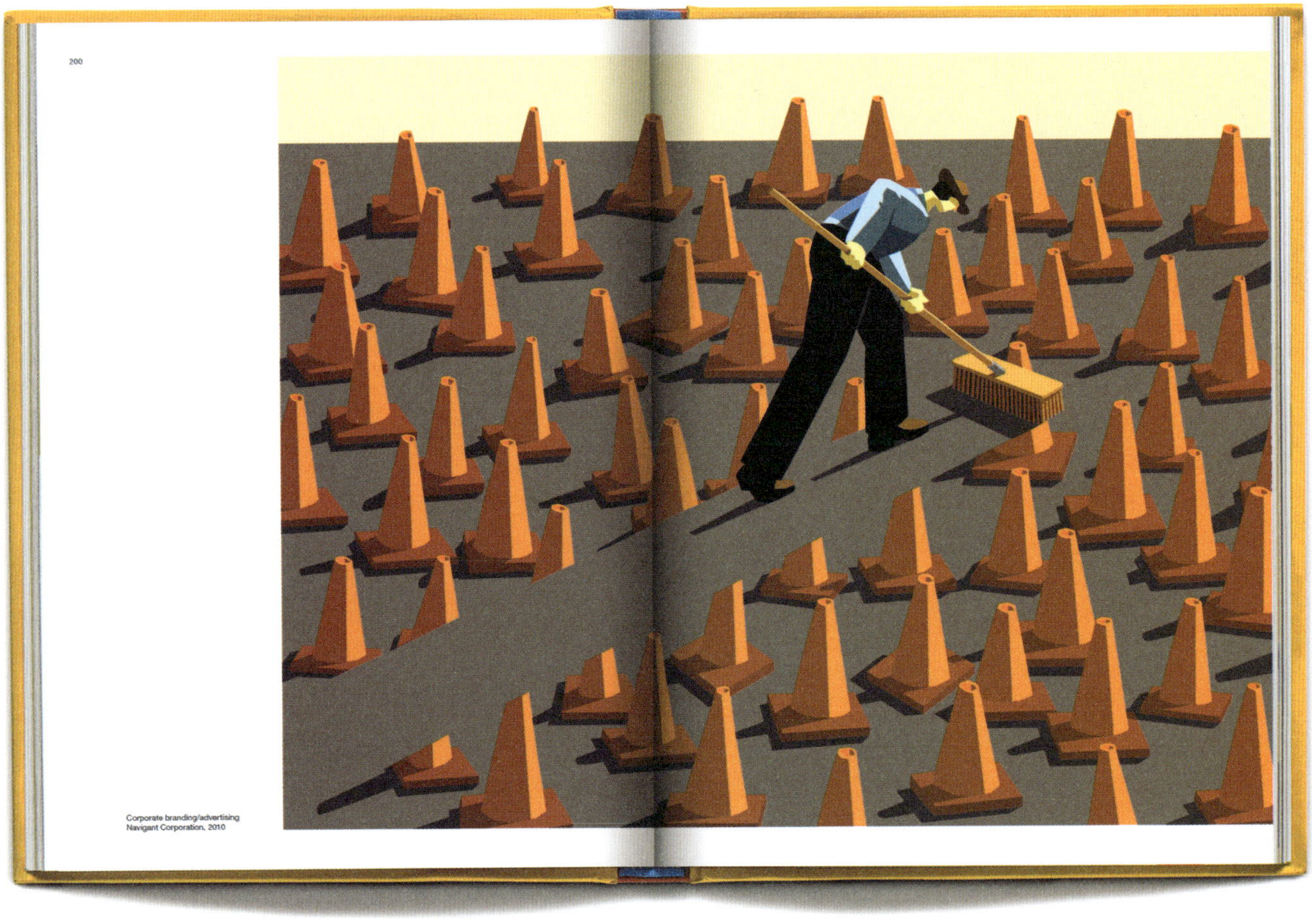

Spreads from Drawn

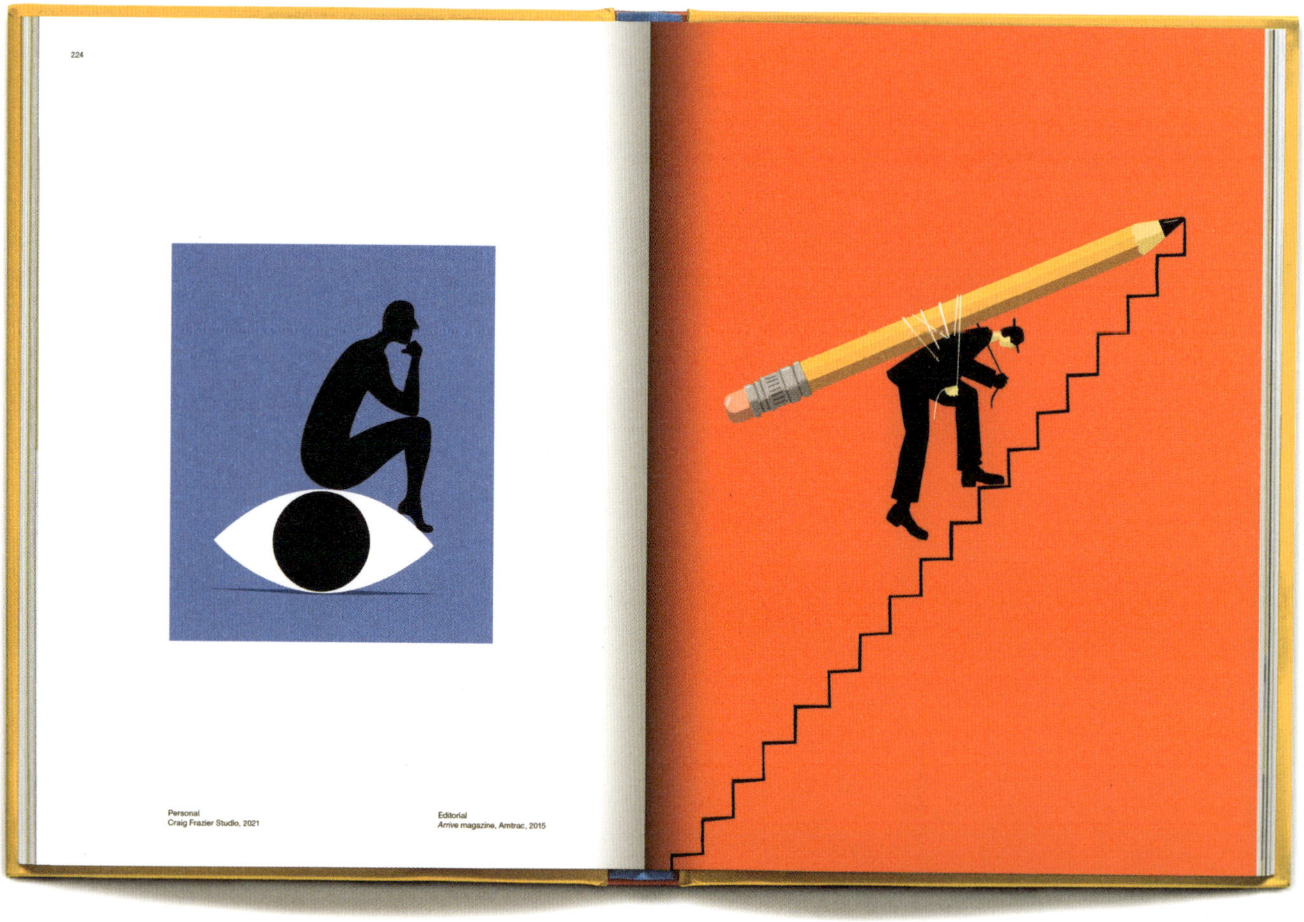

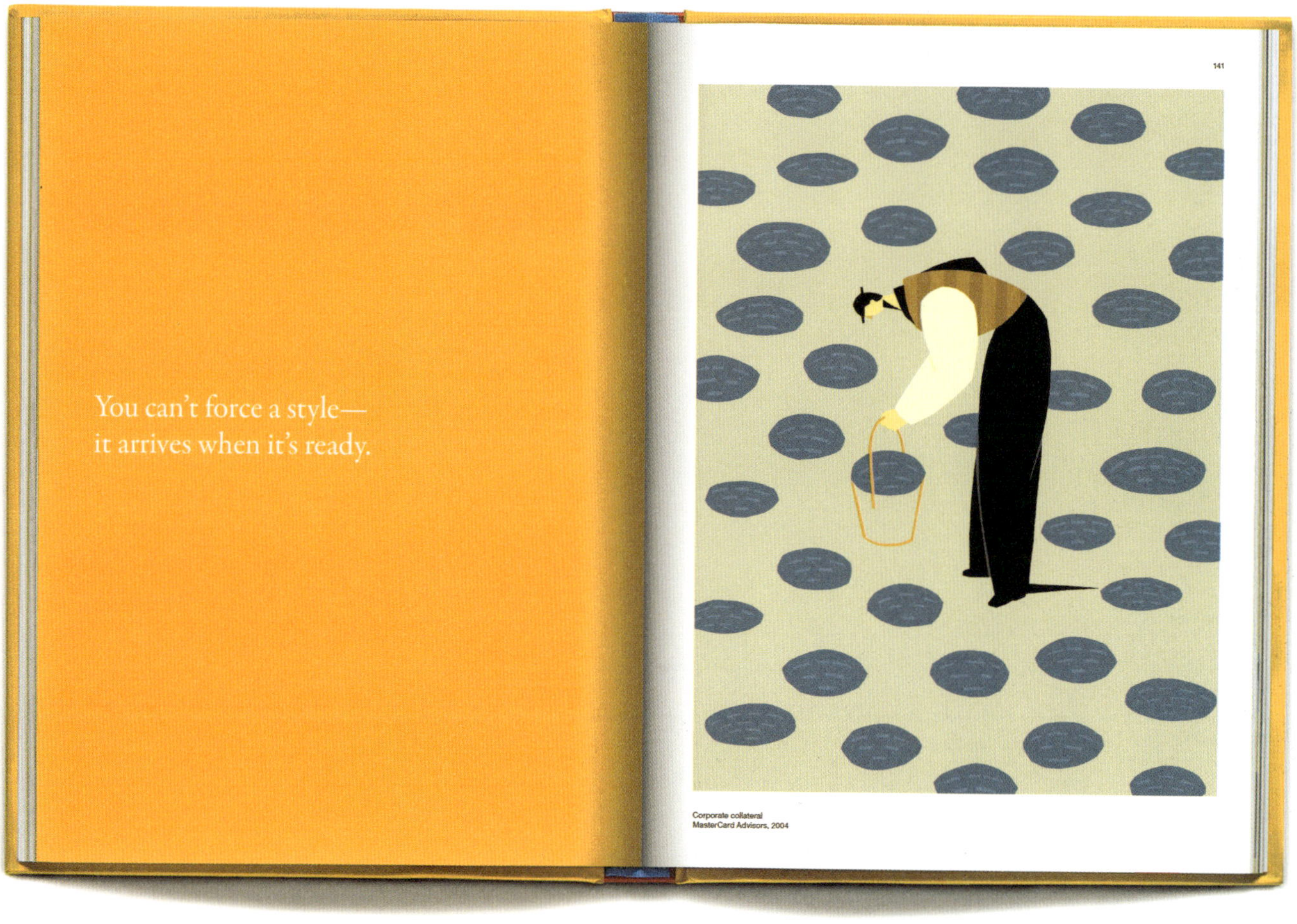

Spreads from Drawn

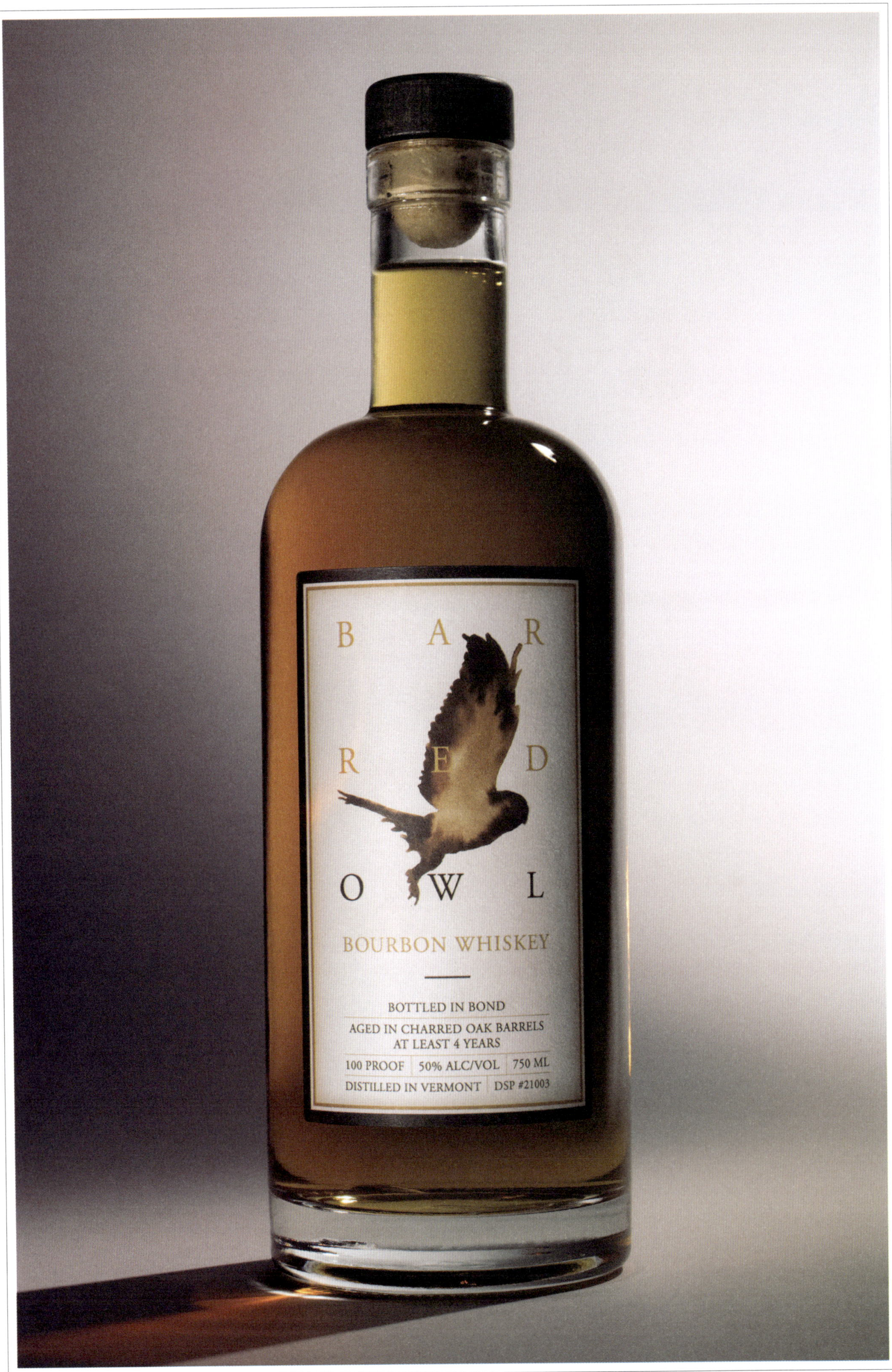

Barred Owl Bourbon Whiskey, 2023, Appalachian Gap Distillery/Olle Lundberg

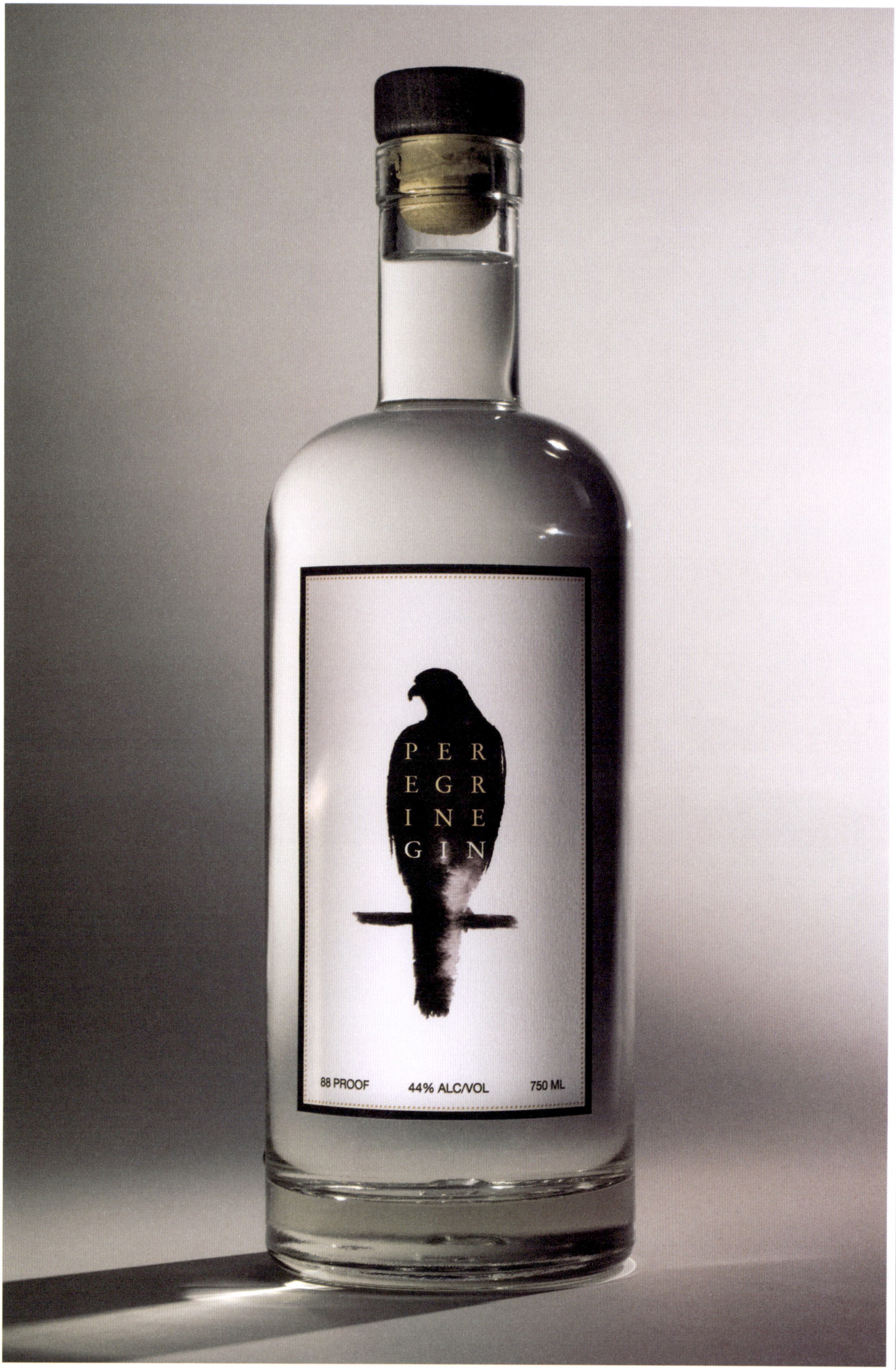

Peregrine Gin, 2018, Appalachian Gap Distillery/Olle Lundberg

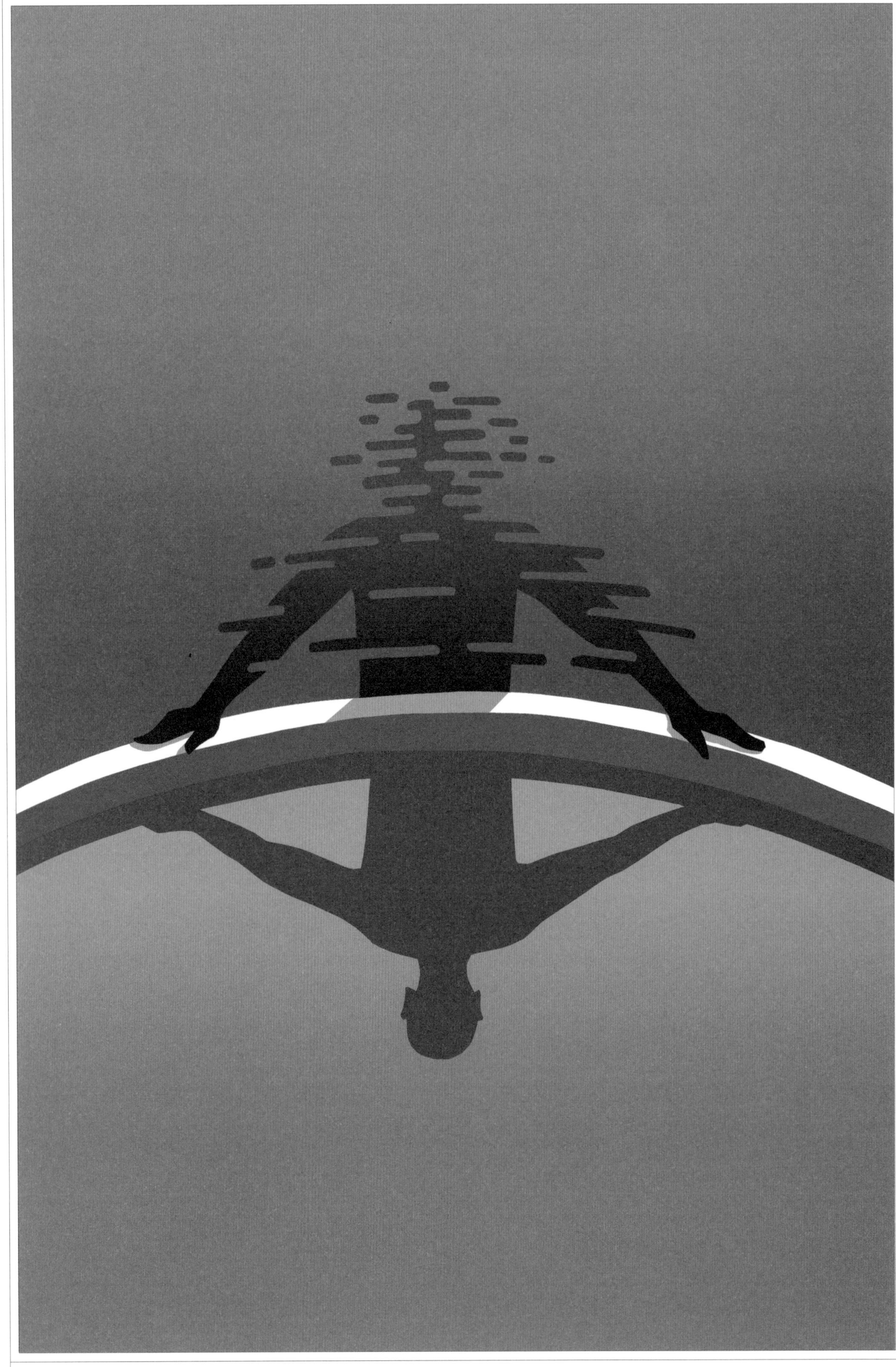

Reflecting Pond, 2021

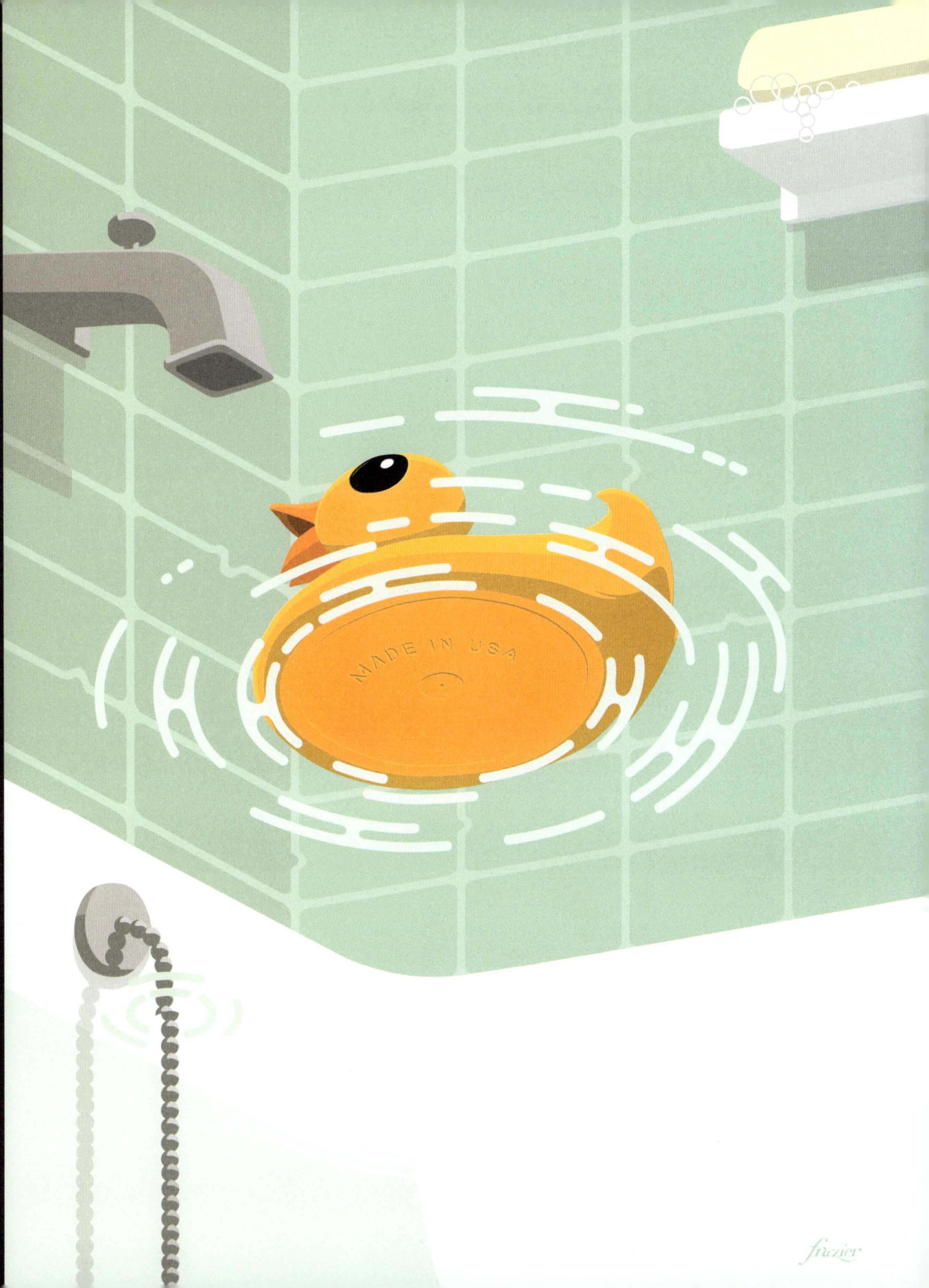
MADE IN USA
frazier

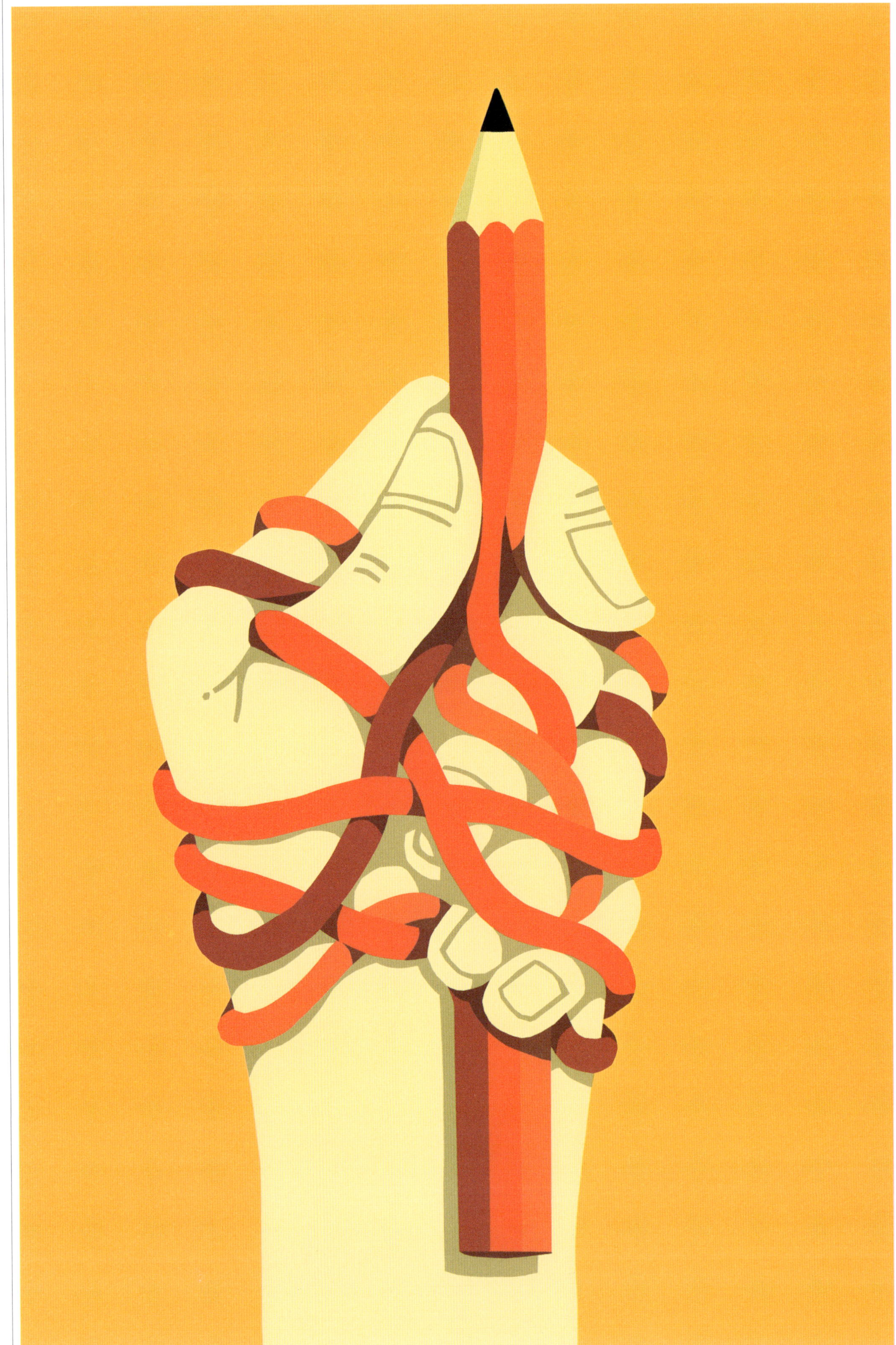

Pencil Pasta, 2018

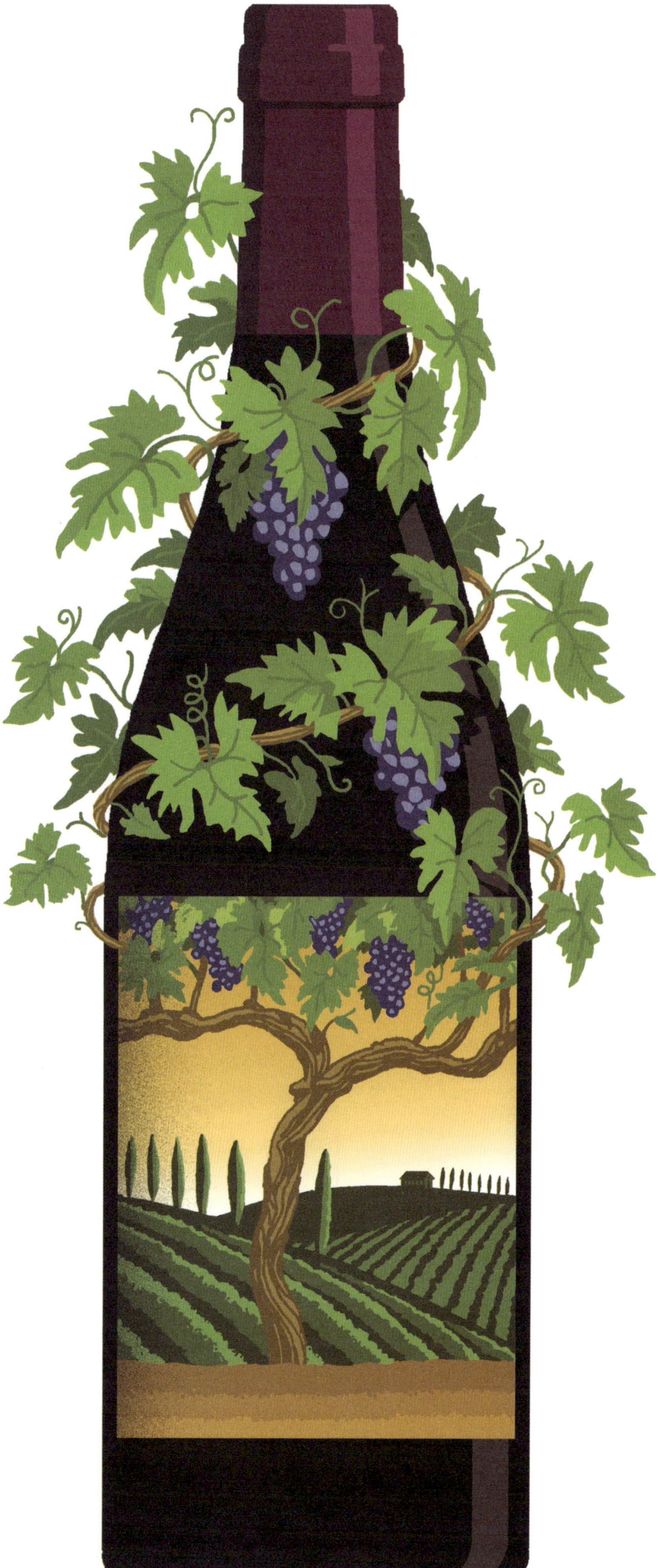

Winevines, New York Times, 2024

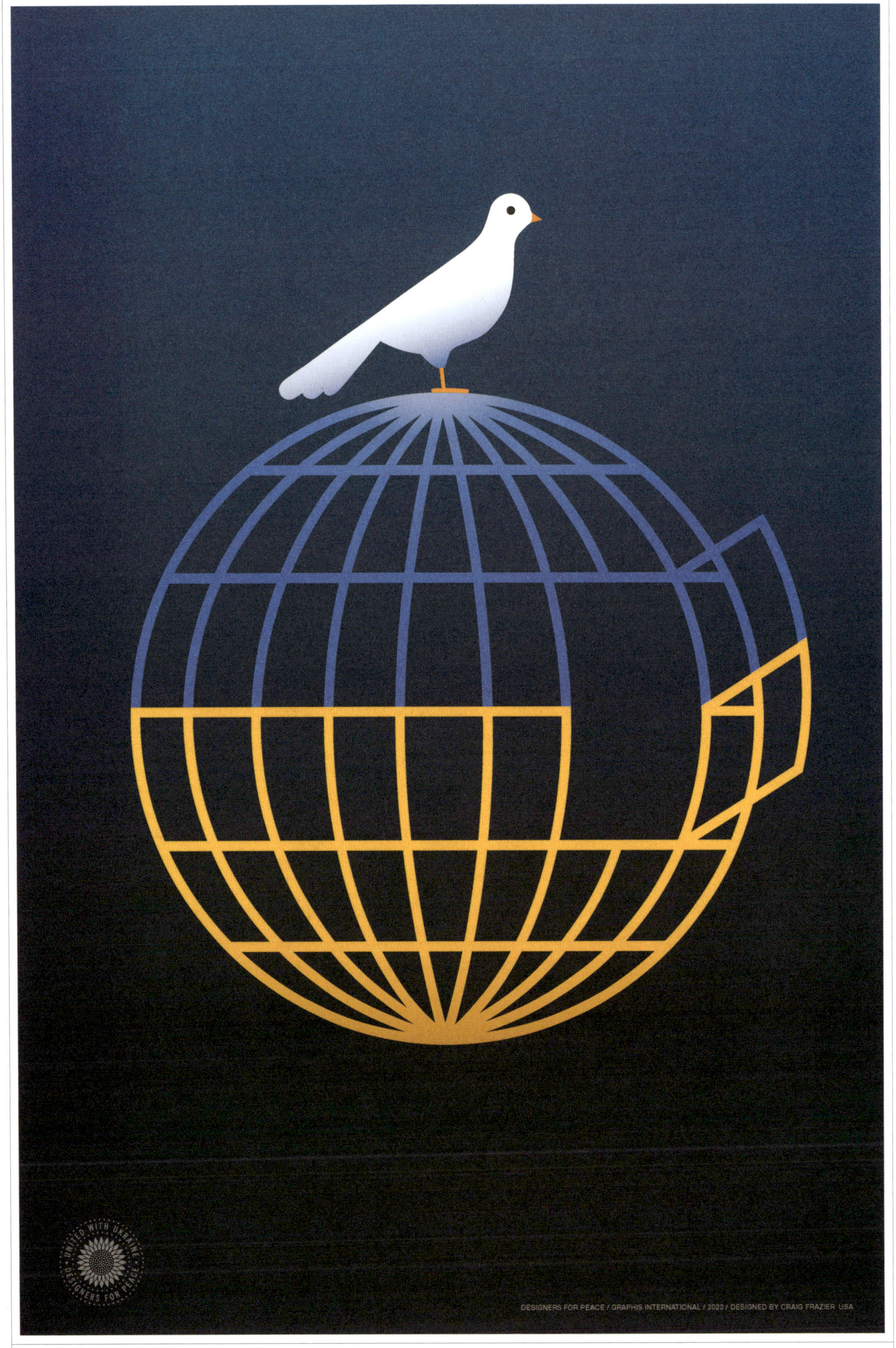

United with Ukraine poster, 2022. Designers for Peace series

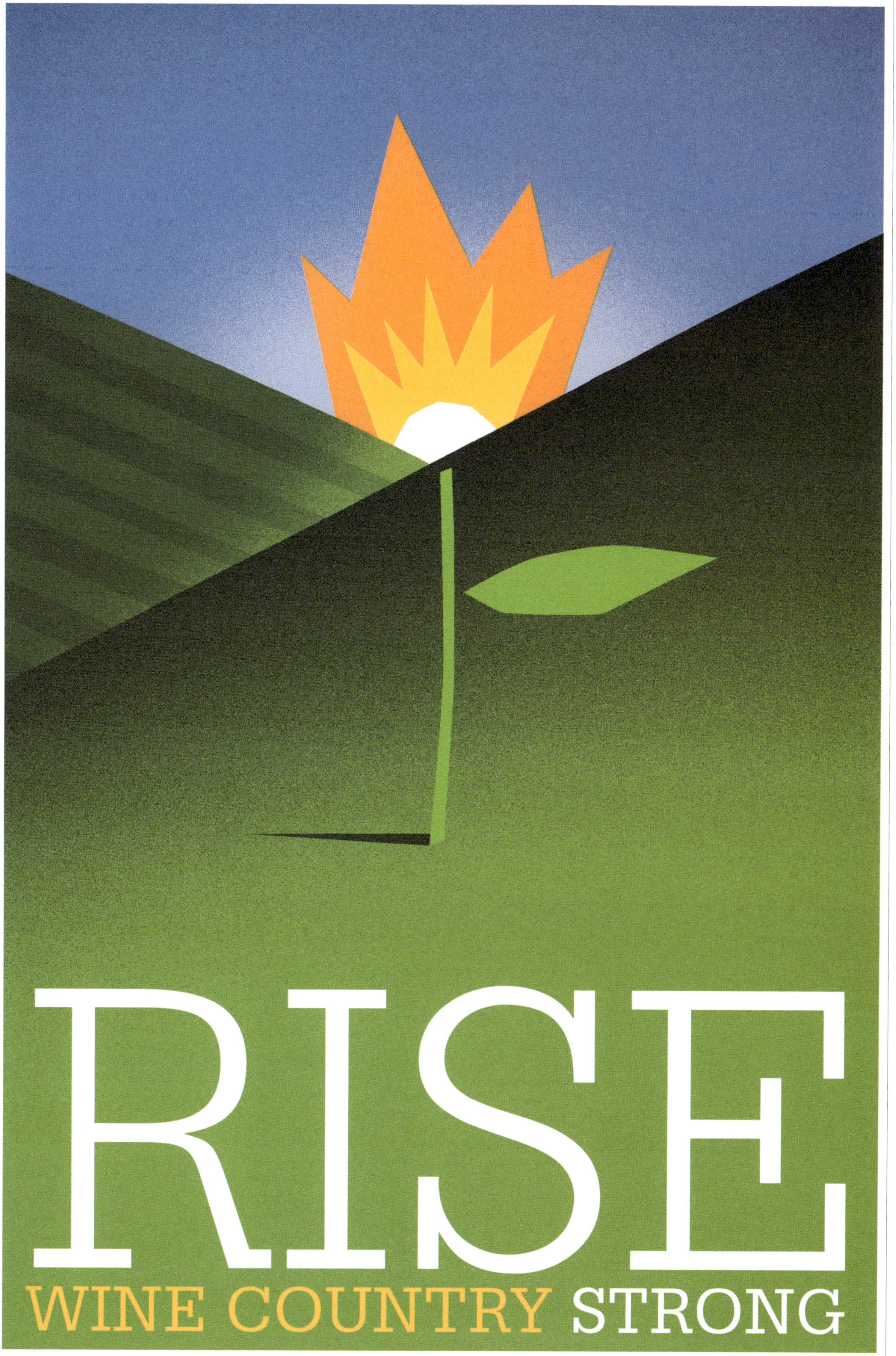

Rise poster, 2017, commemorating the wine country fires.

P

PRODUCT & INDUSTRIAL DESIGN

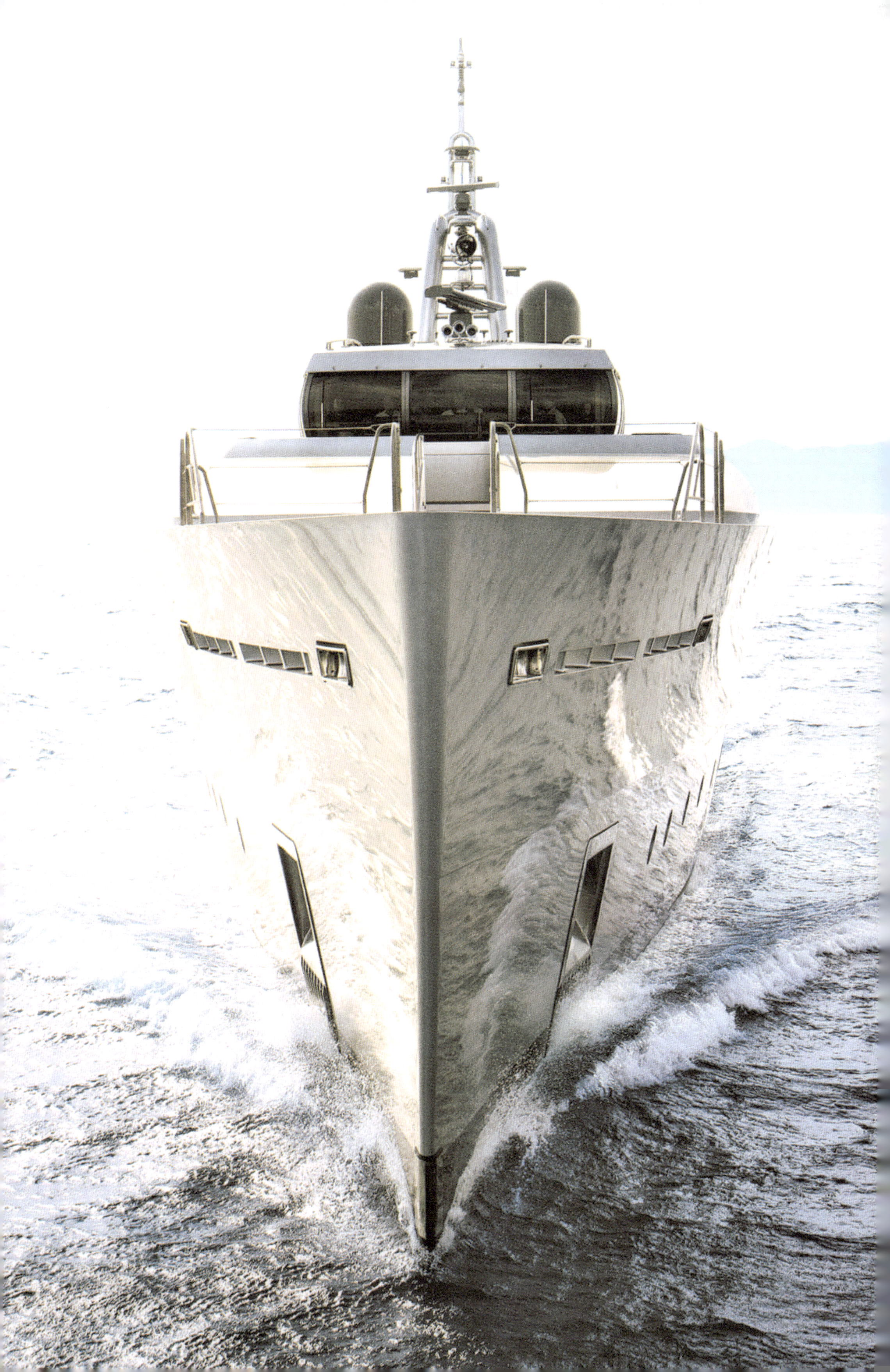

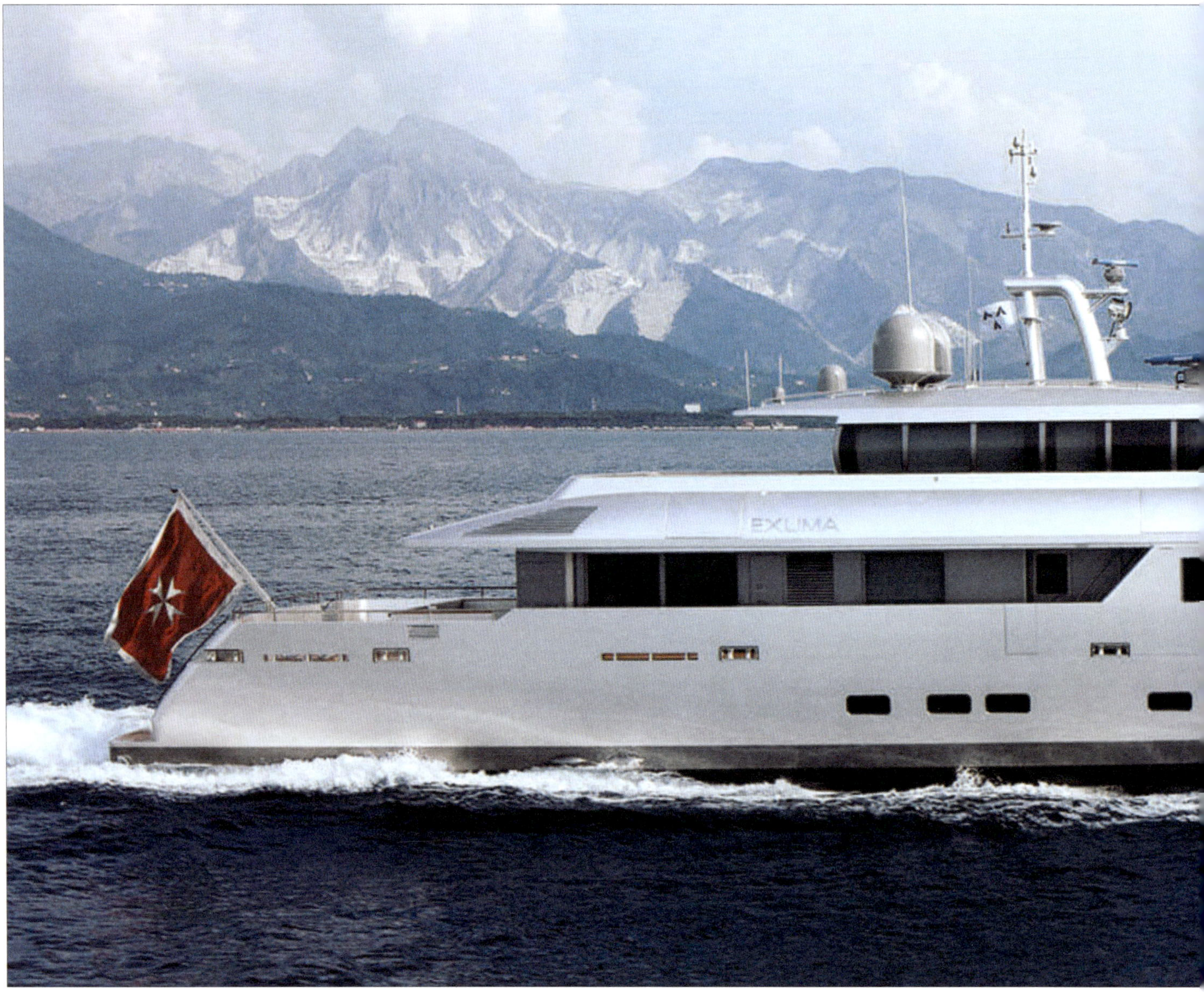

Length overall: 164 ft (50 m)	**Draught (loaded):** 7.5 ft (2.30 m)	**Gross tonnage:** 497 t
Beam (max): 31 ft (9.50 m)	**Hull and superstructure:** Aluminum	**Main engines:** CAT C32 Acert 2 x 970 kW@ 2.100 rpm

The imposing hull of the My Falco Moscata superyacht makes a major statement, no matter how dramatic its surroundings may be. It conveys that this vessel has been built with a commitment to durability. The individual who originally commissioned the vessel, under the name Exuma, requested a yacht that had the hardiness to traverse the entire globe. It's easy to believe that such a formidable-looking vessel could do so, even in the harshest conditions.

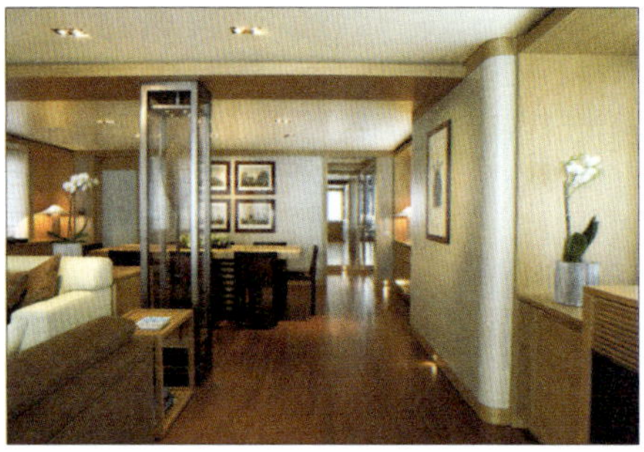

Appropriately, the My Falco Moscata has proven that it can manage rigorous journeys with aplomb. Data from the vessel's first worldwide trip revealed that it had a range of 6,500 miles at a 12-knot cruising speed. Or, to put it another way, it could sail from Los Angeles to Tokyo on a full tank and still have enough fuel left over to reach South Korea easily.

At a distance, it could be easy to mistake the My Falco Moscata for a naval vessel. But upon closer inspection, telltale signs of civilian-centered luxury become apparent. Instead of weaponry, the exterior section of the bridge deck is adorned with a spa pool. This bridge deck extends to the rear, functioning as a gazebo to shelter the outdoor dining area below. Couch frames that are part of the vessel's construction rise up from this lower deck, lining a dining space that far outshines any militaristic mess hall. Toward the boat's bow is another spacious exterior deck, which often houses sunloungers and other outdoor furniture. Despite the high-end features, nothing about this exterior is fragile, with the most robust materials being utilized. For instance, the My Falco Moscata's external handrails are made out of titanium.

Within the rugged exterior is a living space that could pass as a penthouse room at The Ritz, with only the low ceilings betraying the charade. Perini Navi, the organization that designed the interior, should be applauded for crafting such an elegant layout. The materials used in the decor are certainly worthy of a luxury hotel, comprising Italian marble, natural oak, and the finest teak.

Even the windows on all but the lowest cabin level are huge for a yacht. The bridge deck's double-curvature bombe windows are particularly impressive, providing a full-circle panoramic view of the surrounding environment. Picchiotti Yachts, the company that collaborated with Vitruvius Yachts and Philippe Briand to devise the My Falco Moscata, claims that the

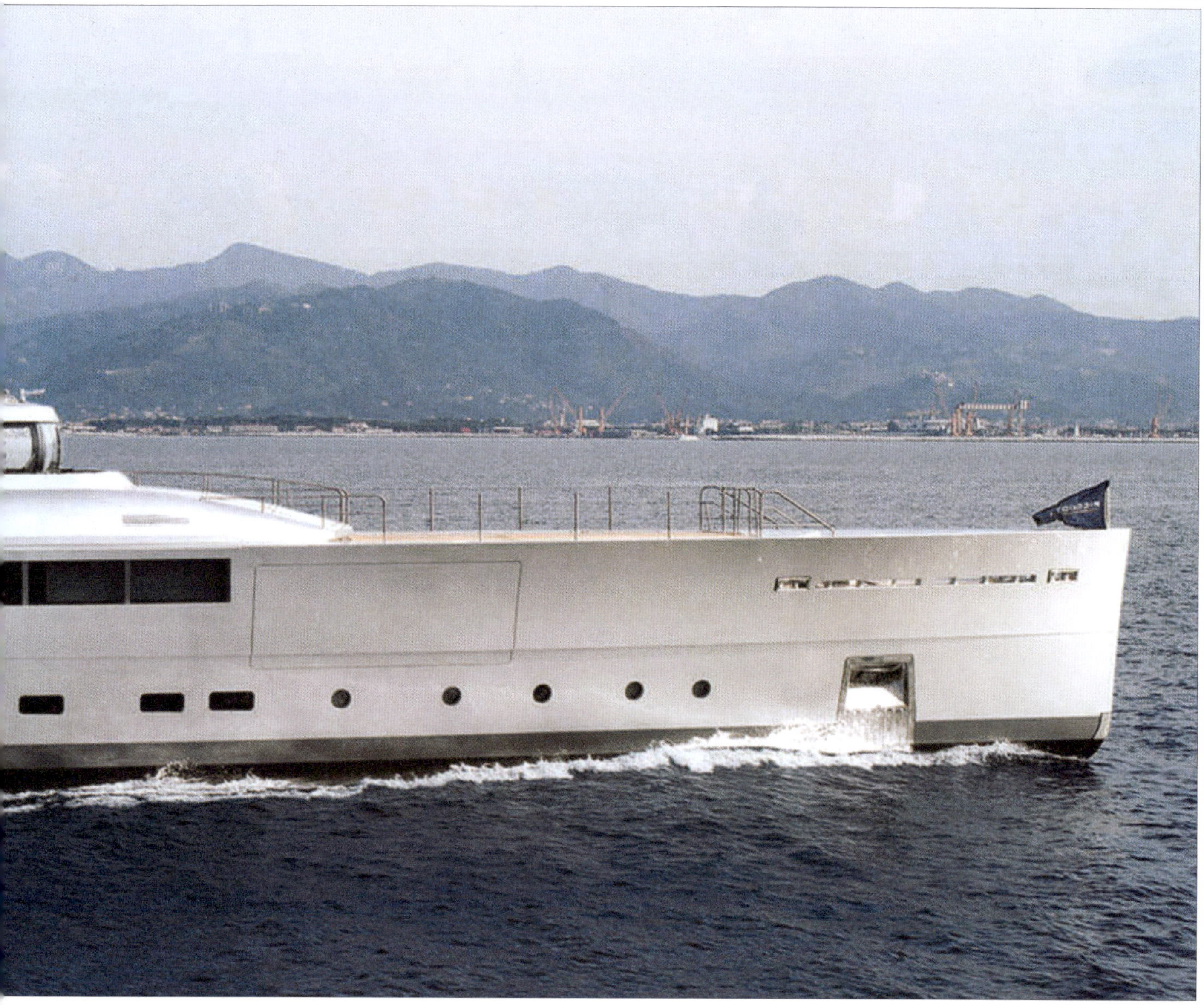

Picchiotti Yachts

Speed under power (maximum/cruise): 16.5/12 kn **Number of owner/guest cabins:** 2 owner and 3 guest cabins **Number of crew cabins:** 4

vessel has revolutionized the design process of explorer yachts, with the expansive windows being just one example. Briand has even referred to the ship as an ideally proportioned superstructure. This statement holds up to scrutiny. The sleekness of the hull lines, the extended nature of the water line, and the optimal balance of straight and curved lines all make the My Falco Moscata one of the most efficient vehicles ever to sail the seas.

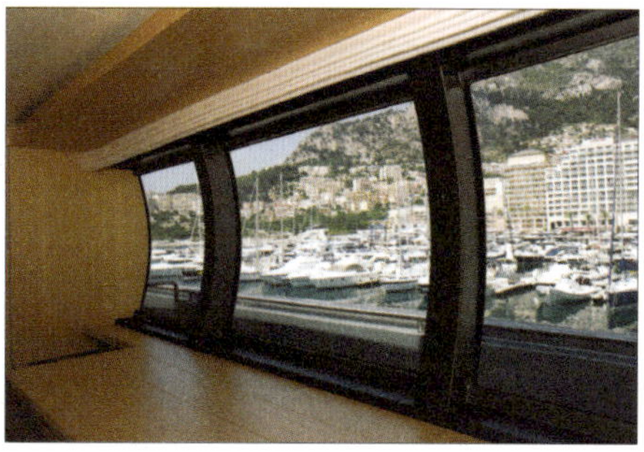

Perhaps the biggest testament to the ship's design is that, with the sheer boldness of the exterior and extravagance of the interior, it's easy to overlook all of the extra vehicles within. Below the spacious forward deck are two garages containing a 12-foot hovercraft and a 16.5-foot amphibious vehicle. A third garage is just behind the transom door at the vessel's stern, housing a 21-foot jet tender. Elsewhere within the ship are a 14-foot rescue tender and a jet ski. These ensure that anyone lucky enough to access the vessel can explore to their heart's content.

Indeed, the My Falco Moscata sets a new standard in maritime adventure.

THE RESULT IS THIS REVOLUTIONARY HULL, MAKING THE TRAWLER CONCEPT OLD-FASHIONED IN COMPARISON. **Philippe Briand, My Falco Moscata Designer**

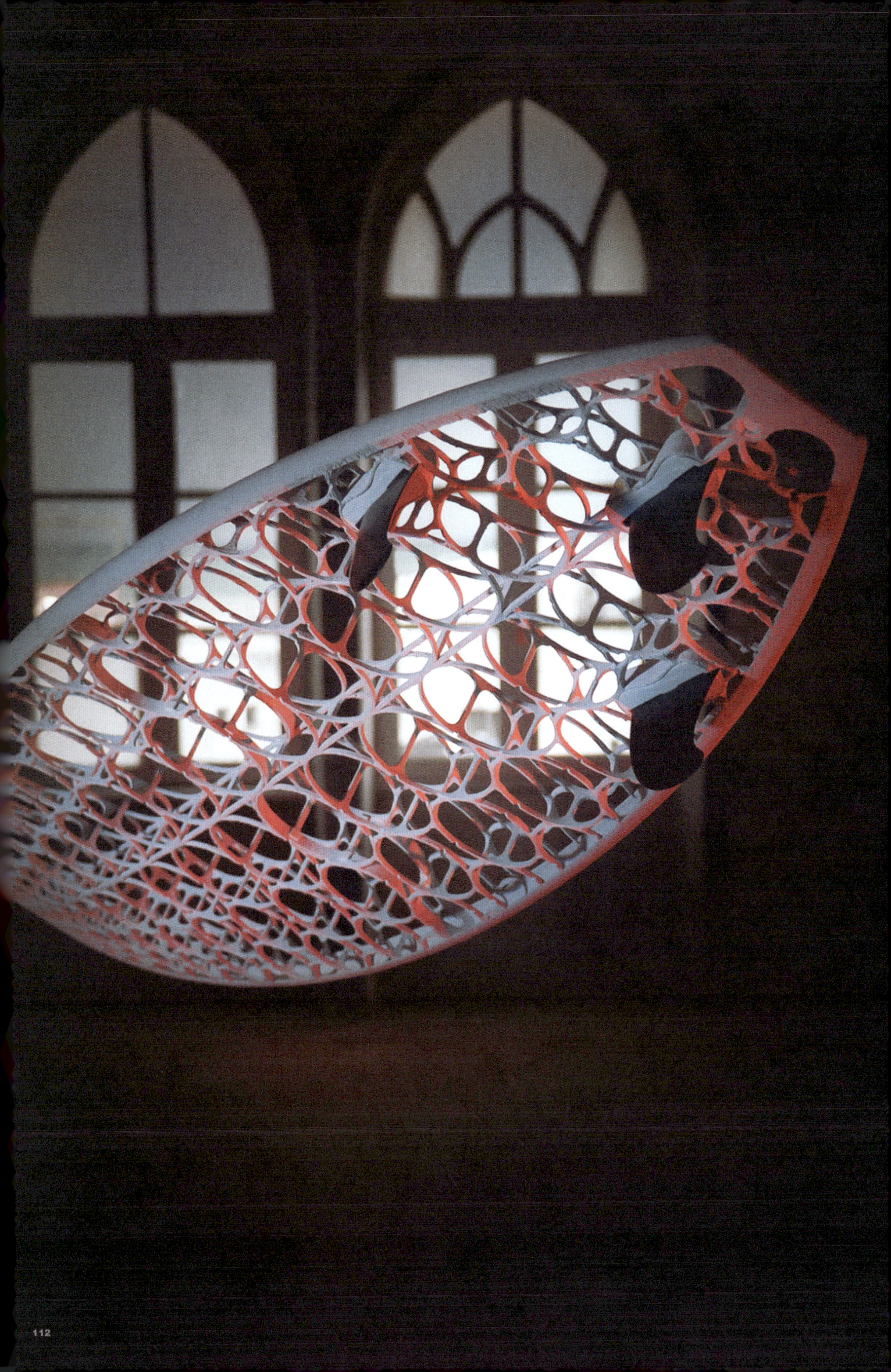

THE 3D-PRINTED SURFBOARD BY PARADOXAL SURFBOARDS $1,600

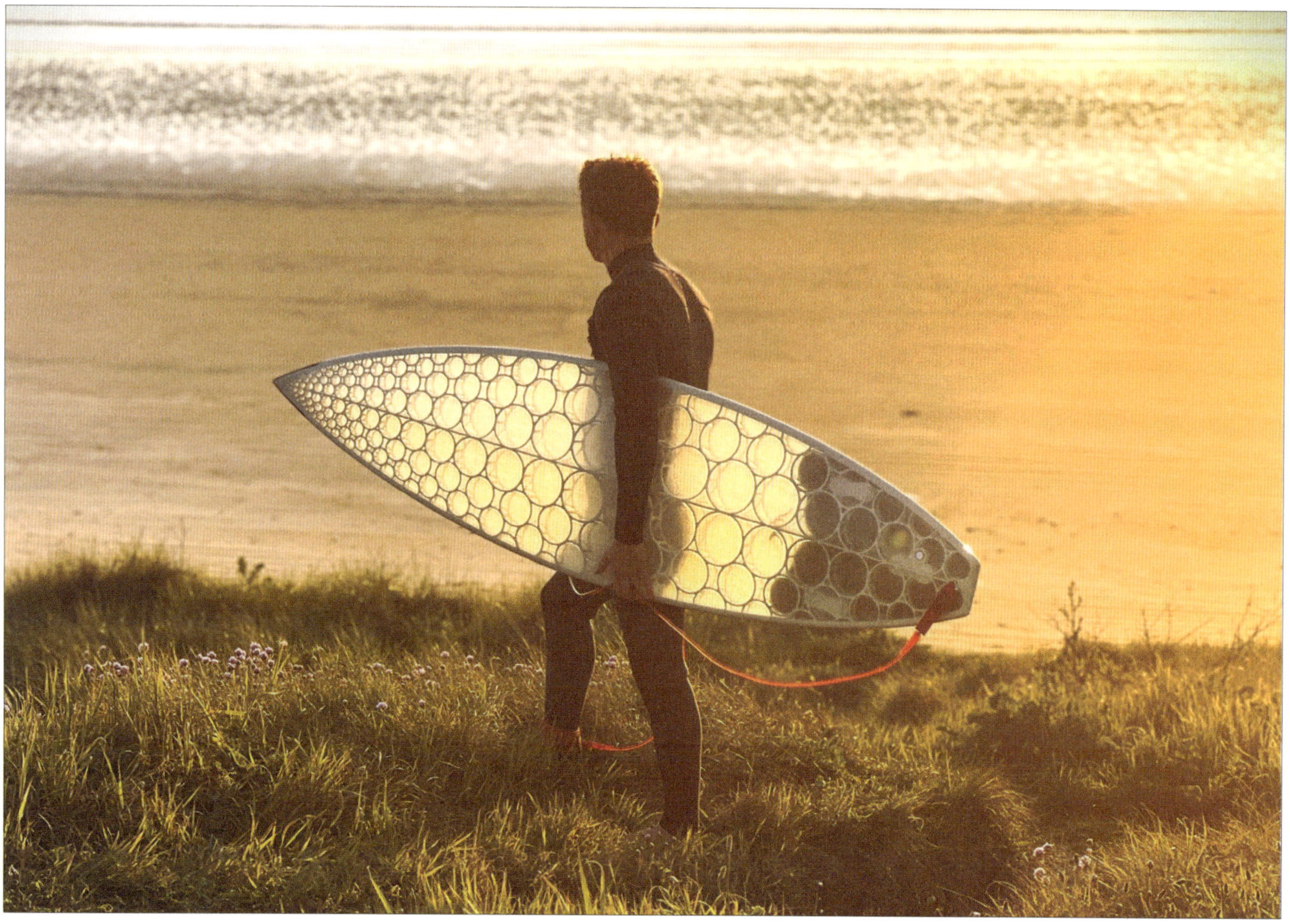

Paradoxal Surfboards

Length: 5 ft 10 in (1.8 m)
Width: 1 ft 10 in (0.5 m)
Height: 2.5 in (6 cen)
Volume: 9 gal (33 L)
Material: 3D printed algae

Many entrepreneurs have used the expression, "When life gives you lemons, make lemonade," to create exciting products. Few have applied this philosophy as literally as Paradoxal Surfboards's founder, Jérémy Lucas, who is converting algae into surfboards via 3D printing.

When discussing design, it's easy to state how curves, colors, and composition convey a specific feel. What's often harder to elaborate on is the ethos behind these physical characteristics. Luckily, with the 3D-printed algae surfboard, the concept is as clear as the product itself. After all, surfing and the hippie-esque eco-conscious spirit often go hand-in-hand.

Frequently, this lifestyle gets conflated with delusionalism. Paradoxal Surfboards shows that this is, in many cases, a misconception. No one can realistically claim that the 3D-printed algae surfboard is the product of a deluded mind. Instead, it's an incredibly innovative solution that the company's founder formulated after conducting significant work on biodiversity, ocean preservation, and 3D printing practicalities.

However, the circumstances surrounding Jérémy Lucas's lightbulb moment did involve one delusional action. Jérémy admits that the idea first emerged after ignoring the prohibition of swimming at Ris Beach in Douarnenez due to an abundance of green algae. As a result, he spent the next two days ill in bed. During this recovery, the idea came to him. He had previously used plant-based plastic in 3D printing and realized that the algae itself could be adapted for the same purpose, removing the hazard and putting it to good use as a material. Essentially, the problem could also be the solution! Like many of the best ideas, it seems so obvious in hindsight.

And, as it's plain to see, the surfboard's appearance is also arresting. Its translucency certainly makes it stand apart from competing products. Many designers will also have ascertained that the inner product's circular honeycomb pattern is utilized to optimize strength while keeping production costs low. This practical element undeniably also gives the board a pleasing aesthetic. Jérémy states that a microscopic image of a diatom algae provided this inspiration. Yet it's easy to imagine that these circles also serve as an expression of the board's overall essence. The act of removing algae, a pollutant, from the environment has resulted in the prevention of the pollution that goes into the production of a conventional surfboard. This using-the-planet-to-save-the-planet approach can definitely be said to be circular. It's precisely the sort of thing that many customers are likely to ponder while using one of these surfboards in the ocean as they wait for the next good wave.

Growing up on the south coast of Britain, I distinctly remember an instance when my father's friend criticized magazine surfboard reviews as a concept because "How much variation can you have in a board?" This highlights why the 3D-printed algae surfboard is incredibly inspiring. These boards prove that there is plenty of room for innovation, and the solutions can literally be floating right in front of you!

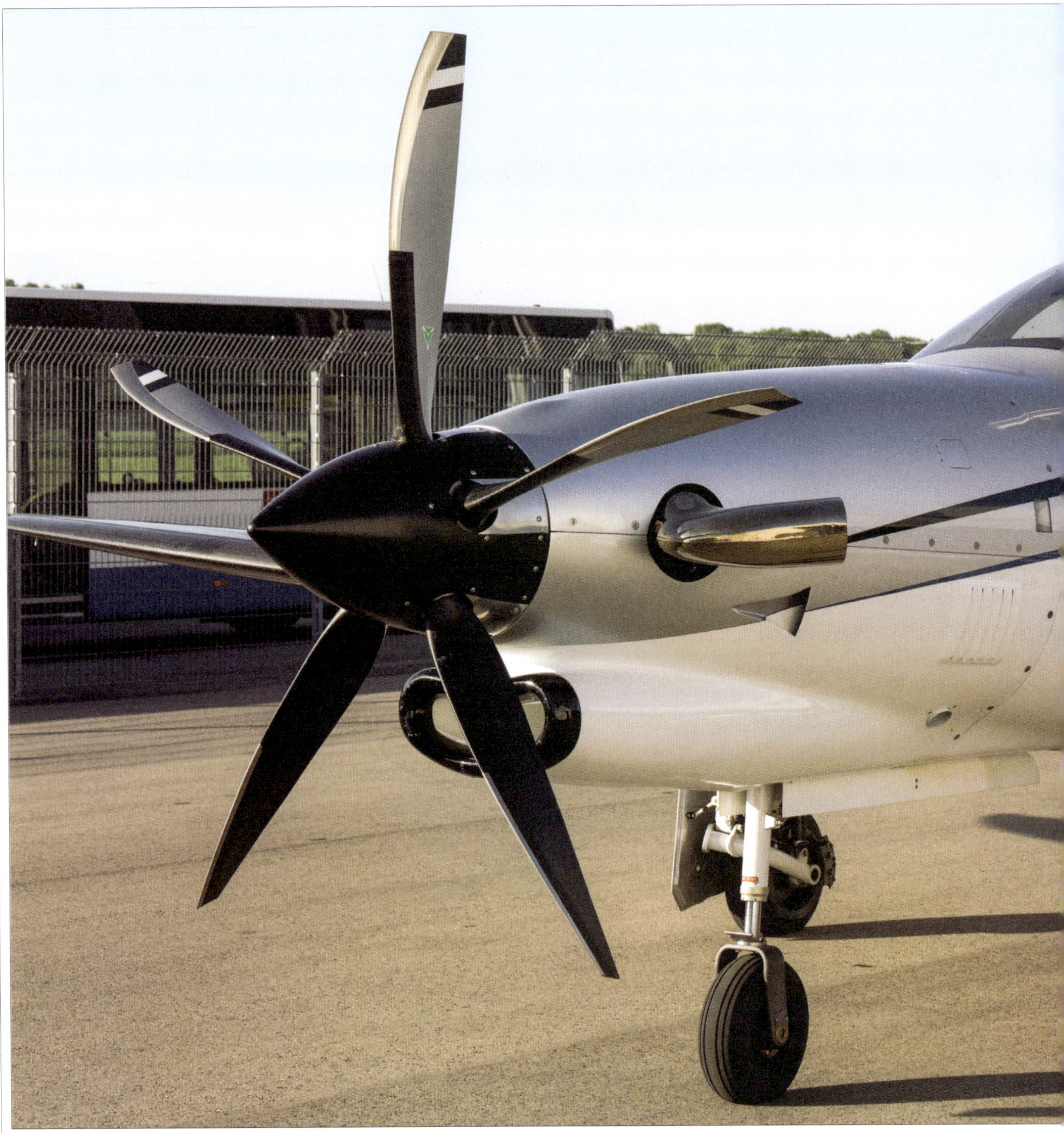

Take off: 1,500 ft (457 m)
Landing: 1,200 ft (366 m)

Best rate of climb: 4,000 ft/min (1,219 m/min)

Max cruise speed: 290 KTAS (334 mph)

Stall speed: 61 KIAS (70 mph)
Vne: 256 KIAS (295 mph)

Engine: Pratt & Whitney PT6-135A
Horsepower: 750 hp

A word that almost, but not quite, describes the Evo is cartoonish—the reason why can be hard to detect initially. Then, a familiar image shines through. The curve of the grill underneath the propeller blades gives the impression of a mustachioed smile. This and the frowny eyebrow-like shape of the cockpit window subtly convey vast amounts of character that, say, 747s never could. Essentially, the plane is smirking, challenging all who see it to take to the skies in search of adventure.

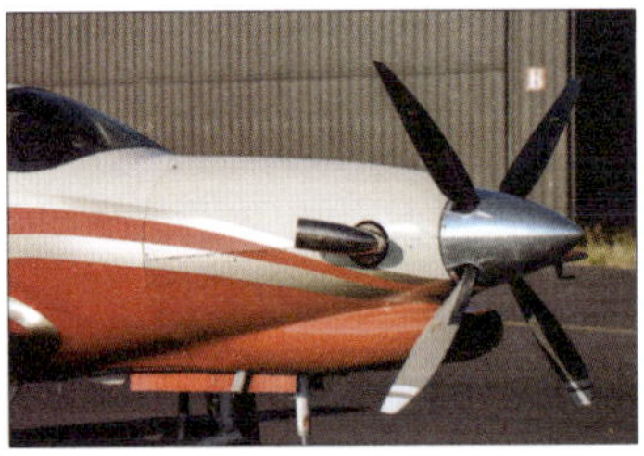

Much like the My Falco Moscata superyacht featured in this issue, the Evo is the result of cross-nation collaboration. Until recently, there were two light aircraft on the market named Evolution: JMB Aircraft's two-seater VL3 Evolution and US entrepreneur Robert Wolstenholme's four-seater kit-built Evolution. In 2022, JMB Aircraft and Wolstenholme decided to partner up, realizing that together, they could improve the overall quality of their products. Basically, they agreed that, by joining forces, they could evolve the Evolutions. This collaboration primarily consists of Wolstenholme reworking the vehicles through conducting research and design, with JMB Aircraft applying its manufacturing expertise to these proposed improvements.

JMB Aircraft's two-seater Evolution model, which is now referred to solely as the VL3, is still on the market. Yet those

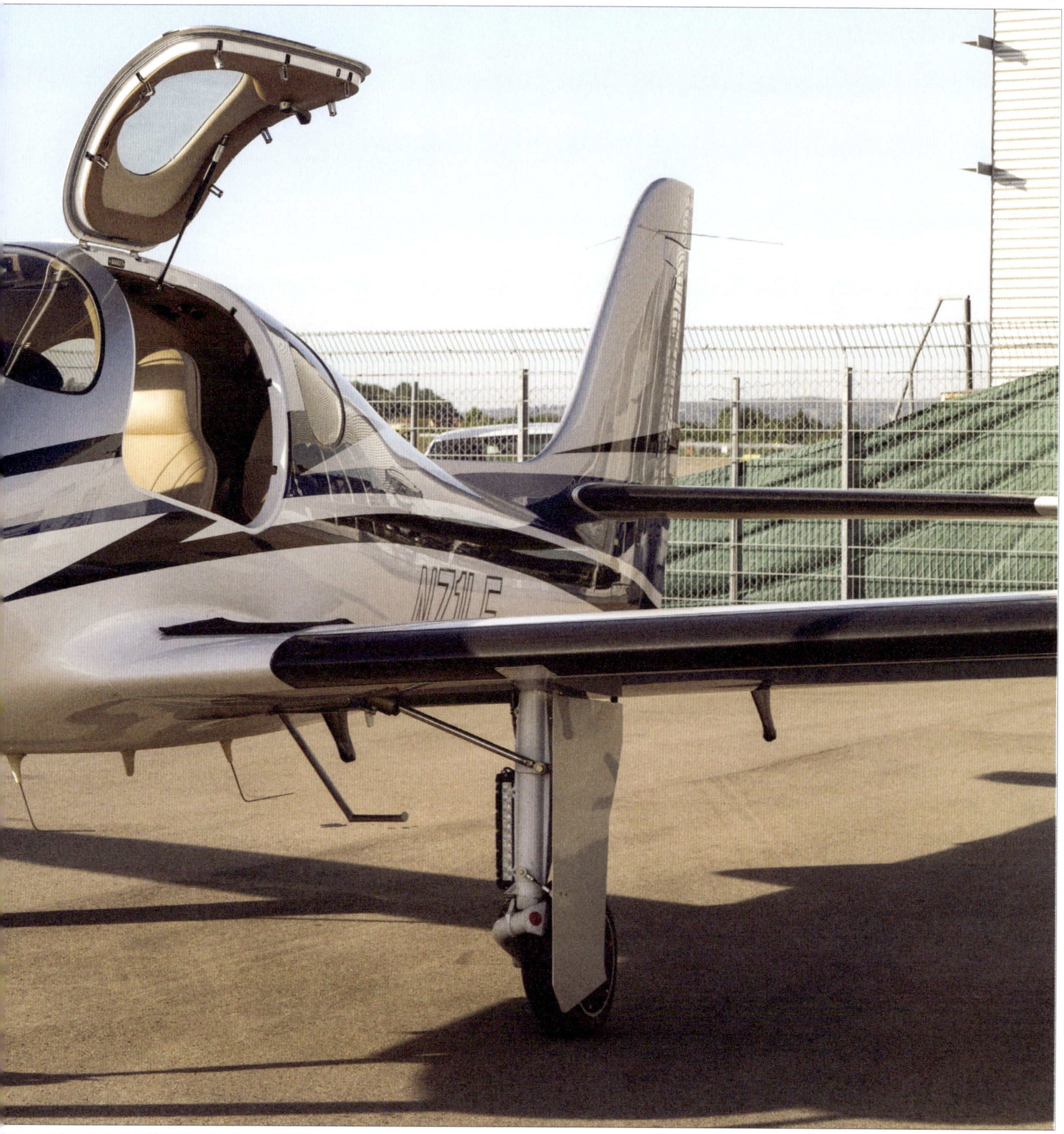

JMB Aircraft

Wingspan: 37 ft (11.3 m)	**Height:** 10 ft (3 m)	**Fuel tanks:** 168 gal (635 L)	**Useful load:** 1,898 lbs (861 kg)
Length: 30 ft (9.1 m)	**Cabin width:** 3 ft 9 in (1.2 m)	**Empty weight:** 2,650 lbs (1,202 kg)	**MTOW:** 4,550 lbs (2,063 kg)

looking for superior performance should only consider the four-seater Evolution, now renamed the Evo, as it offers a number of advantages in addition to the two extra seats. For example, the Evo comes with a 750 horsepower engine, while the most powerful VL3 has a 160 horsepower engine. Similarly, the Evo's fuel tank has a capacity of 168 gallons (635 liters), while the VL3's maximum fuel capacity is just 37 gallons (140 liters).

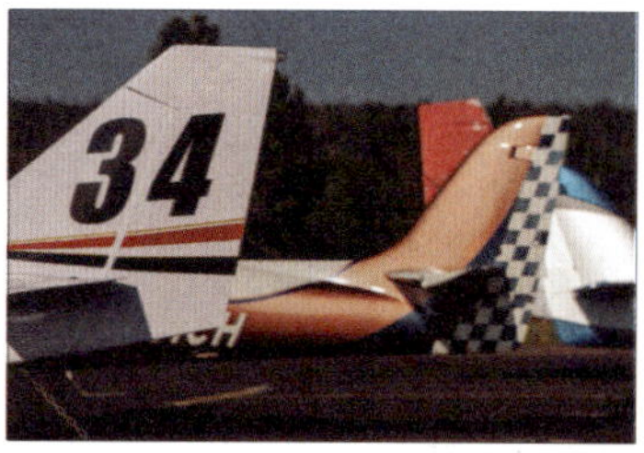

The bones of the interior design can only be discussed because, as JMB Aircraft proudly boasts, "Every cabin is custom upholstered to your design and desires." Unless a customer has an incredibly idiosyncratic request, the four chairs that fill the Evo cabin have incorporated generous amounts of legroom. It's just about possible for the two passengers at the aircraft's rear to tilt their chairs far back enough to feel as if they were lying down, as long as they aren't unusually tall individuals. Technically, this cabin may not meet the standard that someone who always flies in first or business class would demand, but anyone else will be delighted with the space. Again, this refers strictly to the layout of the cabin. Anyone who is offended by the decor of any individual Evo should know that this is a reflection of the original purchaser's customized taste, with JMB Aircraft personnel merely following instructions!

MXL II SPORT LIGHT SERVICE AIRCRAFT BY QUICKSILVER AIRCRAFT $31K

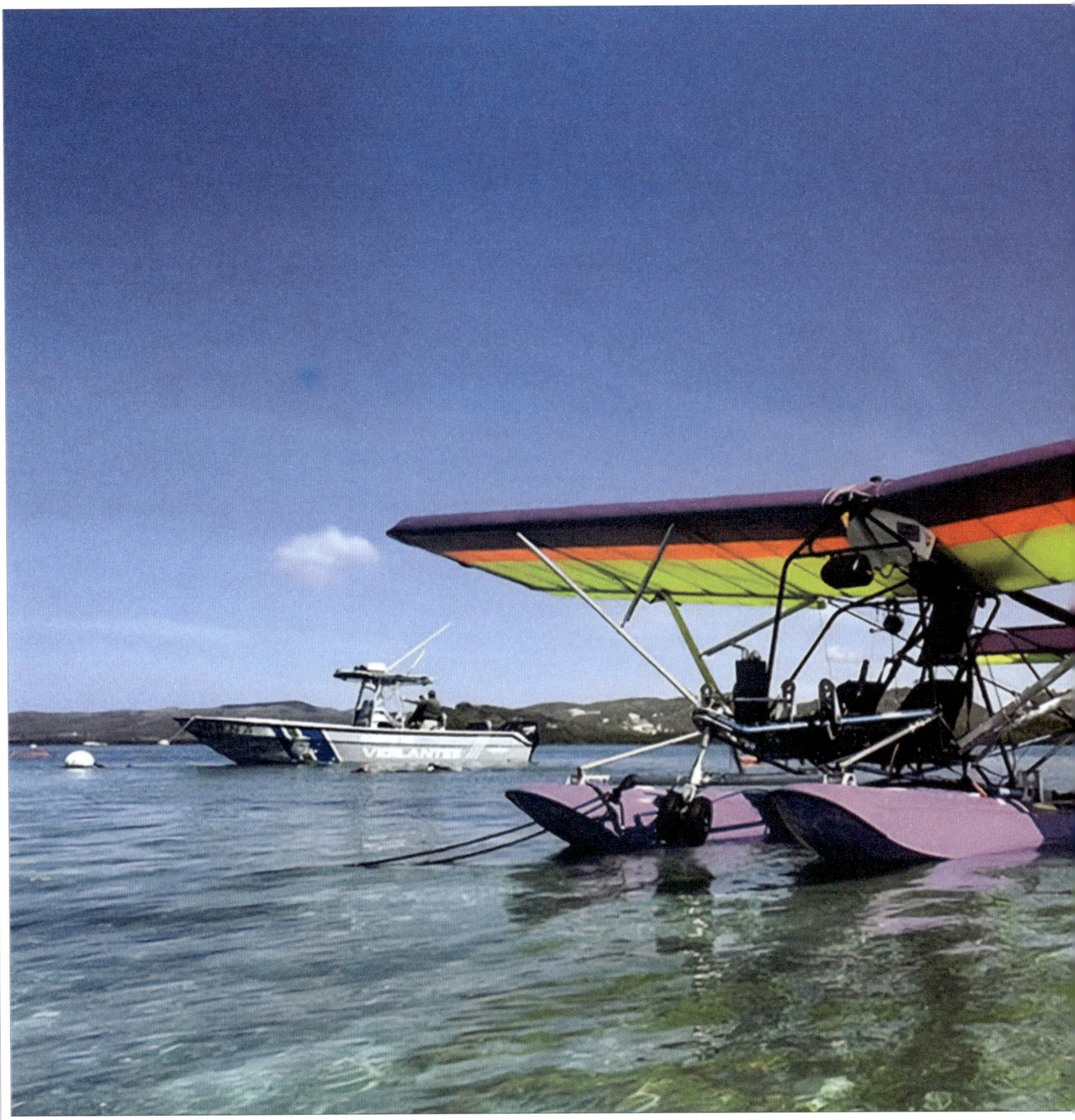

Number of seats: 2	**Wingspan:** 32 ft 9 in (10 m)	**Height:** 9 ft 4 in (2.8 m)	**Engine:** Rotax 582/B
Landing gear: Tricycle	**Length:** 17 ft 6 in (5.3 m)	**Wing area:** 180 sq ft (16.7 sq m)	**Horsepower:** 64 hp

That the MXL II Sport has the appearance of a modernized version of the world's first functional airplane, the Wright Flyer, is apt because it holds a similarly important place in the history of aviation. Quicksilver Aircraft claims that "more pilots have been trained to fly in the MXL II Sport than all other light planes combined." This fact alone speaks volumes of the plane's superior maneuverability and precise control response. Clearly, anything that can appeal to such a wide range of flying enthusiasts must be well-designed in terms of practicality.

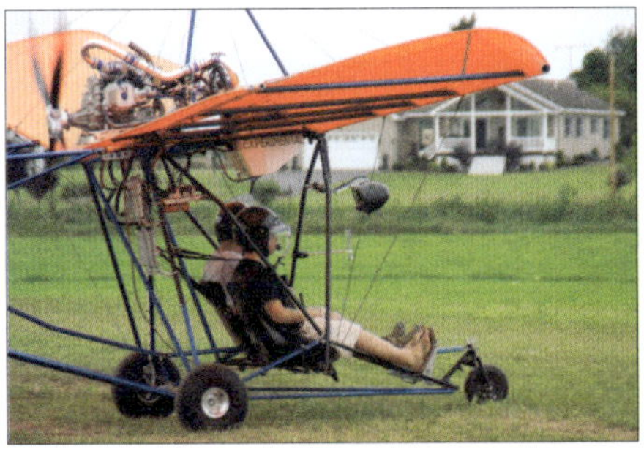

Part of what has made the MXL II Sport so popular is the ease that it offers, and not just in terms of flying. The aircraft is supplied as an amateur build kit, which Quicksilver states is the easiest to assemble on the market. Naturally, it's extremely difficult to prove that these kits are absolutely the easiest to assemble in the entire world. Still, the popularity of the aircraft indicates that, at the very worst, they are at least among the most straightforward to assemble. The simple frame of the MXL II Sport also effortlessly communicates that, for something that can take to the skies, it can be constructed relatively hassle-free. Indeed, some may experience more frustration putting together IKEA furniture than an MXL II Sport.

The MXL II Sport's bare-bones nature is the key to its lon-

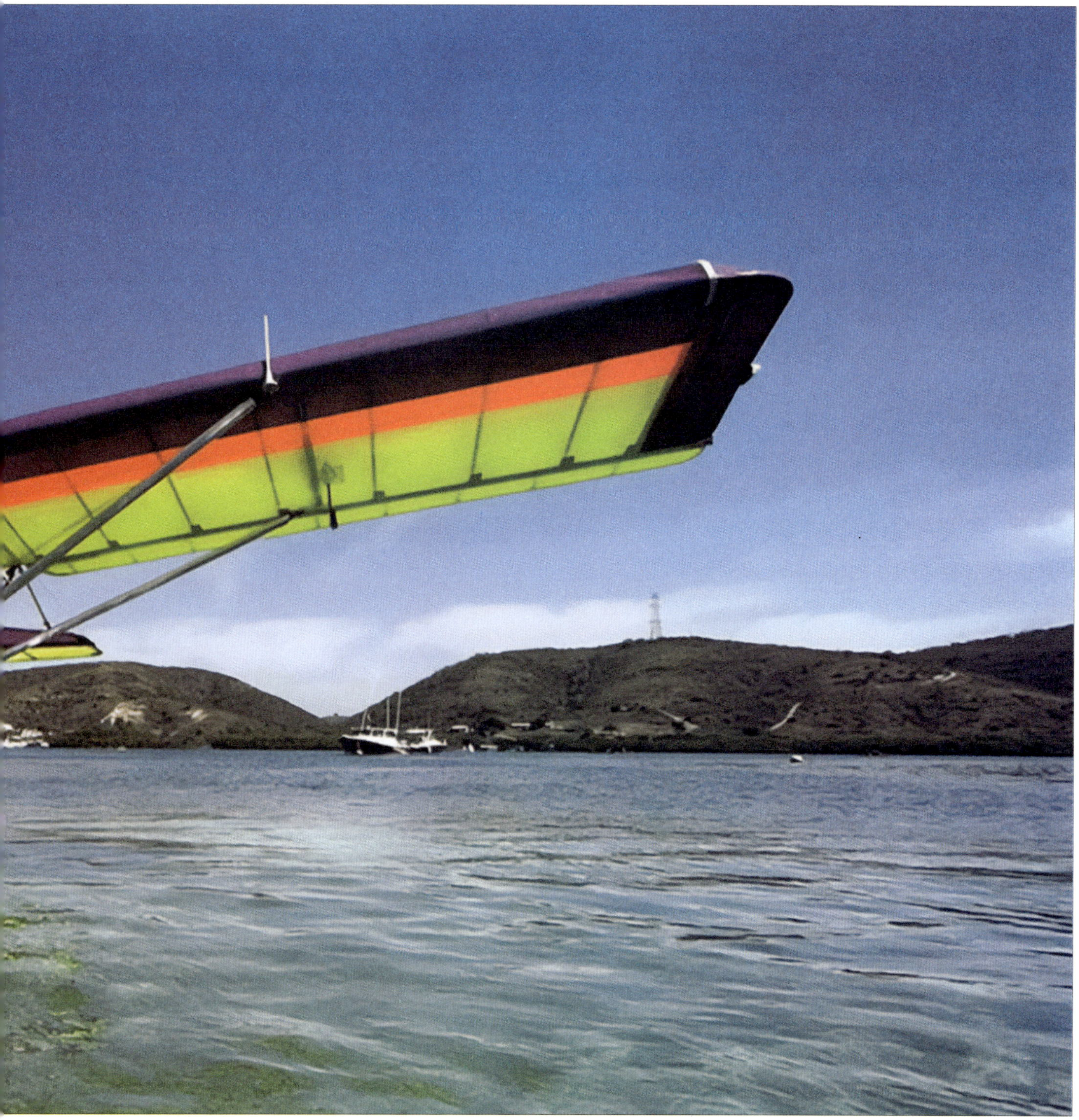

Quicksilver Aircraft

Empty weight: 325 lbs (147 kg)	**VNE:** 75 mph (65 kn)	**Cruise speed:** 40-61 mph (35-53 kn)
Useful load: 395 lbs (179 kg)	**Top level speed:** 61 mph (53 kn)	**Stall speed:** 32 mph (28 kn)

gevity on the market. The prime example of how this spirit is applied throughout the product is its simple steering mechanism. The aircraft is piloted through a single control stick located between its two chairs. Shifting this is all that's necessary to maneuver the plane.

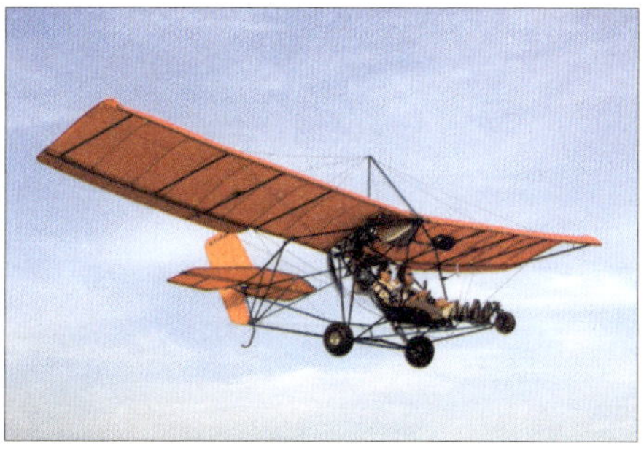

With the aircraft's frame being so minimalist, those looking to add character to the craft must rely on the wings. Overall, purchasers can choose between 14 colors and shades that run the gamut of the visual spectrum. It's even possible to apply seven individual colors or shades to a single MXL II Sport, although many would consider the result quite a clash! A number of optional add-ons ensure further diversity. The photographs on this page go some way toward elaborating both the variance that the colors and optional extras provide. Regarding the additional features, the floats adapting the craft into a seaplane in the main photograph provide a strong example of how individuals can diversify the design. Also on offer to add to the aircraft are electronic instrument systems, radios, wider seats, strobe lights, shoulder harness kits, ballistic parachutes, and much more.

And if anyone still doubts the ingenuity of the MXL II Sport, just ask why over 10,000 people have piloted this aircraft to date. Surely, it must have risen to the top of the ever-competitive aviation industry for a reason!

A

ARCHITECTURE & EXHIBITS

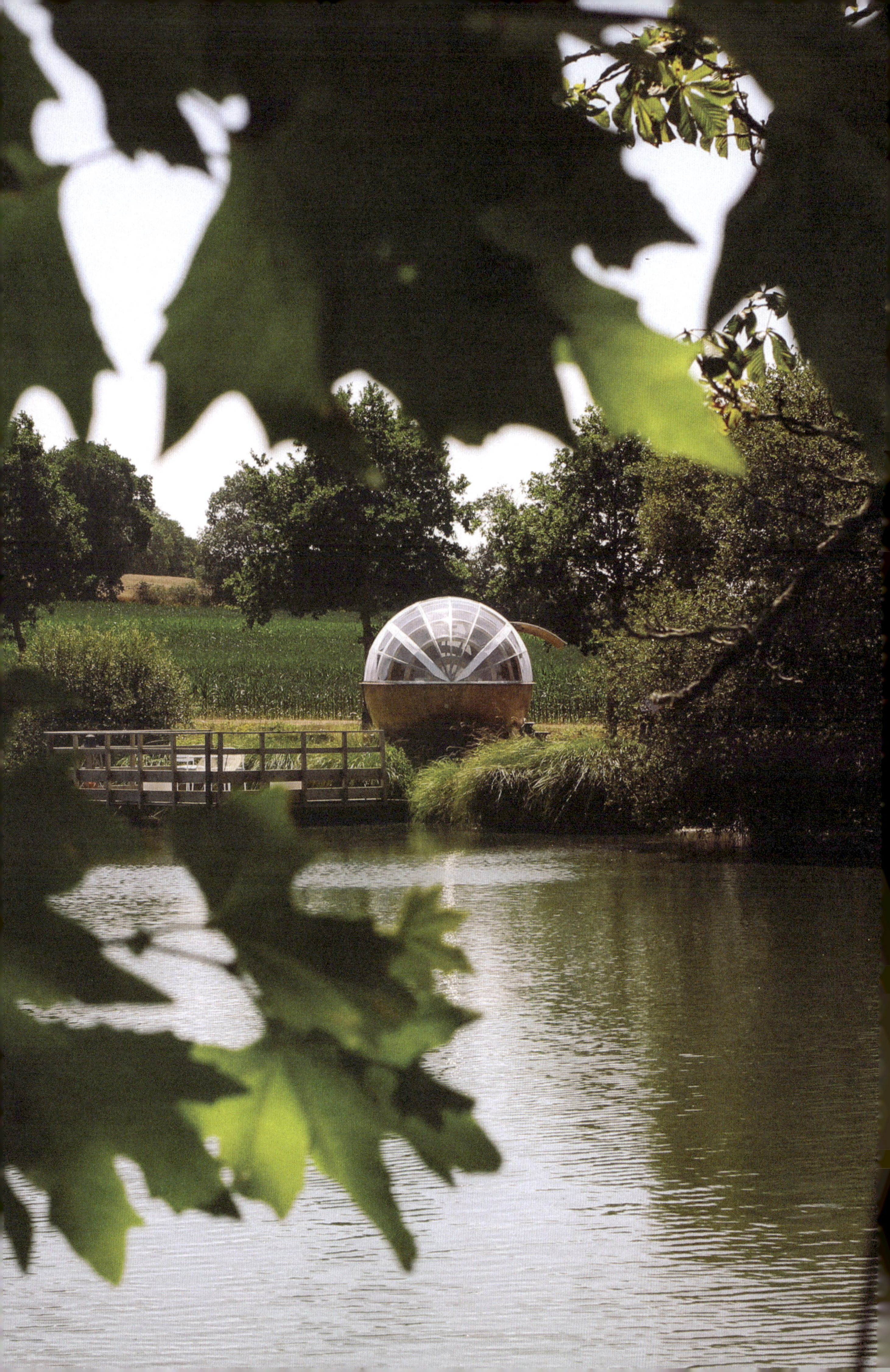

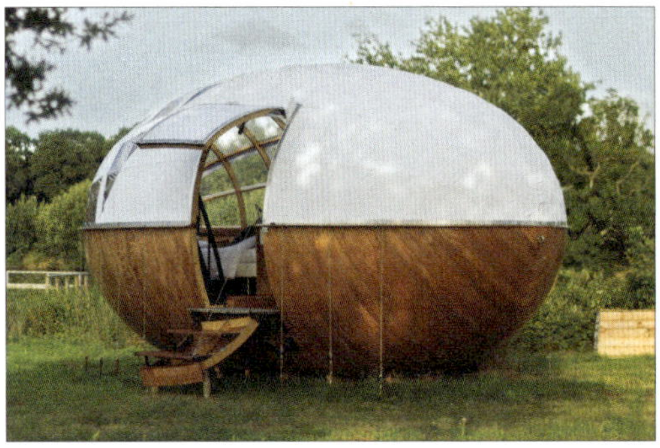

When the sunshine bounces from the oval wooden ribs within Mr. Plocq's Caballon, anyone inside will surely be enthralled. Not only is the sight spellbinding to gaze at, but the transformation in the color of the ribs reveals what must have been the guiding light of the structure: the Golden Ratio. This clever detail proves that Mr. Plocq's Caballon is the work of a team that prizes aesthetic quality above all else.

Naturally, the designers also made an effort to make the Caballon's look just as engaging at all hours, both inside and outside. At night, LED strips within the flooring and a pair of unobtrusive gooseneck lights on either side of the bed provide warm illumination that subtly changes the ambiance of the cockpit depending on how the goosenecks are angled.

Yes, design documents refer to the bedroom space of the Caballon as a "cockpit," revealing the initial spark that led to the structure's existence. A story in France says that one Mr. Plocq constructed a vessel that he used in conjunction with thousands of birds to fly to Africa. The architects sought to visualize what this vessel would have looked like.

The naming of the small bedroom as a cockpit also highlights another astounding effect of the lighting, only apparent from the outside. At night, as the LED illumination emanates from within, the organic tones of the structure are obscured. As a result, the tiny dwelling takes on the appearance of a spaceship that's subtly snuck down to Earth.

Hidden away at the back of the interior is a surprisingly spacious bathroom that further emphasizes the attention to beauty that Mr. Plocq's Caballon proudly boasts. The wooden beams that stand together to form the bathroom door bend in a smooth curve outwards, further imprinting the influence of the Golden Ratio. This doorway rotates in a perfect circle, revealing a small shower space. Beyond this shower space is a small room housing facilities that flow in tune with the structure. Everything immediately visible, except for the sink and a few hinges, is made out of the same wood as the structure's frame.

Both the interior and exterior of Mr. Plocq's Caballon should be shown to anyone considering opening a business in the glamping space. Too often, when people look to profit from a burgeoning industry, they fail to spend time planning how to stand out from the competition. As a result, most glamping locations fill their spaces with one of two tent shapes: A-framed safari-style squares or bell-style cones. Mr. Plocq's Caballon has managed to incorporate all of the materials used in those styles of tents, yet has created something much more unique!

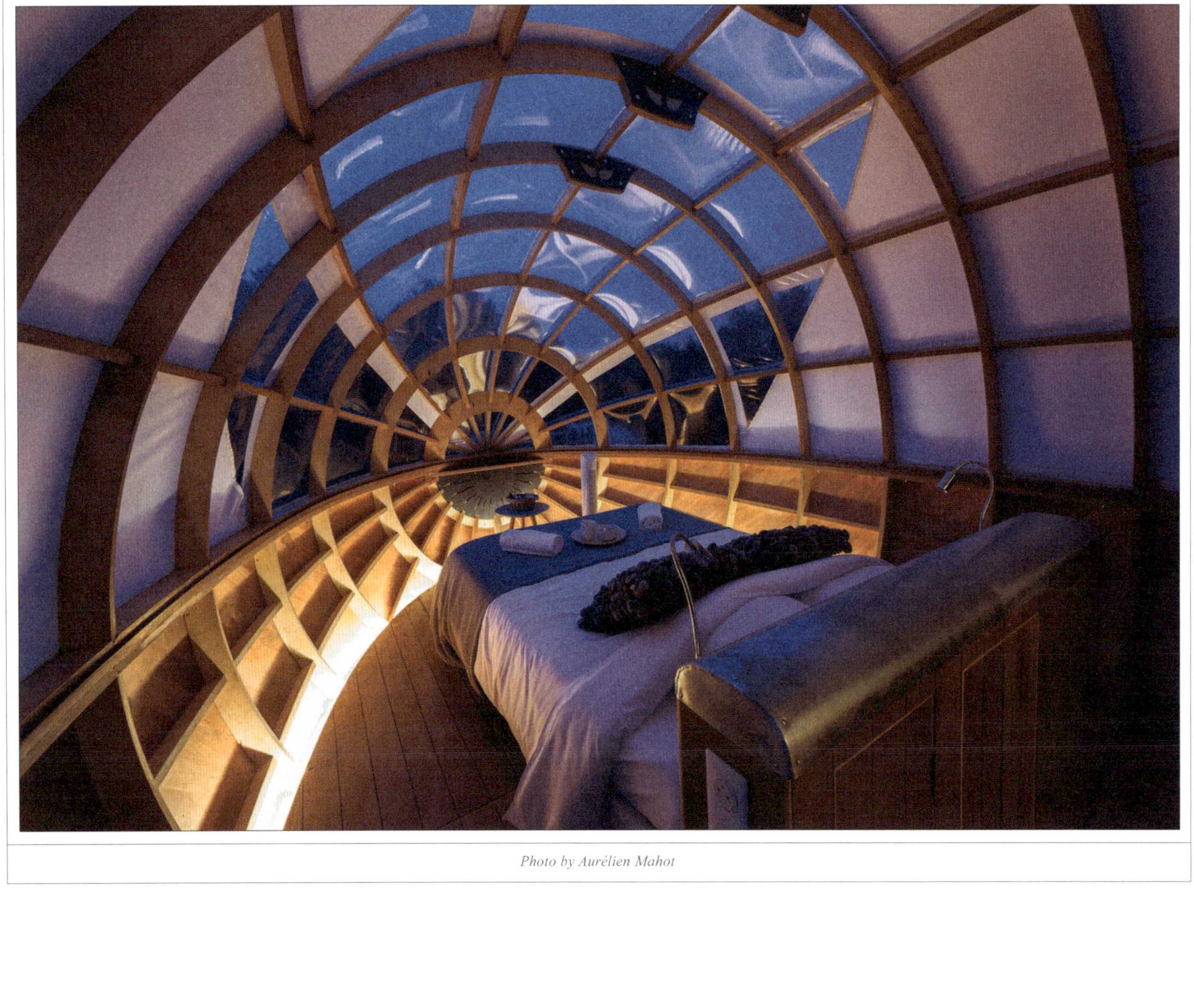

Photo by Aurélien Mahot

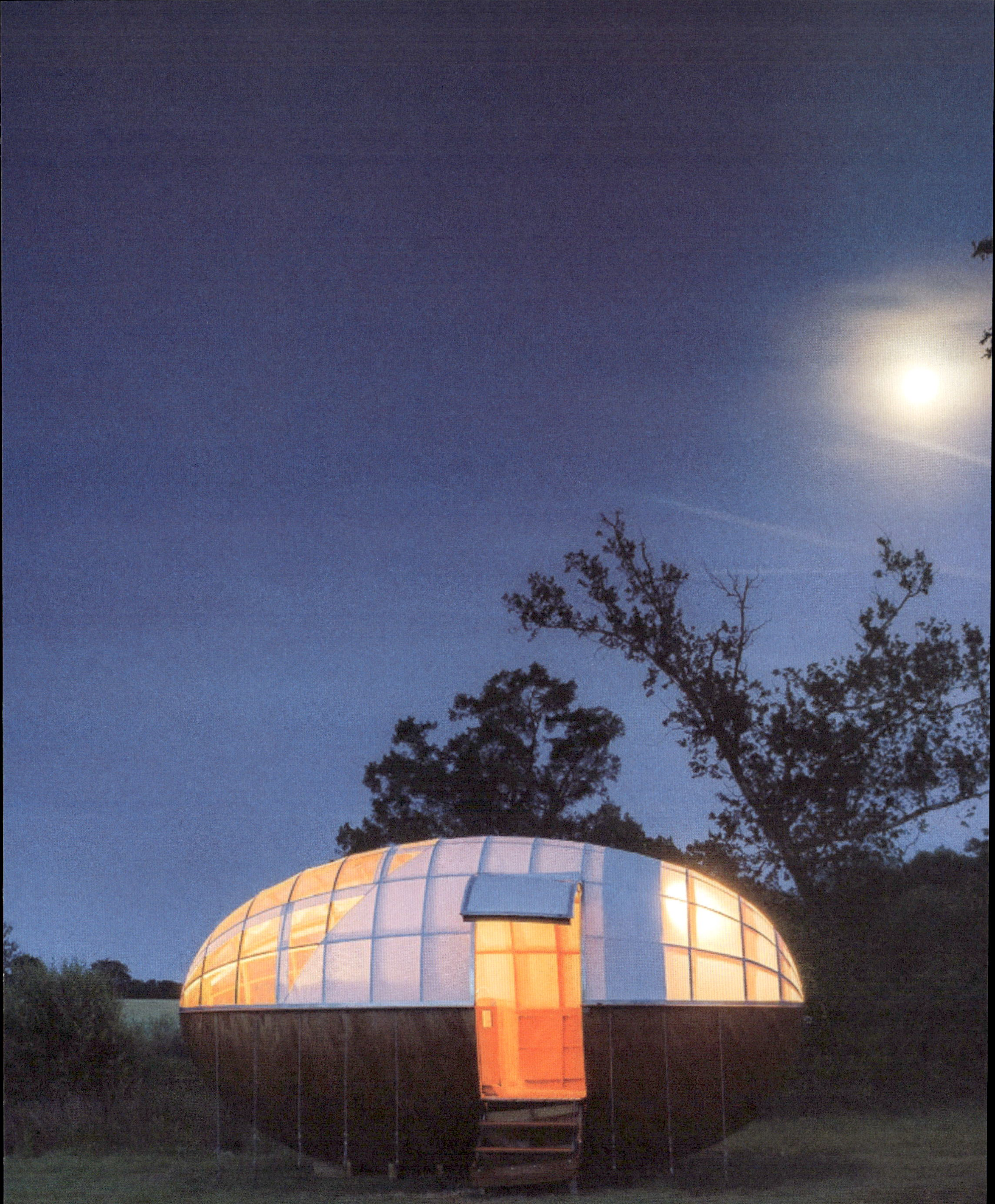

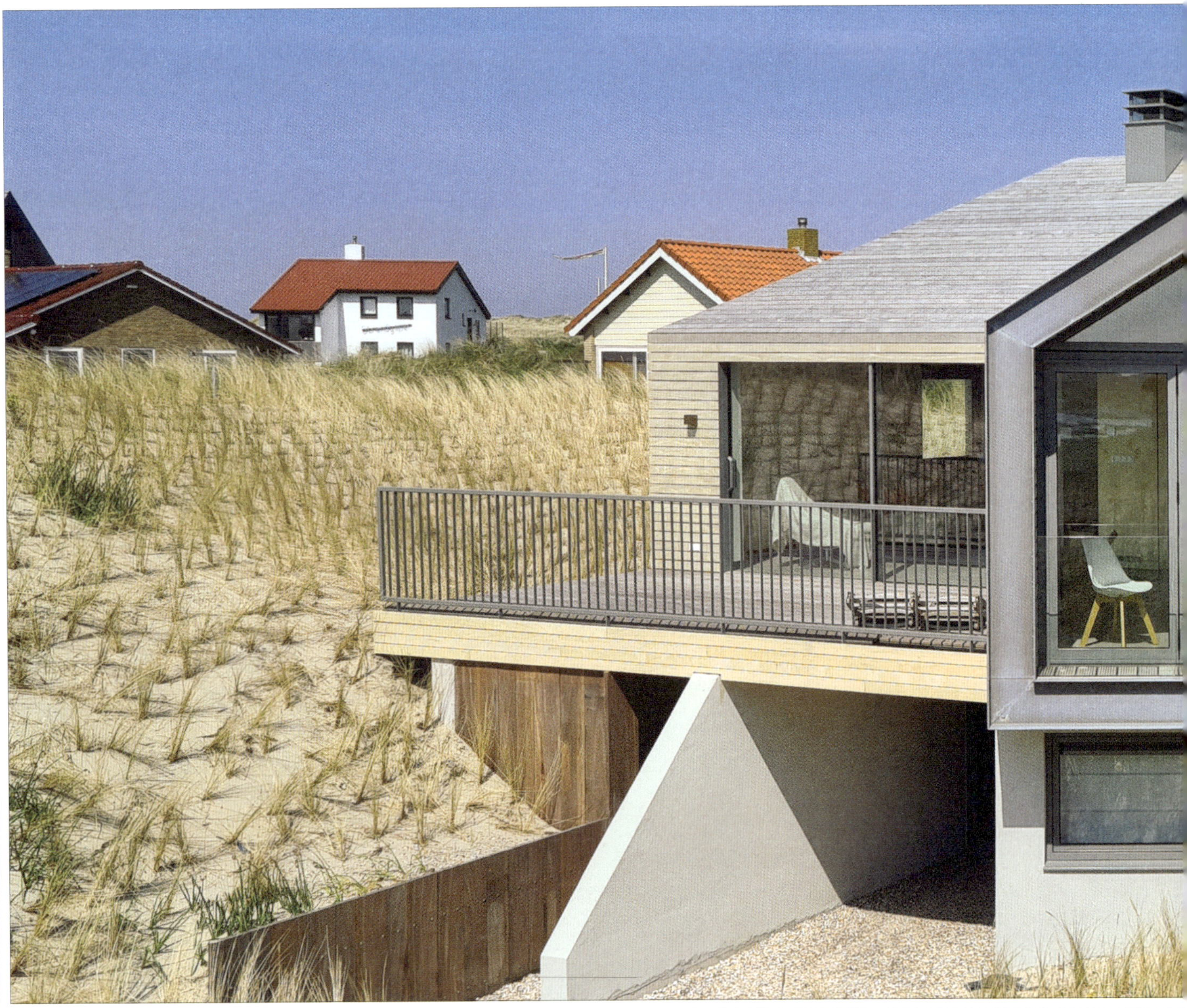

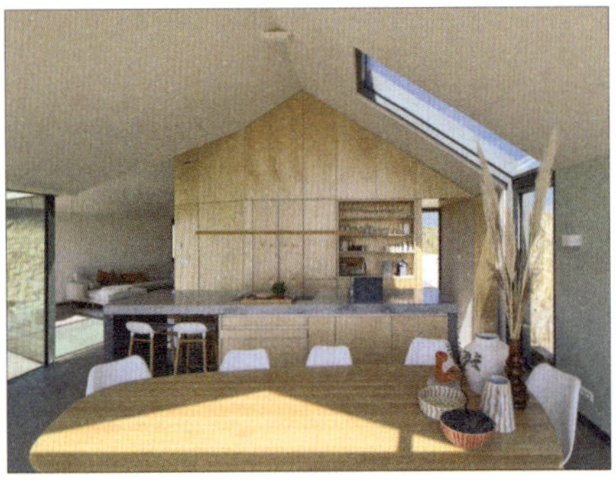

Dune Villa West aan Zee is designed to blend in with its environment in multiple ways. Most notably, the understated hues of the exterior allow the structure to visually align with its sandy surroundings. However, on a much deeper level, the building respects the land it's built on, with 2by4-architects, the firm responsible for this home, dedicating themselves to sustainability throughout the construction project. Thanks to utilizing biobased materials, solar panels, and a range of other environmental-focused measures, the final home has a net zero carbon footprint.

However, the smartest manner in which Dune Villa West aan Zee fits in seamlessly with its environment is how the more ostentatious features are hidden away. From its adjoining street, the villa appears to be an unusually angular sand dune, hence the structure's name. One thin strip of a window, which runs from the basement to the ceiling, and a small chimney make it somewhat clear that this is a man-made structure. However, from the right angle, it's easy to glance at this part of the building briefly while driving and mistake it for a genuine sand dune. On the other side, facing a dramatically gruff rural landscape, are the gigantic windows that take up almost the entirety of two walls. Also revealed at this angle is the clever way that the building seamlessly fits into the curvature of its surroundings. A whole extra level, impossible to see from the road, occupies the dip in the surrounding dune, incorporating a cavernous porch that props up a spacious balcony and a lower floor featuring bedrooms, bathrooms, storage space, and a laundry room.

The tucked-away nature of the home is also a product of the architects working with the keyword "hermit." They knew that this home needed to represent an escape into nature in a manner that was unobvious to passersby. The semi-seclusion of the finished home would undoubtedly make any hermitage within its walls a wholesome experience, with the option of quickly returning to civilization at any point something advantageous to anyone who has to interact with the 21st-century world.

While the Germanic last words are something of a giveaway to the Dune Villa West aan Zee's European location, many could easily mistake this building for a Frank Lloyd-Wright mid-century modern home in the Arizona desert. Instead, it's closer geographically and conceptually to Scandinavia. The home is located on Terschelling, an island to the north of the Dutch mainland.

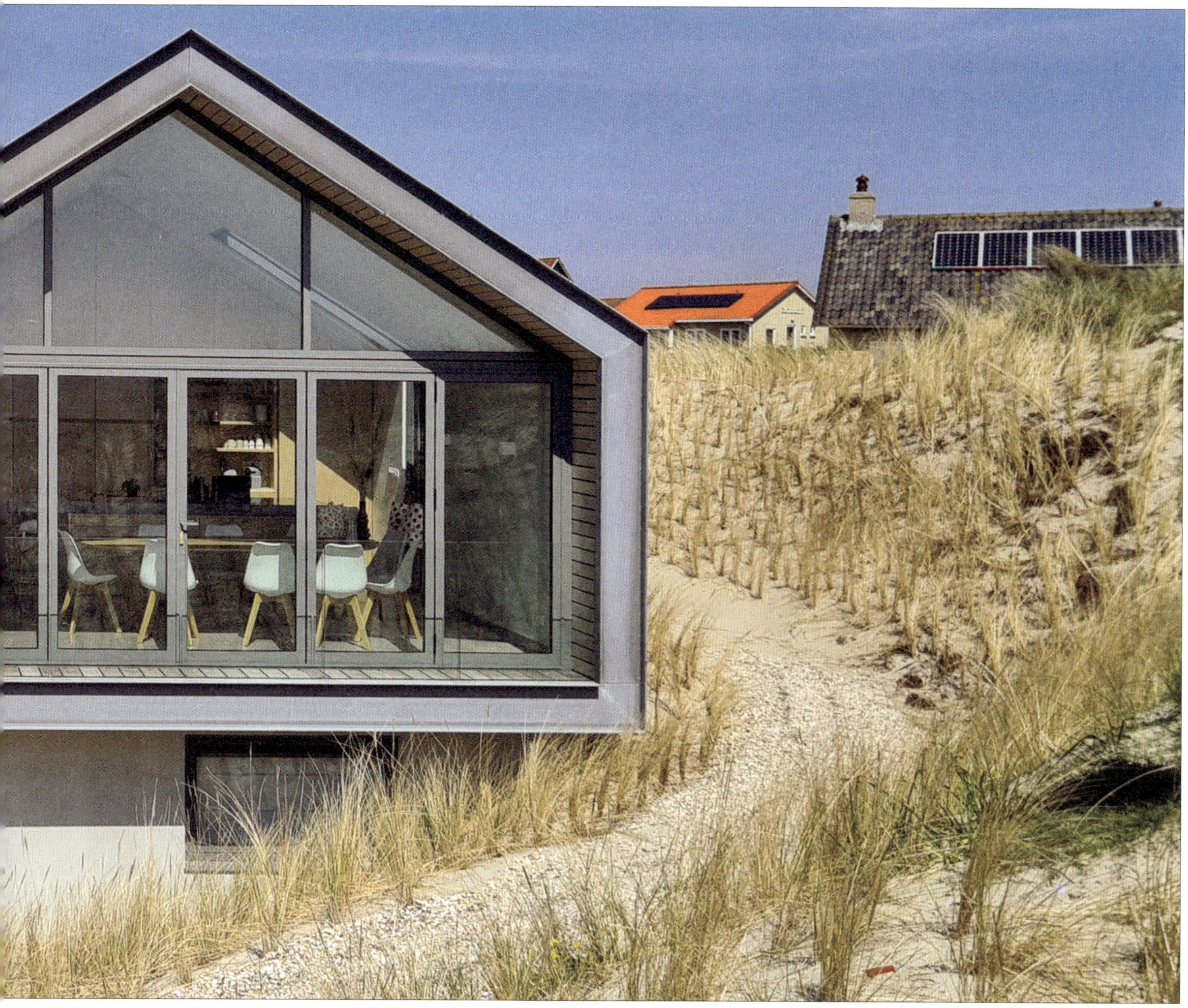

2by4-architects

Certainly, the interior also has touches of both mid-century and Scandinavian design elements. When viewed through the expansive kitchen and dining room window, the most noticeable furnishings are the Eames-style chairs, reinforcing the American mid-century modern mirage. However, the Scandinavian influence is clearly more prominent throughout the rest of the home, such as through the kitchen cabinetry's distinctly Nordic angularity and tone.

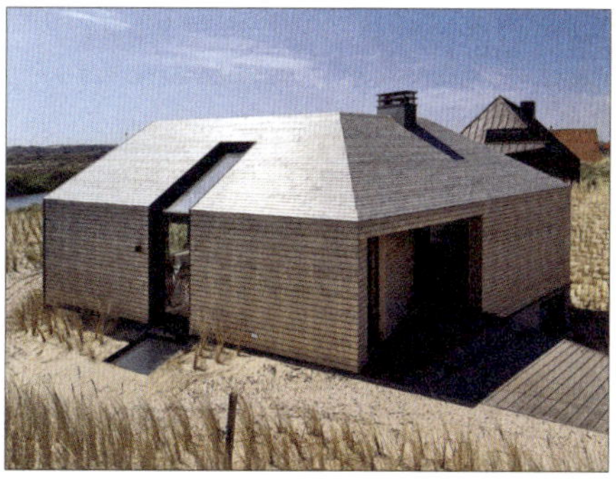

The dedication that 2by4-architects had in undertaking their assignment literally is truly something to admire. When asked to build a structure that blends in with the environment, many other firms would never be bold enough to suggest a home that seems to be embedded within its surroundings. Neither would many consider installing almost all of its windows on a single side to make the rest of the structure fit in with the surroundings. During the planning stages, such an ambitious project must have seemed risky. The outstanding final product proves that this risk has paid off!

THE ARCHITECTURAL CHALLENGE FOR THIS PROJECT WAS TO CREATE A SUSTAINABLE HOLIDAY HOME ON TERSCHELLING THAT HARMONIOUSLY BLENDS INTO THE UNIQUE DUNE LANDSCAPE OF WEST AAN ZEE AND MAXIMIZES THE BREATHTAKING VIEWS. **2by4-architects**

E

EDUCATION

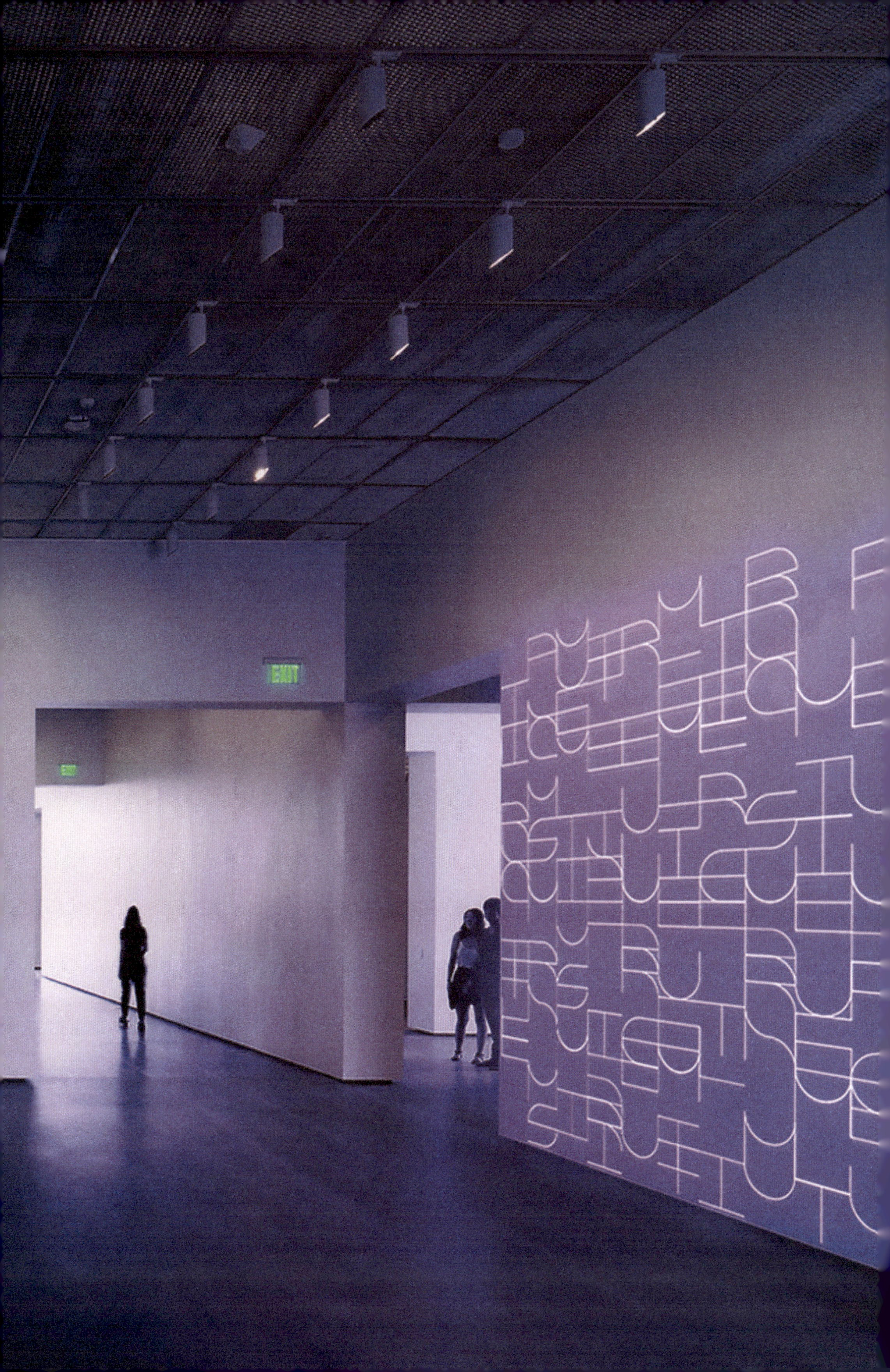
EXIT

NATASHA IS SINCERELY ONE OF THE MOST INTELLIGENT AND FUNNY WOMAN I HAVE EVER MET. SHE WILL NOT DISAPPOINT YOU.

Jean-Marc Joseph, *Filmmaker, Superjeanmarc*

NATASHA JEN IS AN EXCEPTIONAL MENTOR AND A TRUE SOURCE OF INSPIRATION. SHE PRIORITIZES HER STUDENTS' GROWTH AND SUCCESS, DEMONSTRATING GENUINE CARE AND DEDICATION.

Hyun Jung Lee, *Former Student & Junior Designer, 2x4*

LEARNING FROM NATASHA WAS A DISCOVERY PROCESS. SHE HAS THE UNIQUE ABILITY TO MAKE ONE DISCOVER DESIGN; SHE TAUGHT ME HOW TO THINK IN DESIGN RATHER THAN DOING IT LIKE A TASK.

Ipshita Krishan, *Former Student & Freelance Designer*

SHE IS THE MOST POWERFUL DESIGNER I HAVE MET DURING MY ACADEMIC YEARS. SHE SINCERELY CARES ABOUT STUDENTS' WORK AND KNOWS WHAT MAKES THEIR WORK DIFFERENT AND POWERFUL.

Hyowon Kwon, *Former Student & Freelance Designer*

AS MY INSTRUCTOR AT SVA, SHE TAUGHT ME THE IMPORTANCE OF RELENTLESS INQUIRY AND INTENTION. AS MY BOSS, SHE TAUGHT ME HOW TO BALANCE FLEXIBILITY AND RIGOR.

Leo Porto, *Founder & Creative Director, PORTO ROCHA*

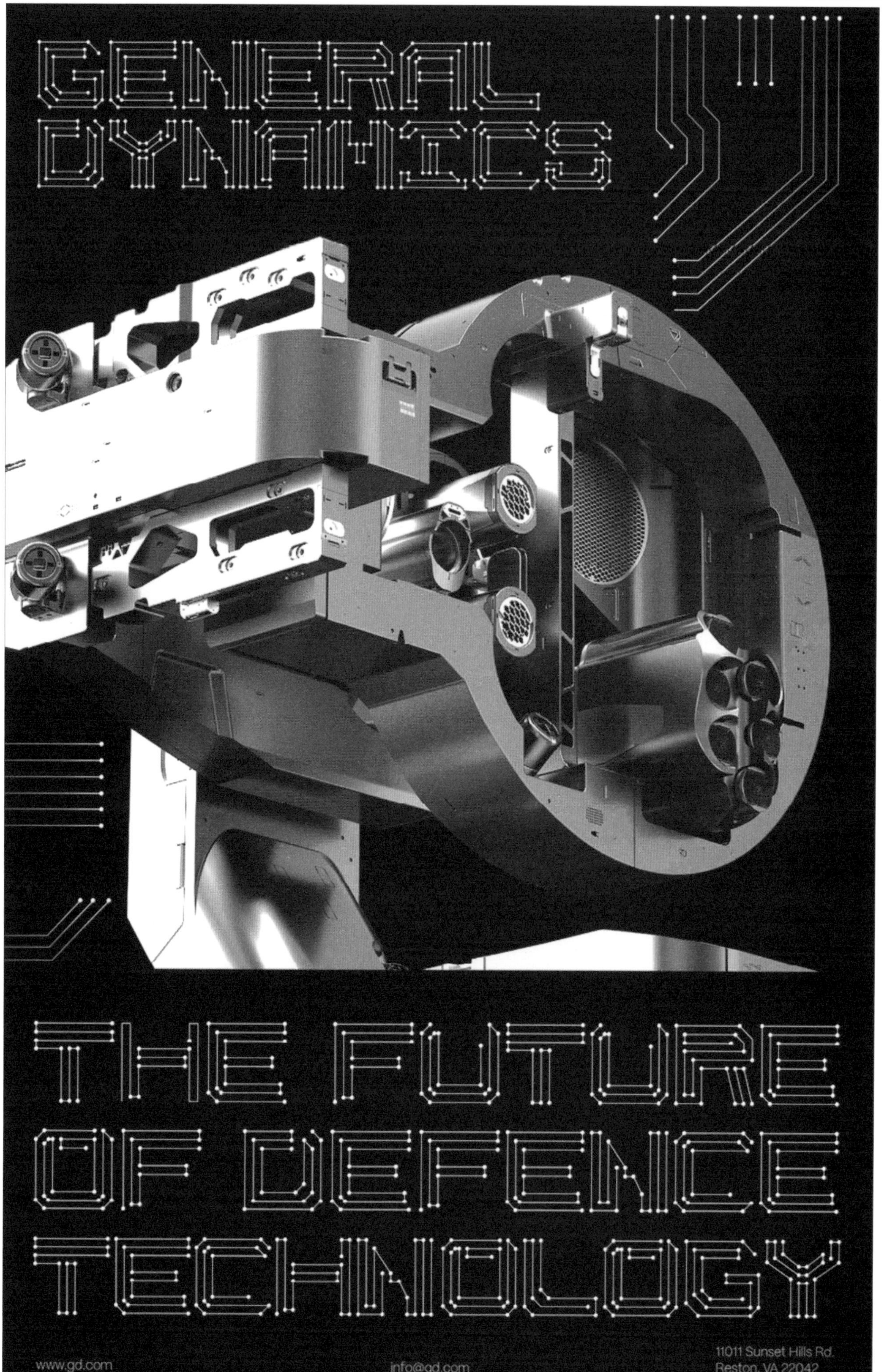

(Page 125) The Light Museum, New Talent Annual 2020. Professor: Natasha Jen. Platinum-winning student: Hansol Jang
(Above) General Dynamics Poster, New Talent Annual 2024. Professor: Natasha Jen. Platinum-winning student: Rachel Pan

Introduction by **David Blankenship** *Partner & Creative Director, CollectiveLA*

In the mid to late 1990s, there were many small design studios dotting lower Manhattan. The one I worked at was busy and spirited, often operating in a hand-to-mouth fashion and with dramatic ups and downs (sometimes in a single day). During these five years, I witnessed a colorful and fascinating array of designers and interns pass through. Natasha Jen stood out. At first, she seemed to be just another meek intern, but this act didn't last long. Yes, she was talented (whatever that means), but what impressed me most were her tough determination and her thoughtful and capable nature. She was a sharp thinker AND a doer. The icing on the cake was her outsized sense of humor, which was something I came to depend on. There was never any doubt that Natasha would go far. It has been a thrill seeing her work and watching her achievements from afar—partner, speaker, educator, fellow, influencer. Thinking back to those early days, it's as if she already knew everything but was patiently lying in wait. Natasha Jen stands out.

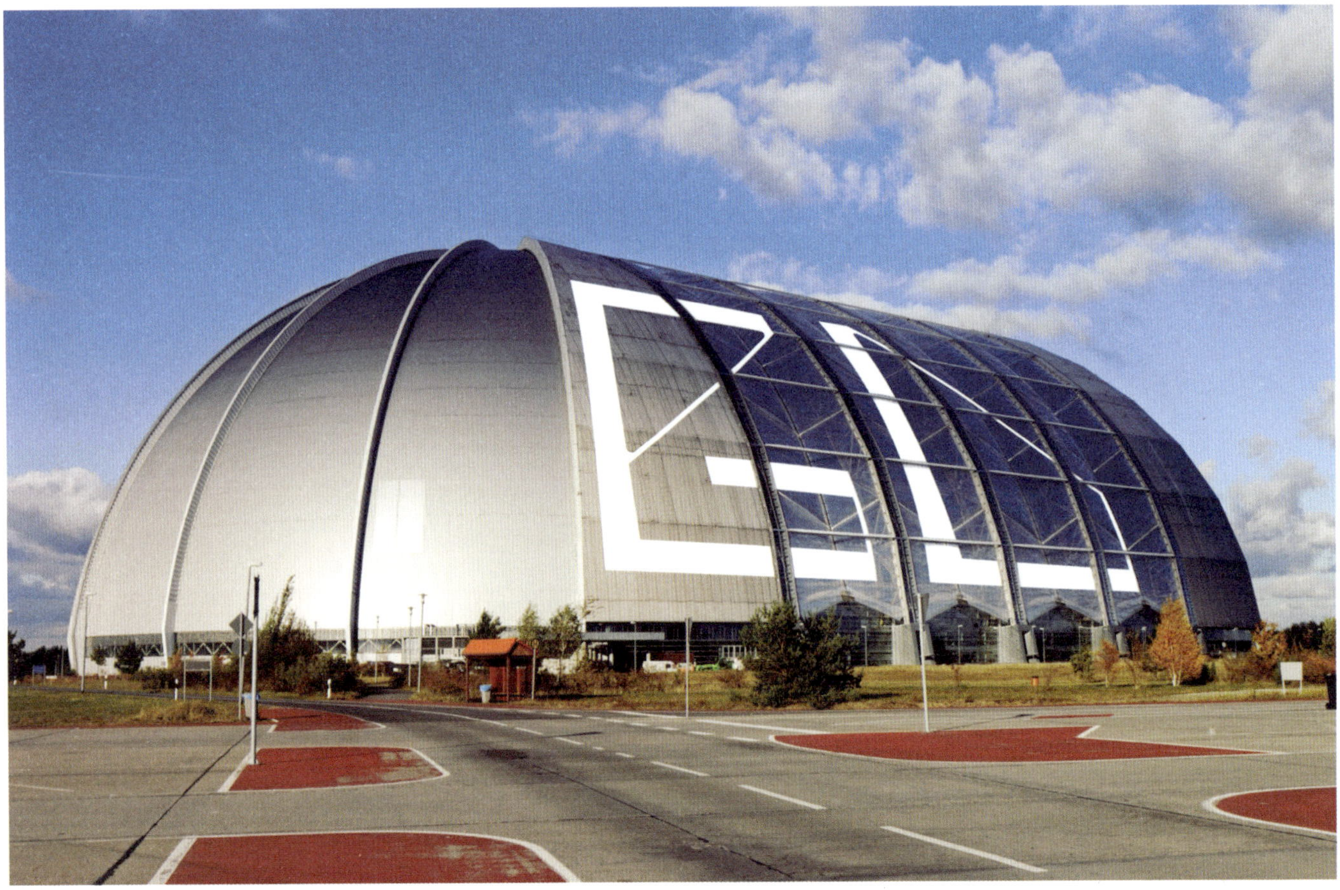

General Dynamics Brand Identity, New Talent Annual 2024. Professor: Natasha Jen. Gold-winning student: Hyowon Kwon

PEOPLE WILL INSPIRE YOU, TEACH YOU NEW THINGS, AND MAKE YOU BETTER. IT'S A KIND OF RIPPLE EFFECT. YOU NEED TO ALWAYS SURROUND YOURSELF WITH THE BEST PEOPLE POSSIBLE.

Natasha Jen, *Professor, SVA, & Partner, Pentagram*

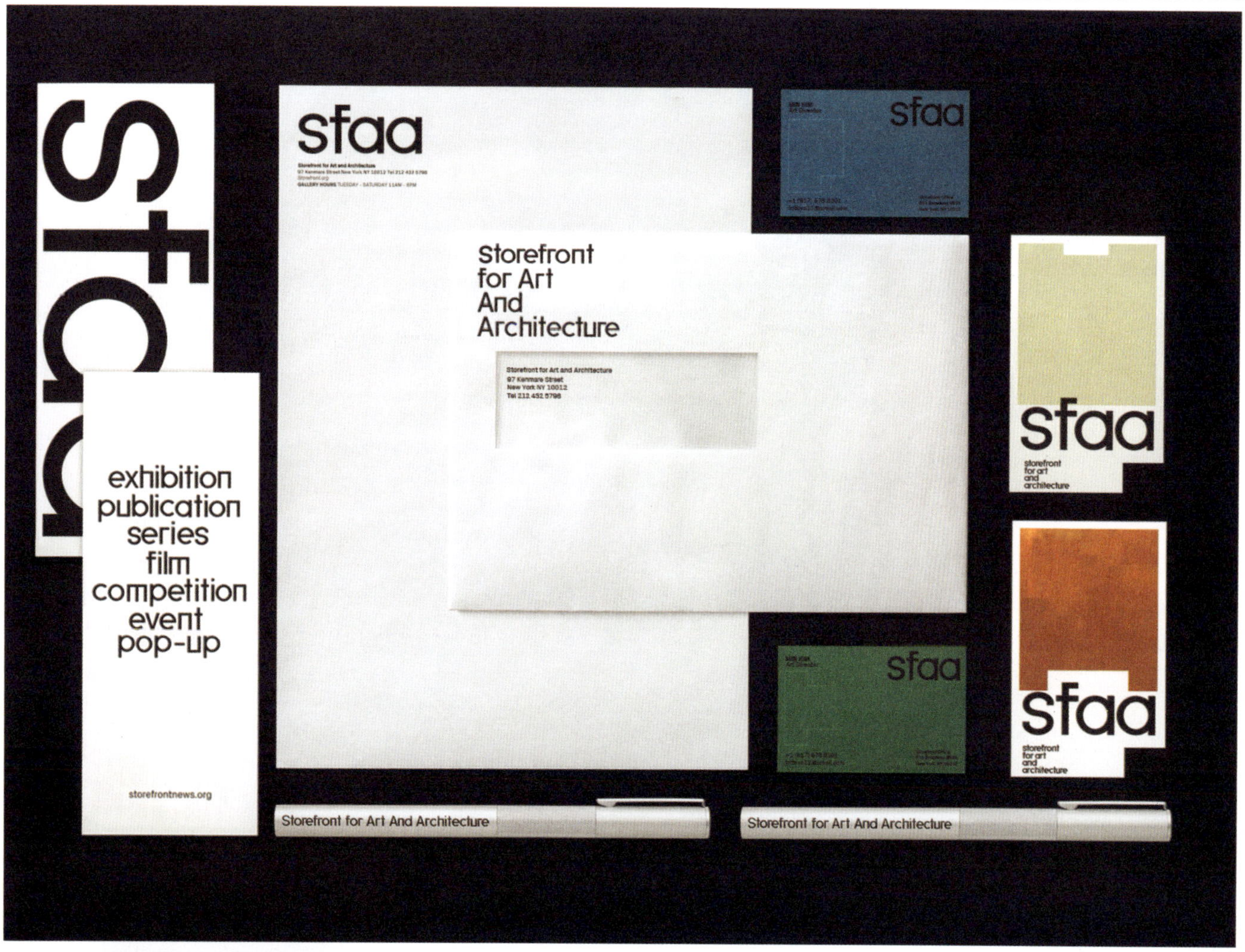

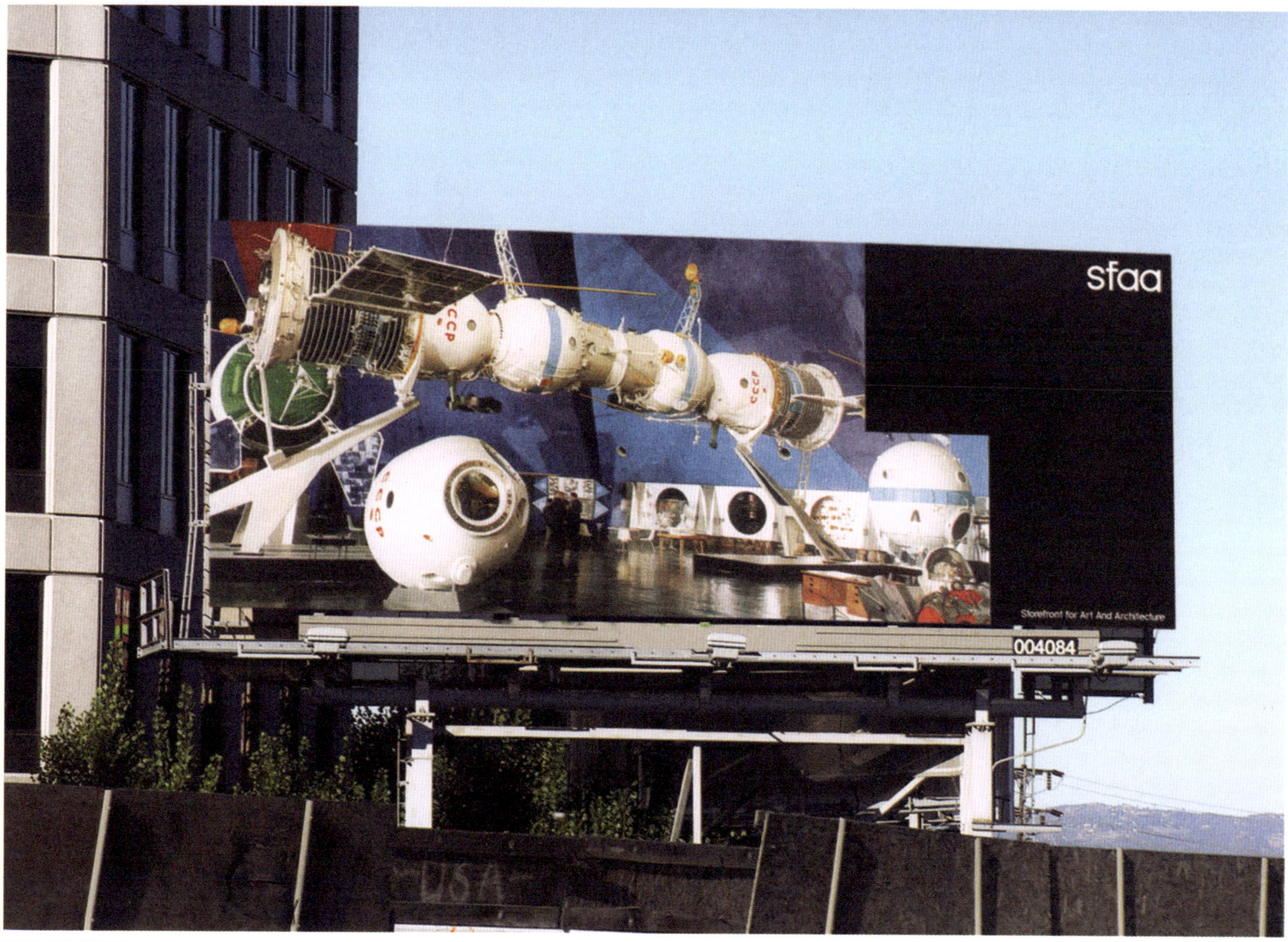

Storefront for Art and Architecture, New Talent Annual 2020. Professor: Natasha Jen. Platinum-winning student: Min Kwan Kim

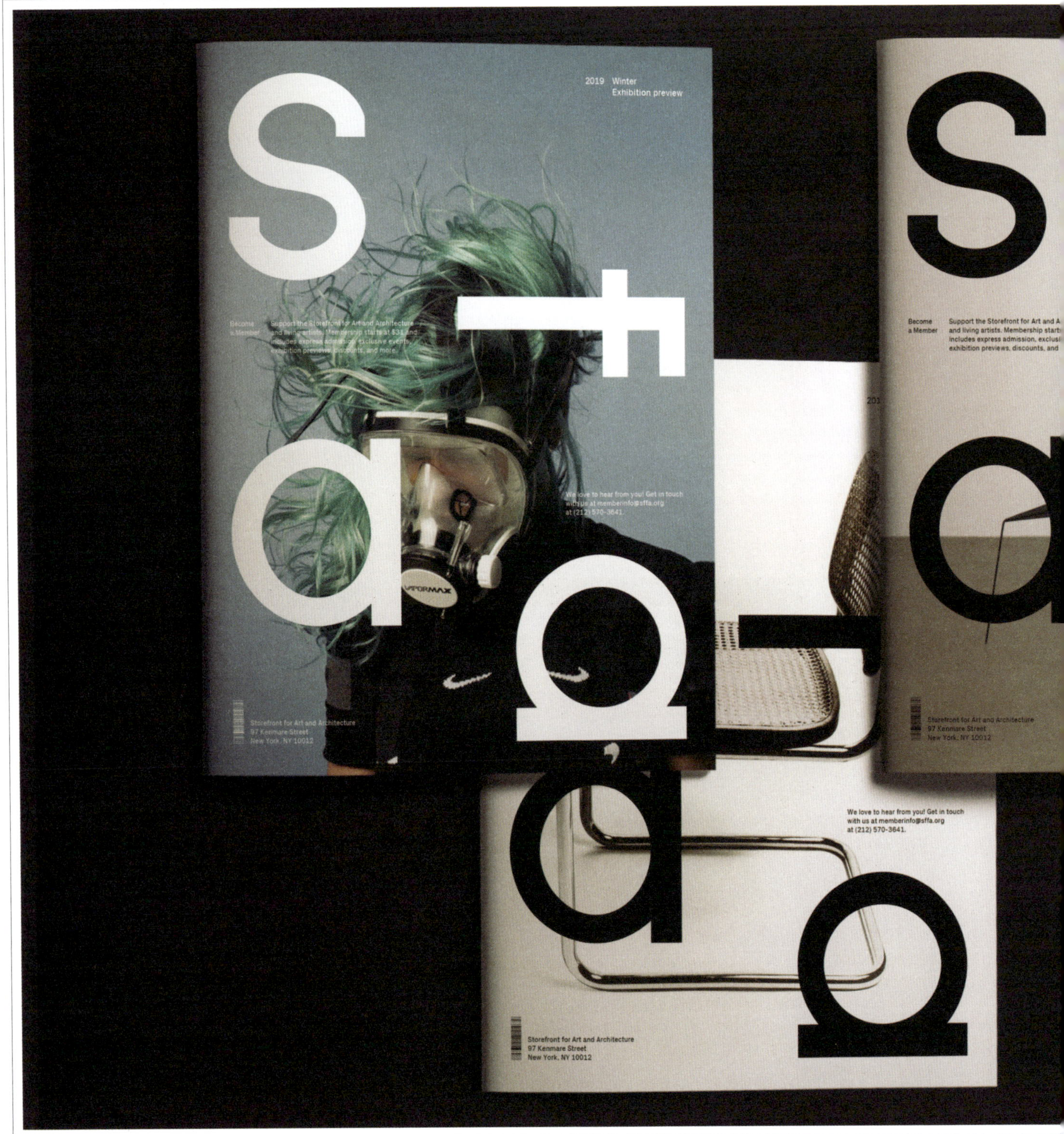

What is your process for selecting students for your classes? Are there certain qualifications they have to meet?
Most of the time, we can't select students, but there's a reason why these courses are structured according to students' level of learning. That's why you would take Typography 101; there's a reason for structuring courses in a very progressive manner. I teach third-year and fourth-year classes, but my class is structured differently from the other courses.

My class is structured as a two-year course. After two years, it allows me to understand a student better because they take the time to figure out their tendencies as a designer. Everybody has very different creative tendencies, you know, impulses. Sometimes, it's something they are particularly talented in.

My principle of teaching is helping my students improve in the field they're interested in or where they already excel. For example, a lot of students tend to lean towards illustration. Graphic design has much more to do with typography, and while its constructive elements may involve illustration, it's never illustration in itself. When encountering a student who is good at illustration, the point is not to kill that interest. The point is to cultivate that, but they must also be introduced to a broader graphic design vocabulary.

I often get a roster of students who have already signed up for the class, but I want to make sure that they can make this class worthwhile, meaning they need to be at a minimum requirement level to learn effectively.

The very principle of education is structured around progressive learning. If you teach something too deep too early on, students will not be able to absorb it or perform well. I want to ensure my students are prepared.

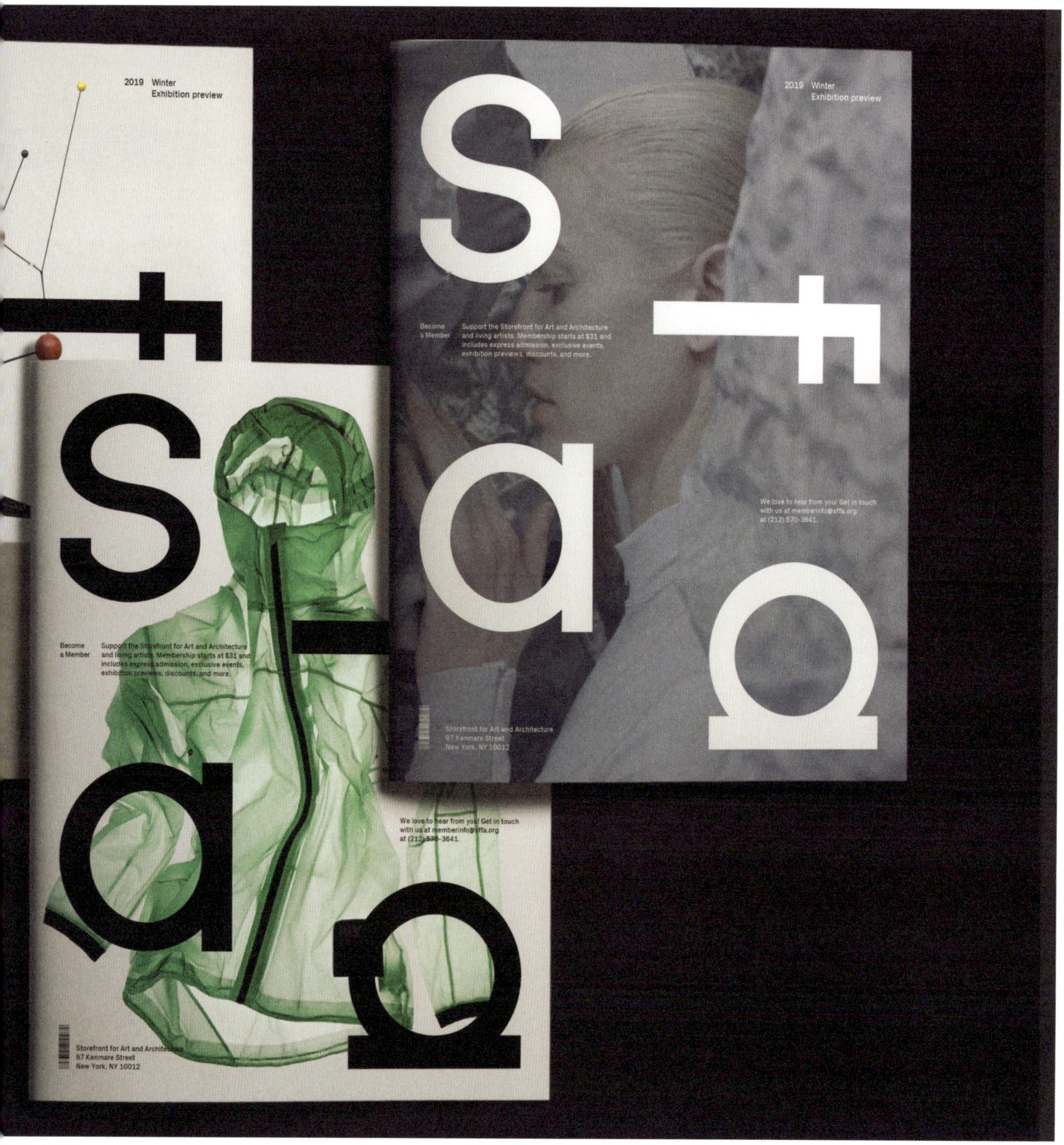

Storefront for Art and Architecture, New Talent Annual 2020. Professor: Natasha Jen. Platinum-winning student: Min Kwan Kim

There are cases with students whose work doesn't feel like they're ready yet. That means they will have to go back and study other courses first to be successful.

What might be a typical first assignment in your class?

It depends. For a third-year student, which is the entry point of the course, they would read a book. For example, they could read *The Little Prince*, a story about a young boy's journey and his encounters with human beings, all with very different qualities. Once they read the assigned book, the following assignments would be given.

The first assignment would be to visualize the story through a diagram or visualization. Visualizations transform a written story into graphic representations of the narrative and characters. This assignment might take three weeks.

The next assignment would be to create a reimagined book design for the assigned story. This is an editorial and typography exercise. The subject matter stays the same, but students practice deciphering and reinterpreting the story through different assignments.

Do you ever have your students work on assignments for real clients?

Never. I find it unethical. Why should students design for real-world clients who are profiting and benefiting from that? Once you get into these questions, that is a big no-no for me. We design for our clients, and we get paid for that. Students should not be involved in this process. However, we can create imaginary assignments for an existing company or organization that doesn't serve anybody. That allows students to encounter certain design problems. But that is not for a client. That doesn't serve anybody.

Do you ever ask your students to include something they're passionate about in their work for your class?
Well, "Do what you're passionate about" is never a good assignment because that's too broad, right? What they're interested in can actually be a choice of media or medium. If it's an open medium assignment, that means it can be anything: a song, a book, an exhibit, a toy, whatever. That's open-ended. That allows them to choose the subject or medium they're interested in.

An assignment can also be open-ended in a subject matter, but the ultimate output must be one particular medium. For example, students could design a zine on any subject they like. If they like music—jazz, hip hop, etc.—go ahead! It can also be a zine about food. It can be anything, but it must be a zine. And what is a zine? They have to research. It's more about creating opportunities for students to investigate and answer questions for themselves and not so much doing what they're passionate about. You don't need to go to school to do what you're passionate about. You can do it on your own.

Do you work with students individually, in groups, or a combination of the two?
Our class is structured as a presentation by each student and a group critique. We have a three-hour class with up to 13 or 14 students. Time management is crucial to ensure that every student gets equal time to present and discuss. My role in those critique sessions is to help them measure their own time to structure their presentation better. They must explain what they did, the stories they want to tell, and the work itself. Once they're actually doing the presentation, they're already thinking about how they will present it. That way, they can practice presenting to a group in this class.

How do you develop and raise your students' visual and verbal standards?
That's very hard to answer because there are no describable words about what constitutes good work. It's all very assignment- and context-specific. What I require everybody to do is first structure their work through their research. Research should primarily be images because we don't want an essay on screen while presenting. There should be a rough script in their mind about the research: what they found, what was discovered, what inspired them, and what motivated their concept. Then, they talk about their concept and their design. They have to present ideas and concepts first. All my classes are structured this way, and I want my students to become very familiar with this method of working.

Because design involves creating visual things, it's also largely analytical. You have to think along your design process. Teaching students this work method is meant to help them develop a habit of continuing a creative and intuitive approach to design.

At the end of the semester, what kind of advice do you like to give the class?
I don't want to sound cliché, but the first principle is always to work as hard as possible. Be aware of your hard work, and remember that it will pay off. At one point, the power of working hard will have tangible effects: putting in extra hours, revisiting work repeatedly, and really trying to improve it. Deadlines are created by other people, by instructors in a school situation, and, in the real world, by clients and their situations. But remember that there's never a finish line when it comes to creative work.

My first bit of advice is that you can always improve your work, though you have to work really hard on that. My second piece of advice is to identify people who inspire you and the best people who can be around you. Identify people you can hang out with and learn from within your immediate or adjacent environment. People will inspire you, teach you new things, and make you better. It's a kind of ripple effect. You always need to surround yourself with the best people possible.

Can you name a few of your past students who have gone on to gain success? And if so, where are they now?
I have many, actually. One example is Leo Porto, who runs his own design studio, Porto Rocha. He's an example of a student who went through education and worked hard. He was talented, of course, and he surrounded himself with the best practitioners before he started his own business. AJ Kim, who I believe graduated in 2020 during COVID-19, is currently at Google. She worked with me for years and was terrific in many ways: versatile, independent, and a very talented designer. She's one example of somebody who graduated from school and didn't have much experience with the real world, but she worked hard and figured things out on her own. There's also Hansol Jang, who was in AJ's class. He worked for me for a couple of years and is now at Apple.

What attracted you to teaching at your current school? Were you a student there?
Yeah, I was at SVA. I went to their undergraduate program.

Do you think university-level training is needed in the creative field? How does university-level training help people in the creative field?
That's a question for any field, right? Like, does it need to exist at all if there are people who intuitively know how to do it? I mean, you see those exceptional ones in almost every field. They don't need to go to school, but there is immense value in higher education. I still believe that. If there are people who find themselves successful without higher education, that's fine, too. However, I think the assumption that creative fields don't require rigorous training is false. Creativity is no different from engineering or physics.

On top of being a teacher, you also work at Pentagram, one of the best design firms in the country. How does your job at Pentagram influence your teaching job?
I do work at Pentagram, but it's not a job. I'm actually a co-partner and co-owner of the company. This is my practice. That's very important.

I'm not sure that the specific company defines how I work and how I teach. At Pentagram, we're in a very privileged position where we have clients with exciting assignments who come to us. That exposure is something that we're very thankful for. All design assignments and problems have their own challenges, so it's really up to the designer to make them unique. That has nothing to do with where you work. You must find something attractive, even if the project is seemingly dull or mundane. Once you actually make it interesting, you will likely do much better work.

That applies to the practice as well as teaching, for example, because students are often not interested in certain things. They're like, "I'm not interested in that subject matter. I don't know. I don't like to set type," right? But the point is when confronting something seemingly boring, you have to figure out how to make it interesting to you.

Natasha Jen www.sva.edu/faculty/natasha-jen
See her Graphis Master Portfolio at graphis.com.

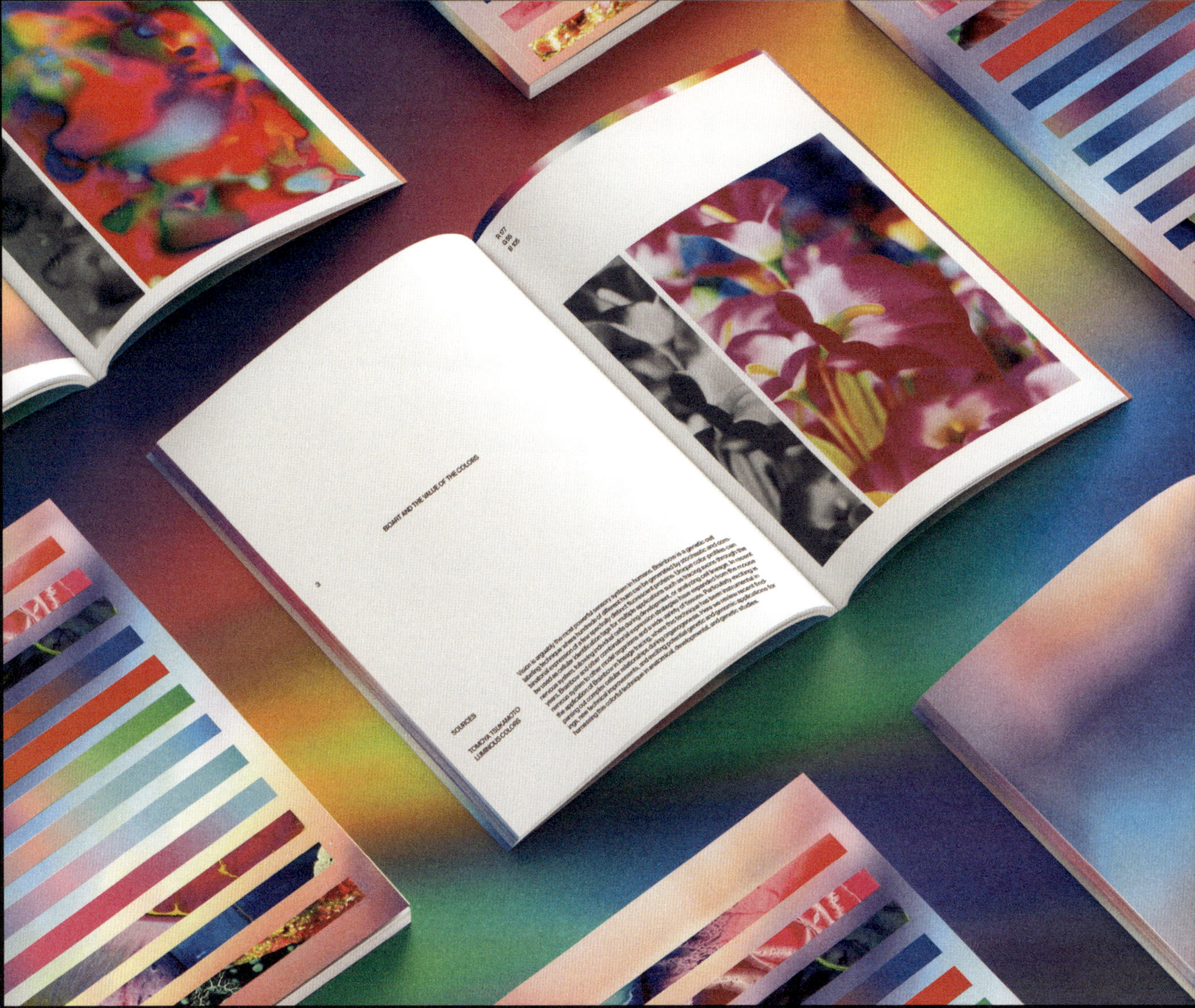

BIOART AND THE VALUE OF THE COLORS
SOURCES
TOMOYA TSUKAMOTO
LUMINOUS COLORS

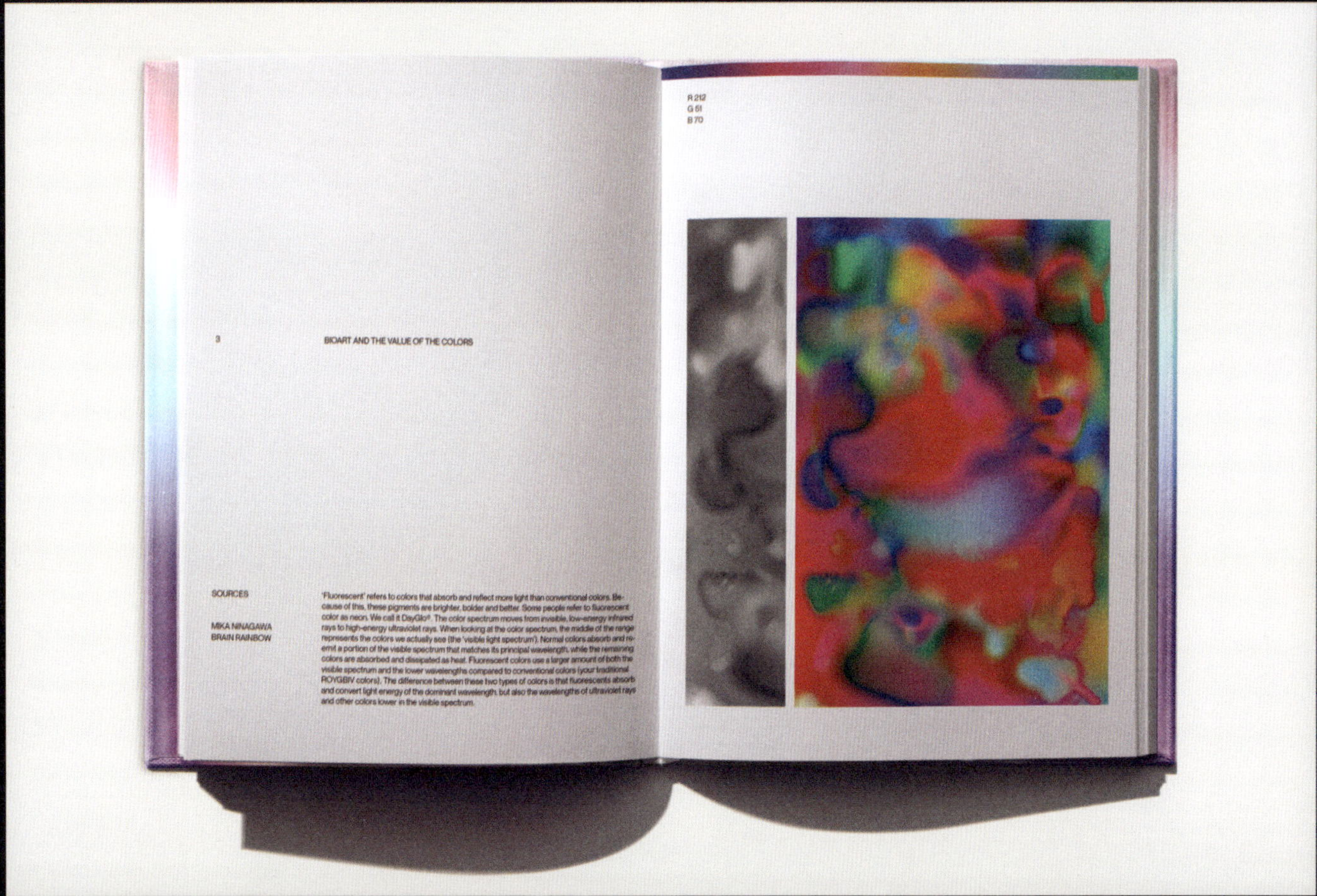

R 212
G 51
B 70
3
BIOART AND THE VALUE OF THE COLORS
SOURCES
MIKA NINAGAWA
BRAIN RAINBOW
'Fluorescent' refers to colors that absorb and reflect more light than conventional colors. Because of this, these pigments are brighter, bolder and better. Some people refer to fluorescent color as neon. We call it DayGlo®. The color spectrum moves from invisible, low-energy infrared rays to high-energy ultraviolet rays. When looking at the color spectrum, the middle of the range represents the colors we actually see (the 'visible light spectrum'). Normal colors absorb and re-emit a portion of the visible spectrum that matches its principal wavelength, while the remaining colors are absorbed and dissipated as heat. Fluorescent colors use a larger amount of both the visible spectrum and the lower wavelengths compared to conventional colors (your traditional ROYGBIV colors). The difference between these two types of colors is that fluorescents absorb and convert light energy of the dominant wavelength, but also the wavelengths of ultraviolet rays and other colors lower in the visible spectrum.

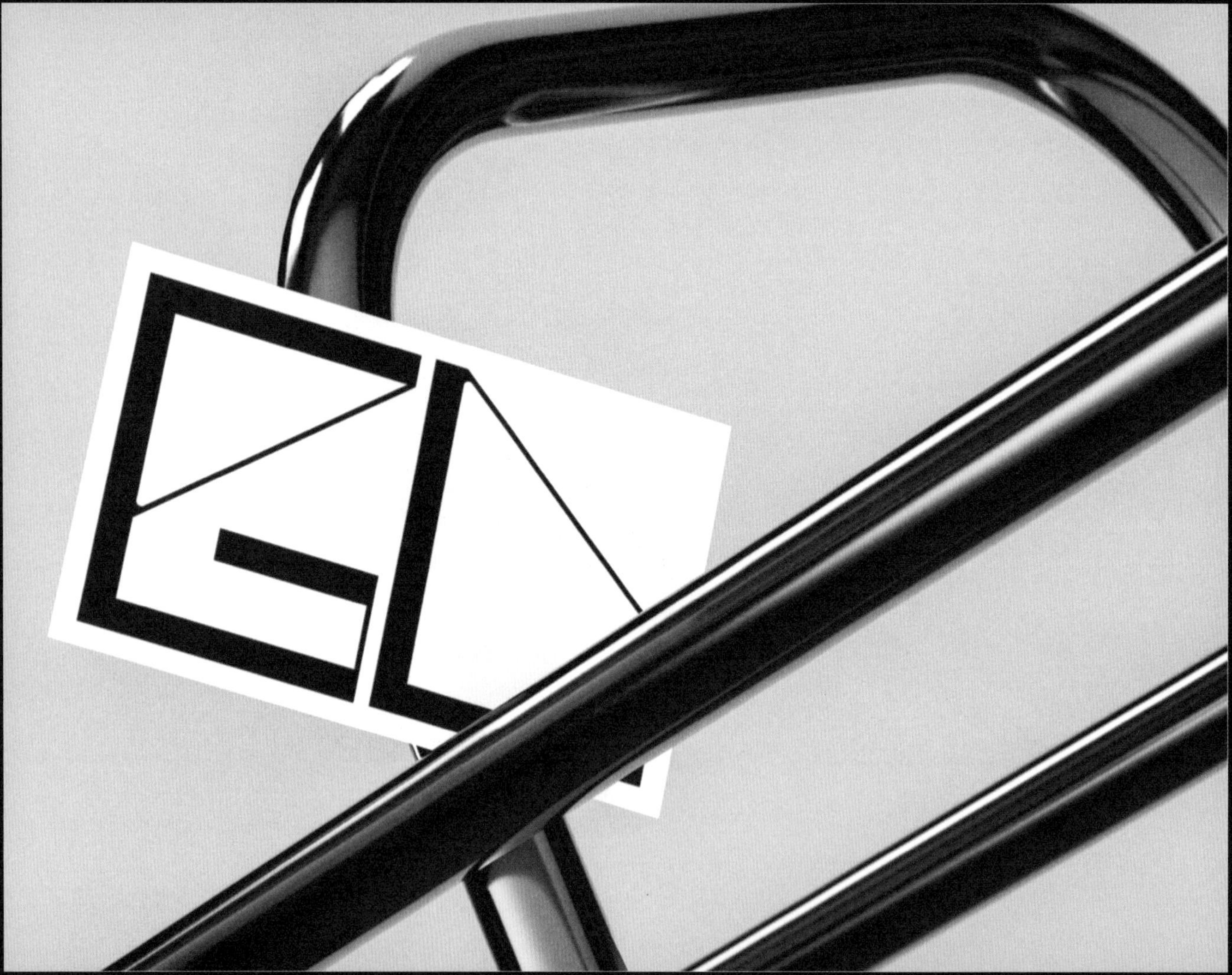

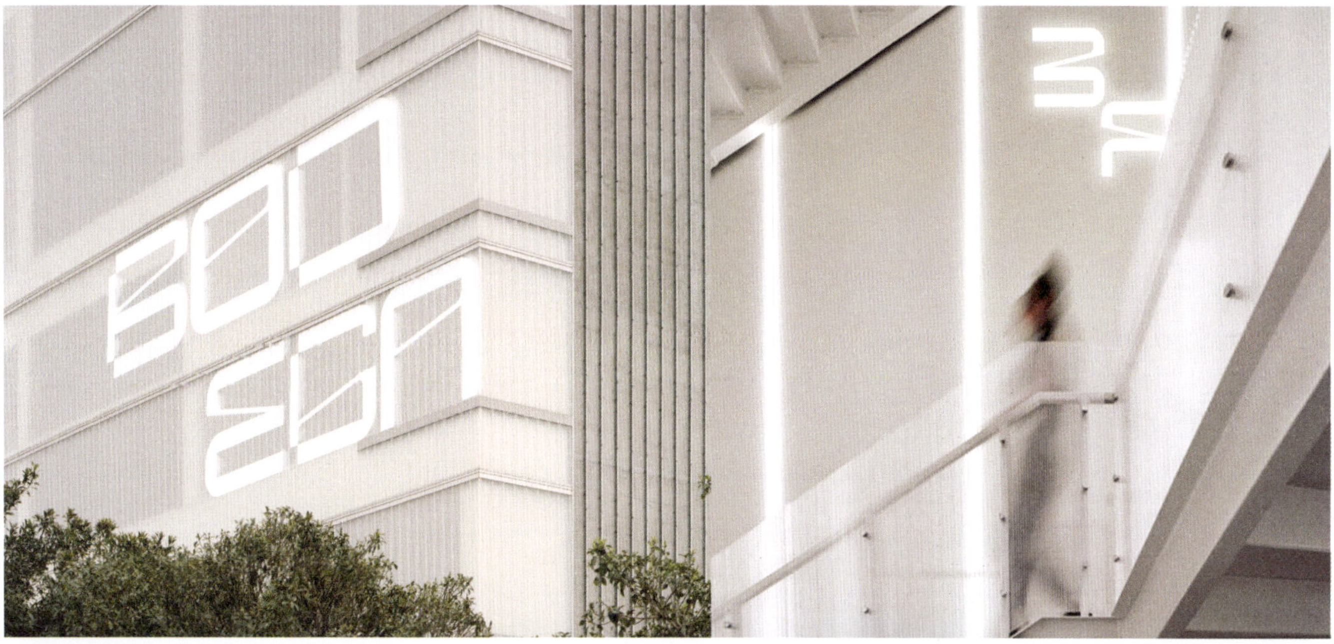

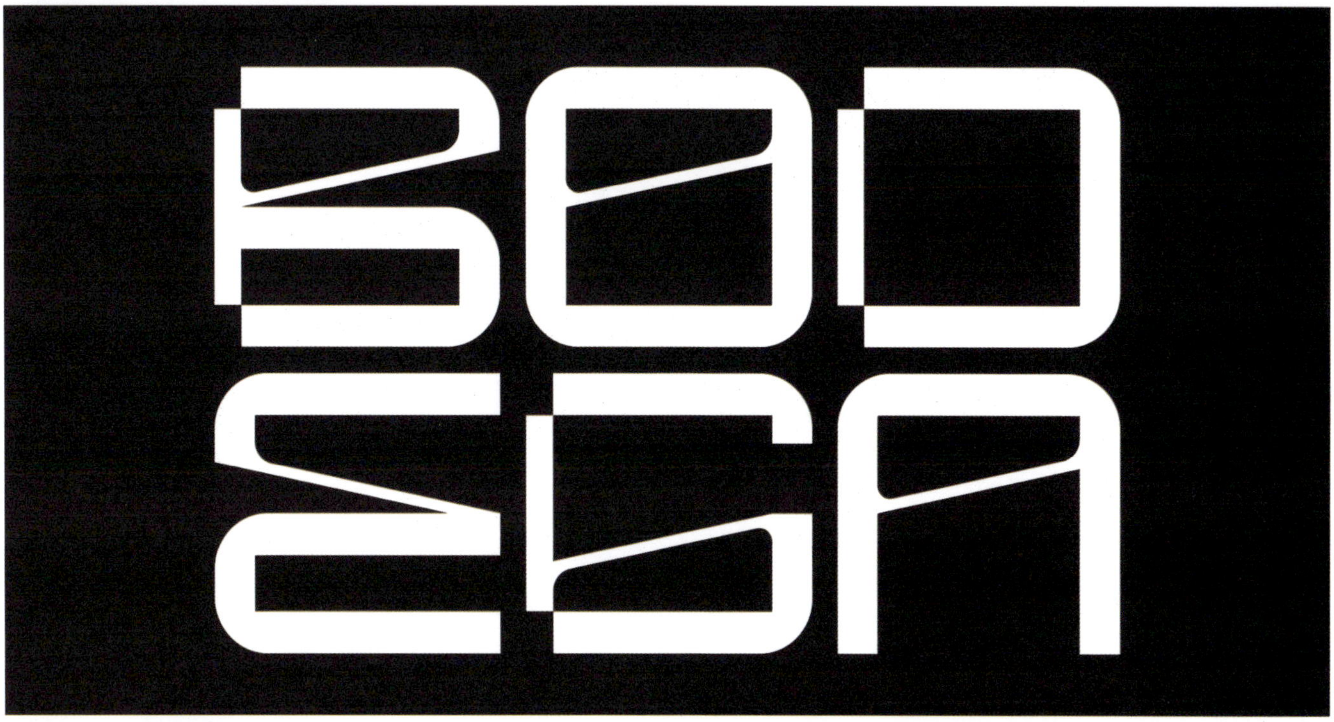

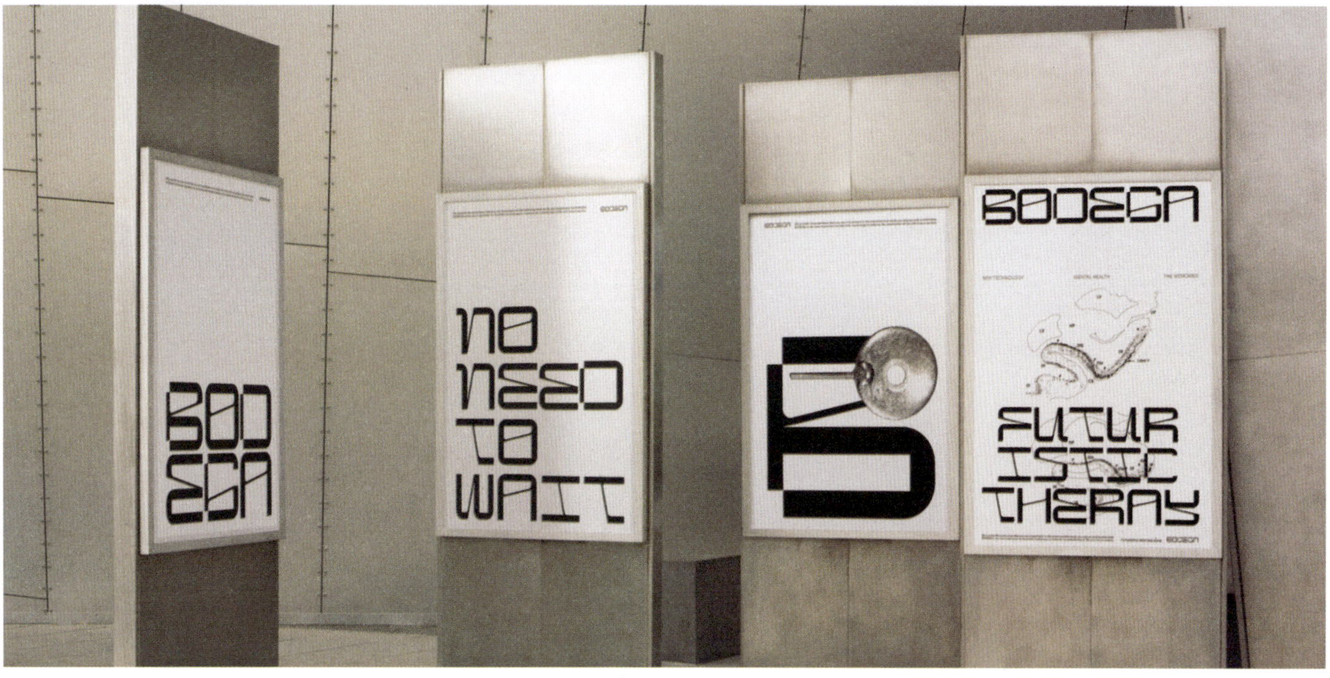

Bodega, New Talent Annual 2024. Professor: Natasha Jen. Gold-winning student: Hyowon Kwon

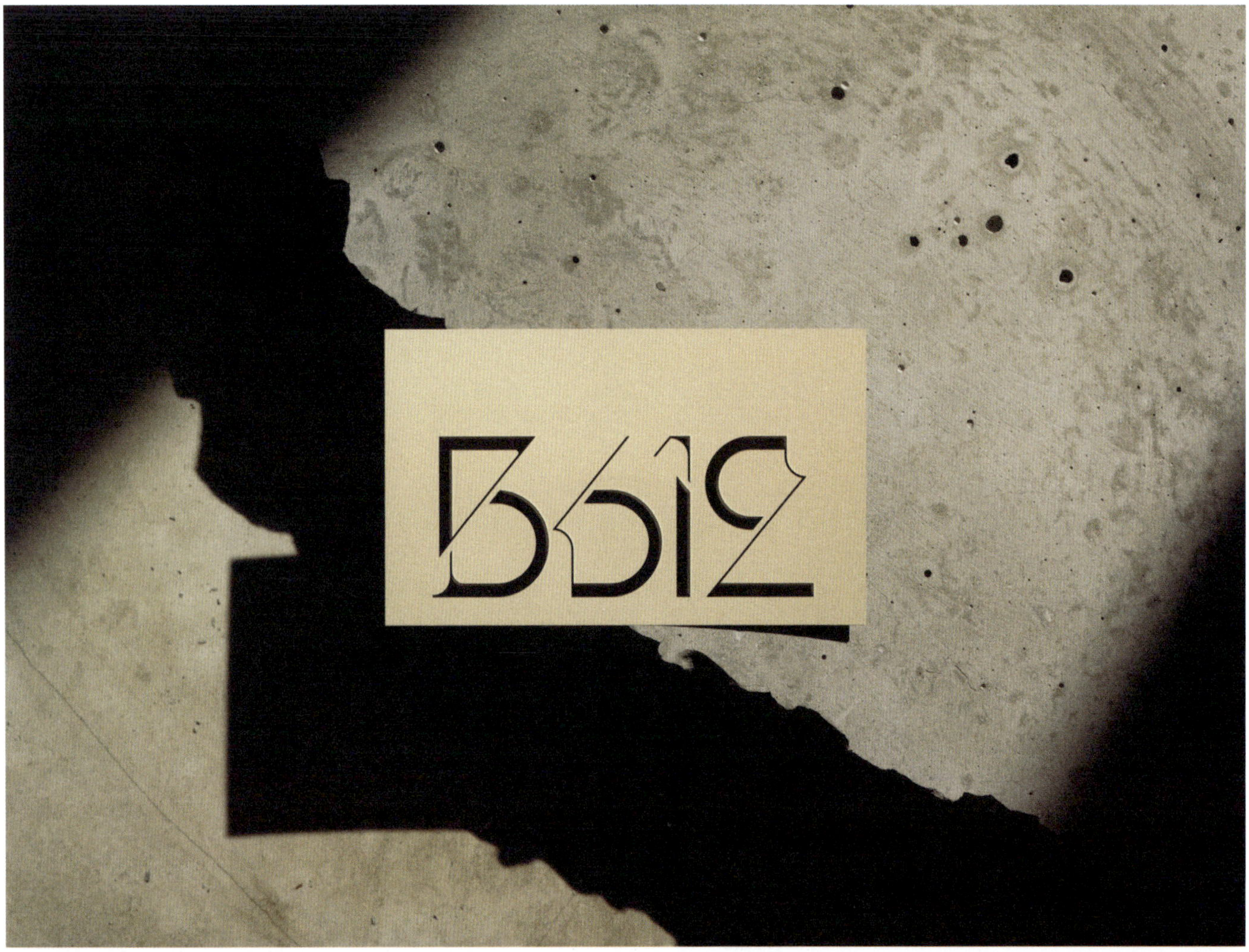

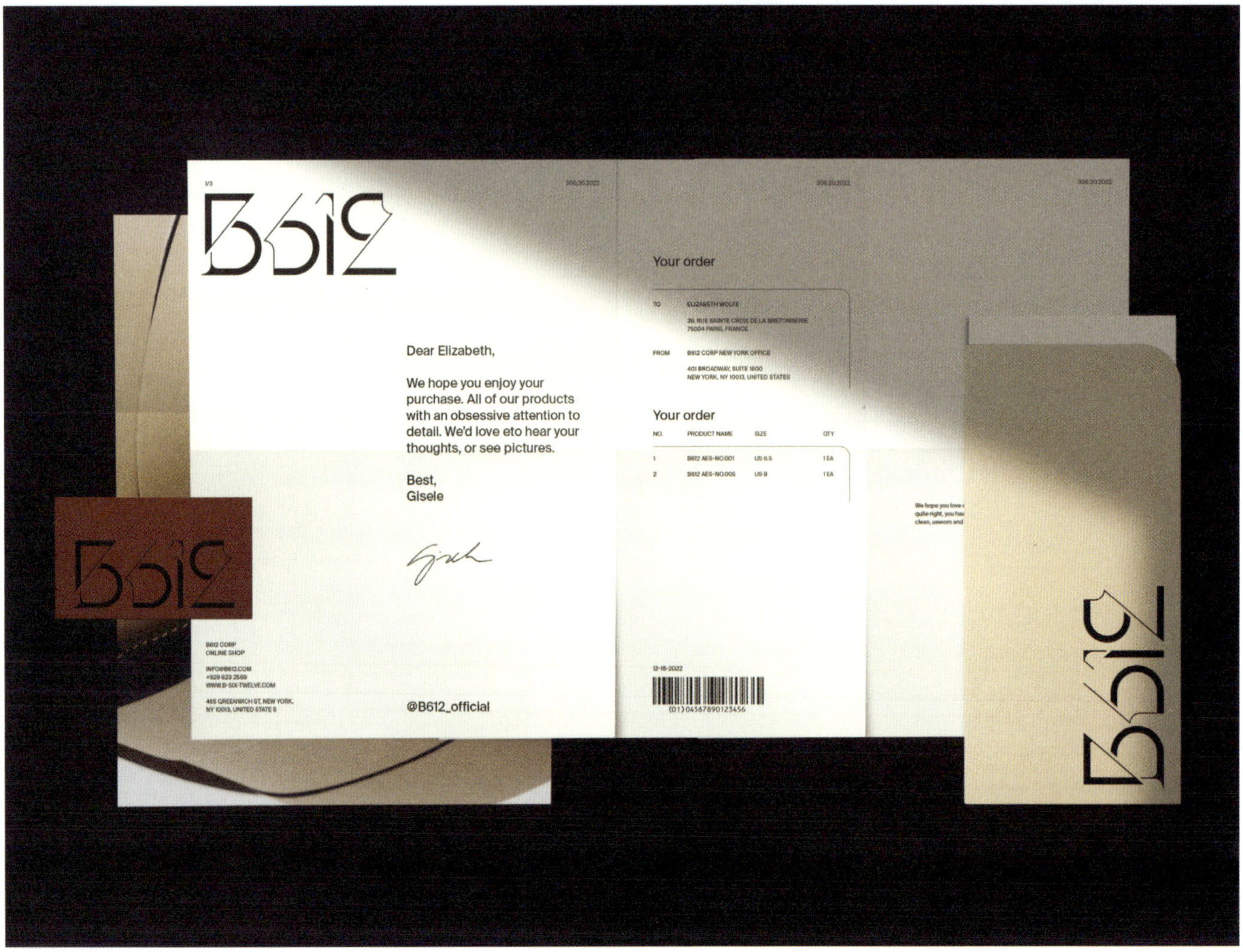

B612 Brand & Type Identity, New Talent Annual 2024. Professor: Natasha Jen. Gold-winning student: Mina Son

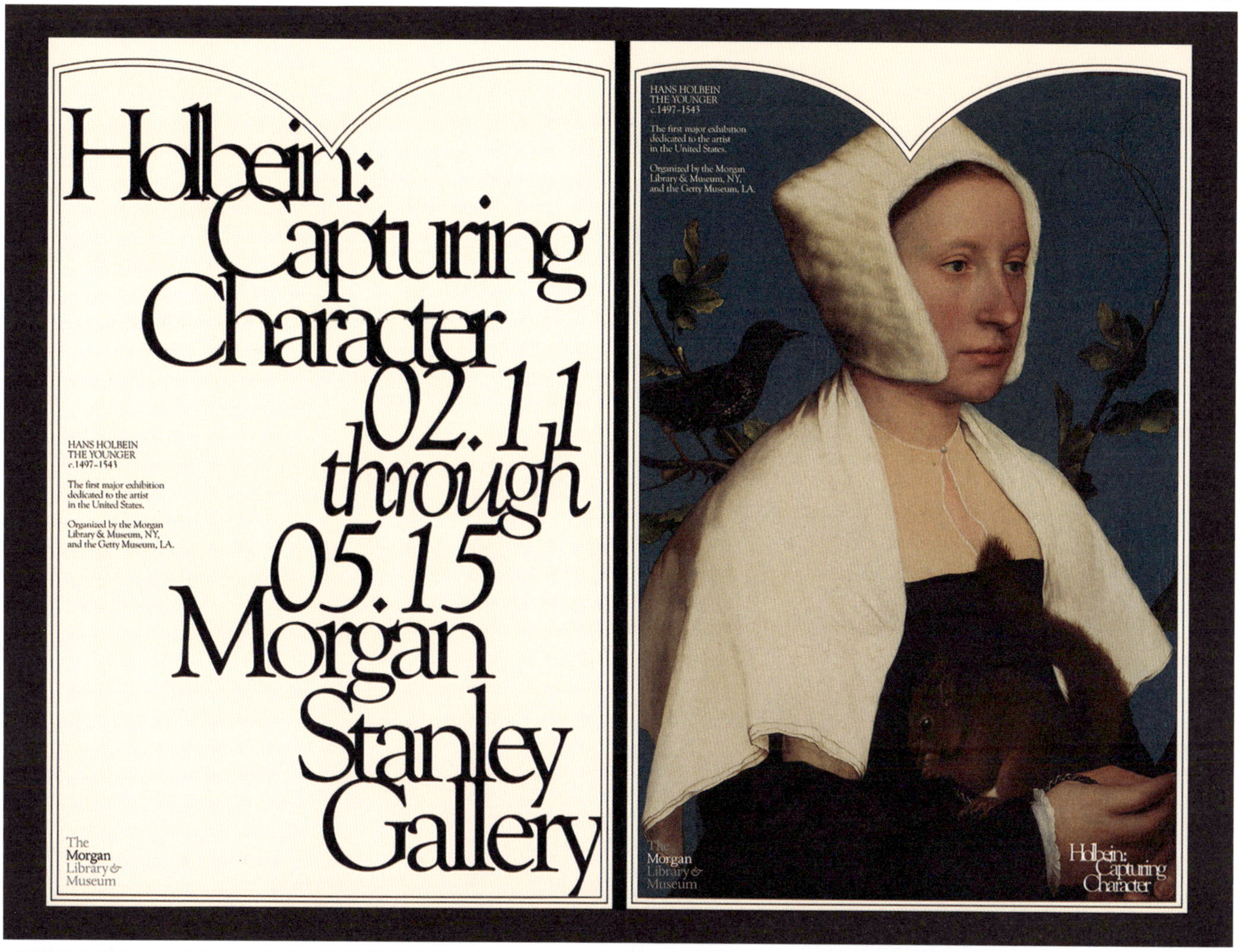

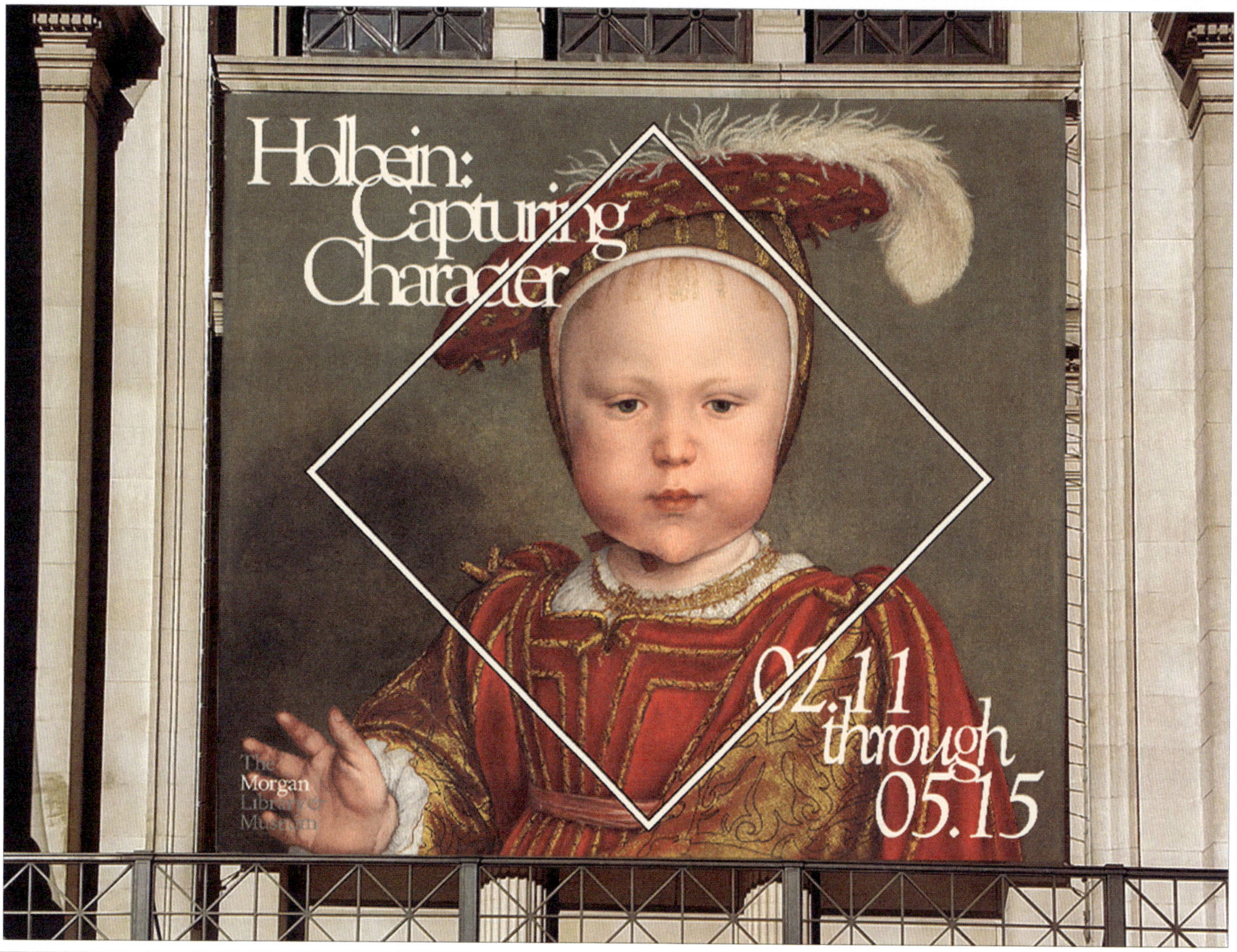

Holbein: Capturing Character, New Talent Annual 2023. Professor: Natasha Jen. Gold-winning student: Hyun Jung Lee

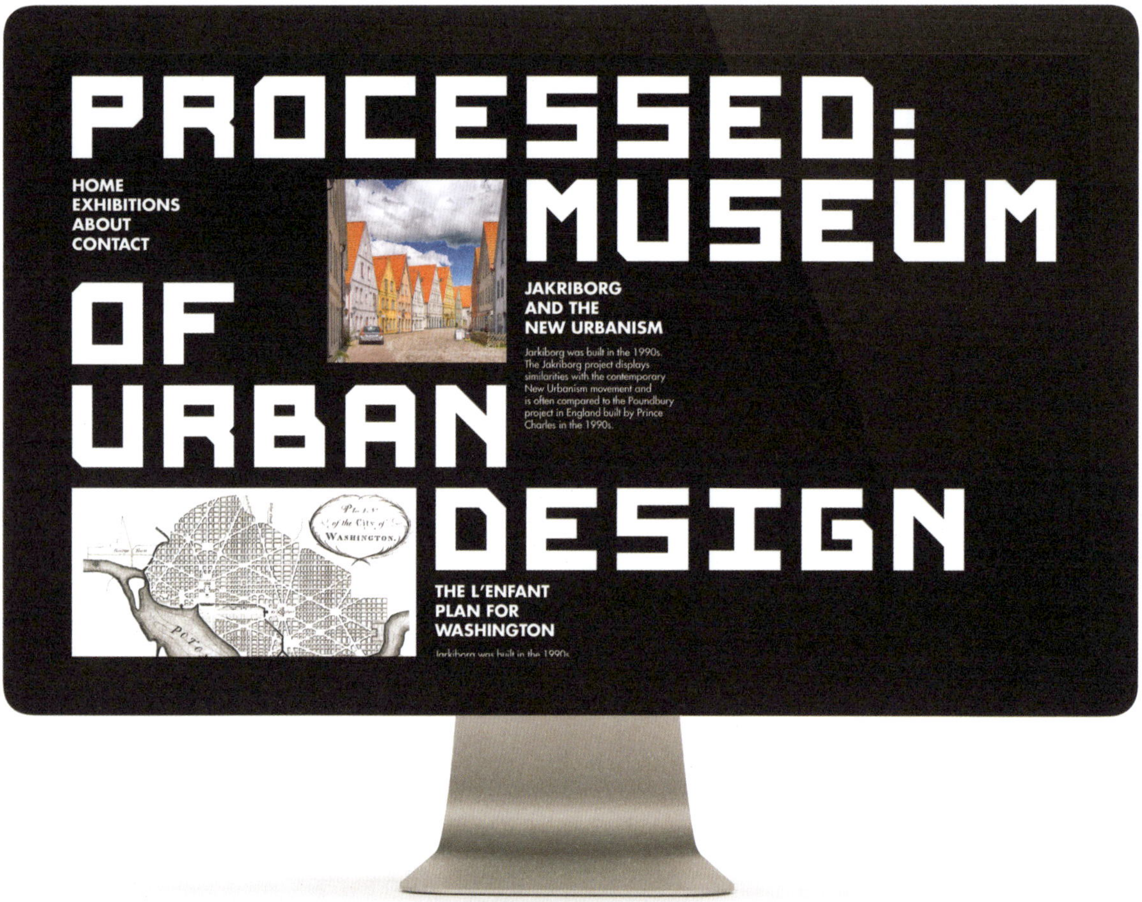

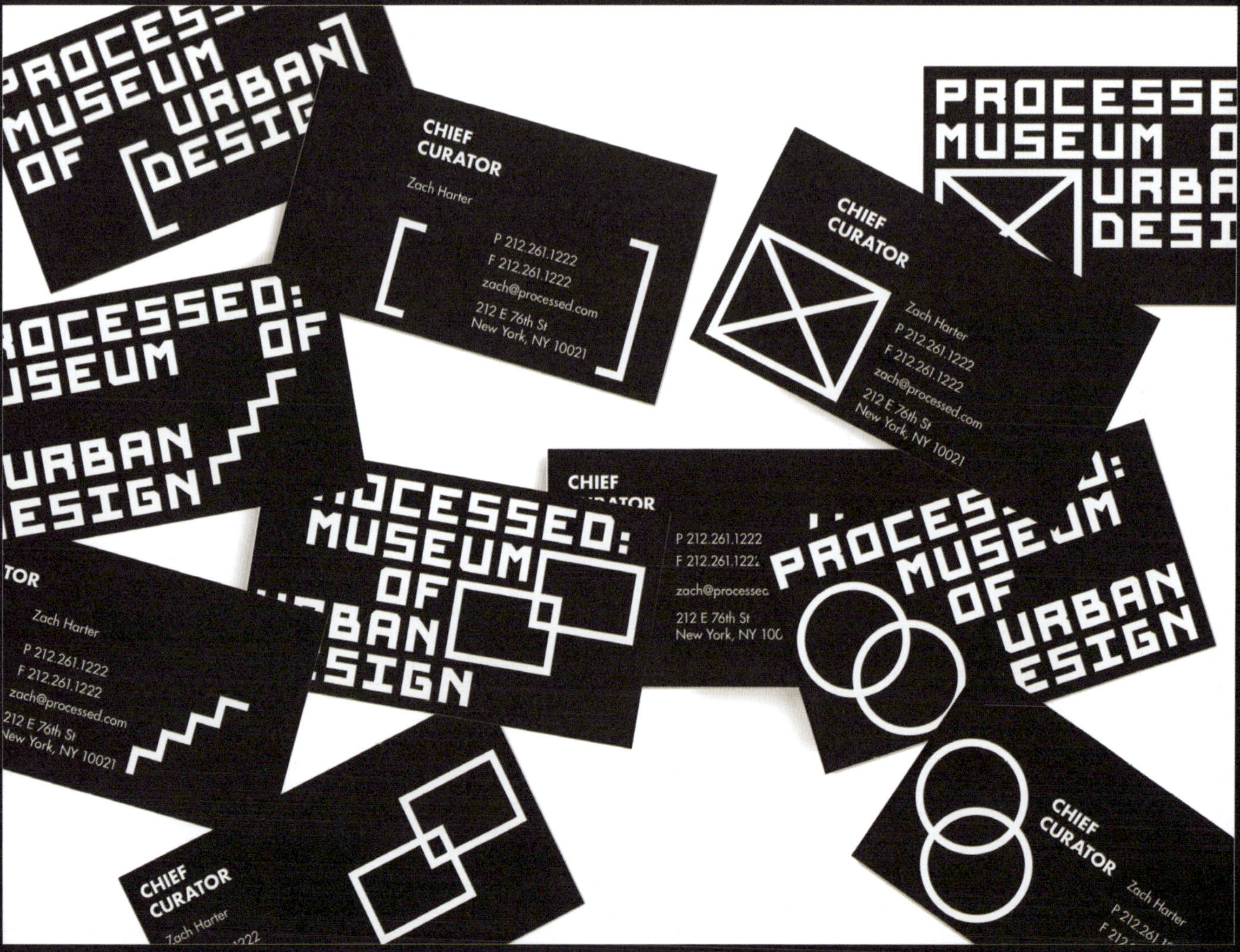

Processed Museum, New Talent Annual 2016. Professor: Natasha Jen. Gold-winning student: Zachary Harter

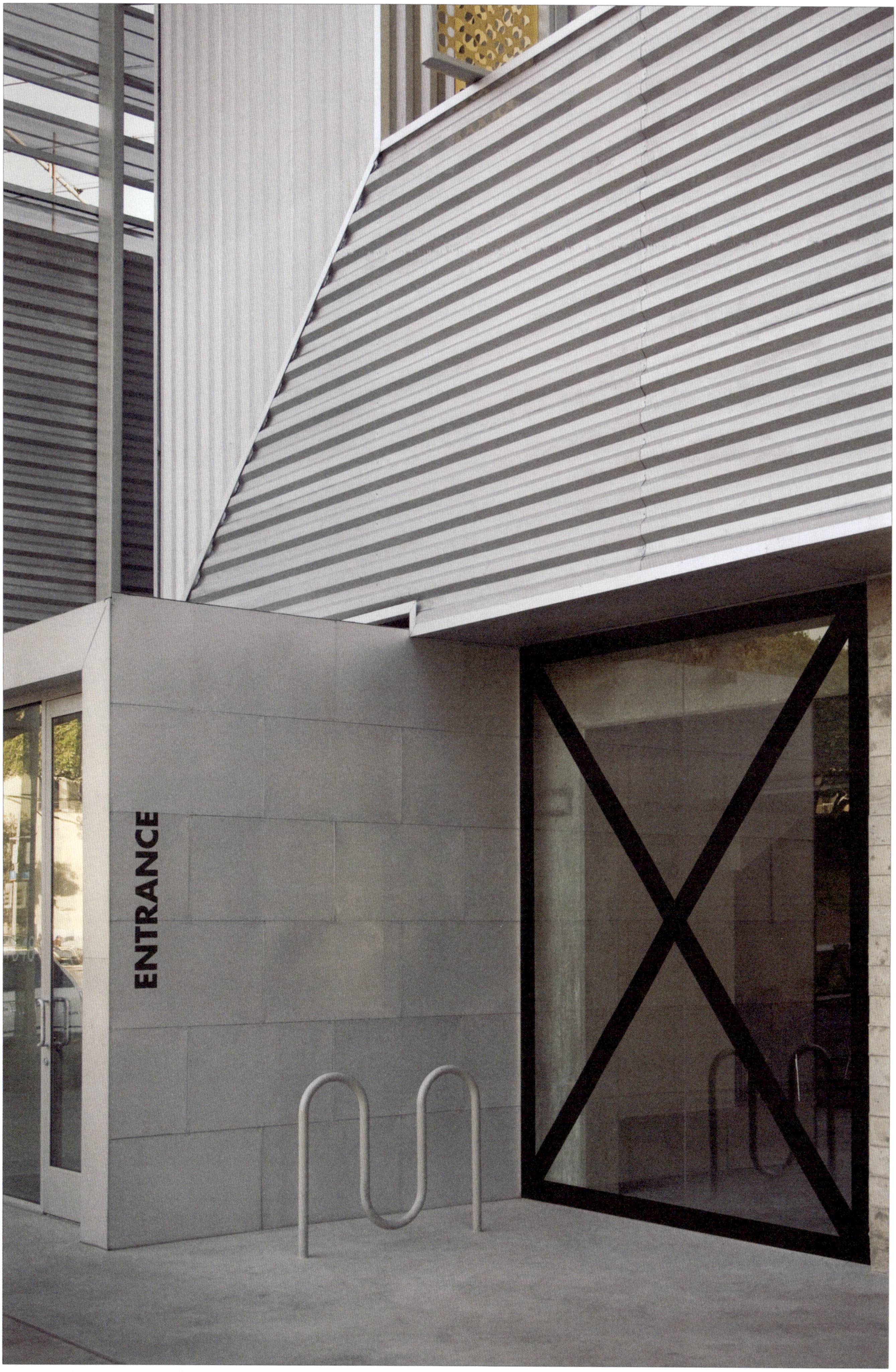

Processed Museum, New Talent Annual 2016. Professor: Natasha Jen. Gold-winning student: Zachary Harter

Graphis Books

POSTER

DESIGN

ADVERTISING

PHOTOGRAPHY

NUDES

TYPOGRAPHY

PROTEST POSTERS

Poster Annual 2025

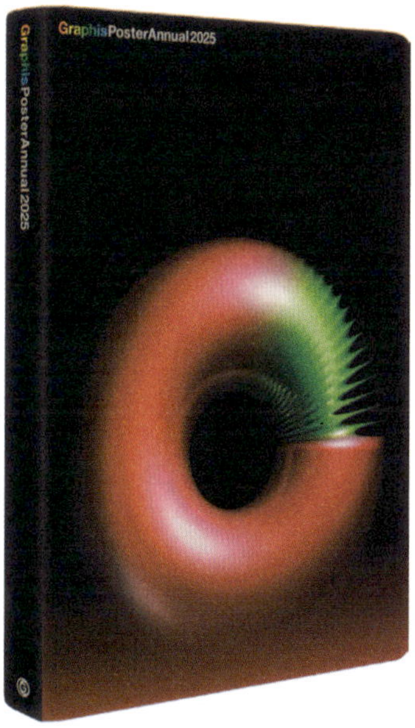

2024
Hardcover: 256 pages
200-plus color illustrations
Trim: 8.5 x 11.75"
ISBN: 978-1-954632-33-2
US $75

Awards: Graphis presents 12 Platinum, 100 Gold, and 328 Silver Awards, along with 90 Honorable Mentions, to many international poster designers who challenged what poster design can be with innovative, creative works.
Winning Entrants: Atelier Bundi AG, CollierGraphica, Dankook University, dGwaltneyArt, Freaner Creative, Gallery BI, João Machado Design, Katarzyna Zapart, Melchior Imboden, Skolos-Wedell, The Union Design Company, and THERE IS STUDIO.
Judges: Liz English, Paul Garbett, Brad Hochberg, Sven Lindhorst-Emme, DaeKi Shim, and HyoJun Shim.
Content: This hardcover book displays full-page images of Platinum-winning work from talented poster designers. Gold and Silver-winning work is also presented, and Honorable Mentions are listed in the physical copy. All work is presented equally on our website. Award-winning work from the judges and a section of Platinum-winning works from 2015 are also included.

New Talent Annual 2024

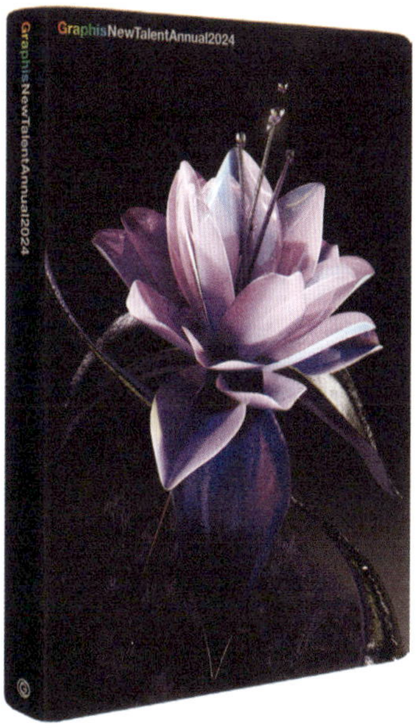

2024
Hardcover: 256 pages
200-plus color illustrations
Trim: 8.5 x 11.75"
ISBN: 978-1-954632-29-5
US $75

Awards: Graphis presents 13 Platinum, 132 Gold, and 587 Silver awards, along with 858 Honorable Mentions.
Winning Entrants: Design: Peter Bergman, Justin Colt, Rob Clayton, Natasha Jen, Simon Johnston, Billy Magbua, William Meek, Richard Mehl, Nathan Savage, Stephen Serrato, Hyojun Shim, Ming Tai, and David Tillinghast.
Judges: David Bernstein, Scott Bucher, Hoon-Dong Chung, Patti Judd, Jim Ma, Kah Poon, Frank P. Wartenberg, Lisa Winstanley, and others listed in the book.
Contents: This book contains award-winning entries in Advertising, Design, Photography, and Film/Video. There are full-page images of Platinum-winning work from talented teachers and students. Gold and Silver-winning work is also presented, and Honorable Mentions are listed. We also present A Decade of New Talent, featuring Platinum-winning works from 2014.

Photography Annual 2024

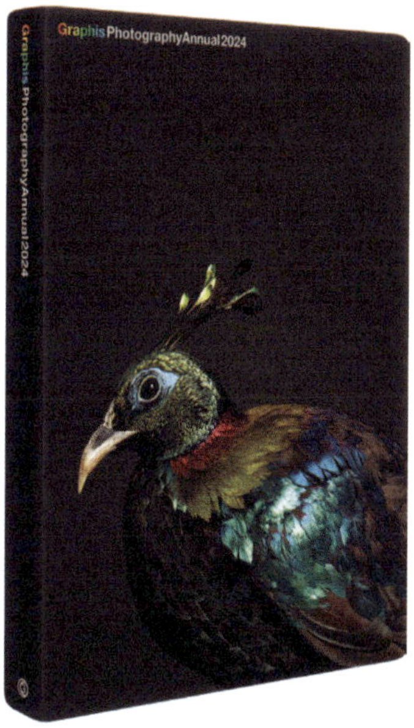

2024
Hardcover: 256 pages
200-plus color illustrations
Trim: 8.5 x 11.75"
ISBN: 978-1-954632-28-8
US $75

Awards: Graphis presents 12 Platinum, 102 Gold, and 216 Silver awards, along with 54 Honorable Mentions.
Winning Entrants: Craig Cutler, Lindsey Drennan, Jonathan Knowles, James Minchin, Artem Nazarov, Peter Samuels, Howard Schatz, John Surace, and Paco Macias Velasco.
Judges: Per Breiehagen, Nick Hall, Takahiro Igarashi, RJ Muna, and Hadley Stambaugh.
Content: This book is full of exceptional work by our masterful judges, our Platinum, Gold, and Silver award winners, and our Honorable Mentions. It also includes a retrospective on our Platinum 2014 Photography winners, a list of international photography museums and galleries, and an In Memoriam list of photographers who have passed away this past year. The digital copy has an extra 52 pages of additional content for you to peruse.

Advertising Annual 2024

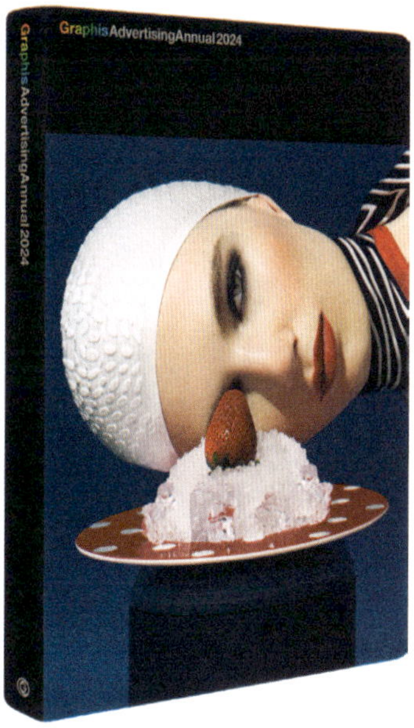

2024
Hardcover: 224 pages
200-plus color illustrations
Trim: 8.5 x 11.75"
ISBN: 978-1-954632-25-7
US $75

Awards: Graphis presents 15 Platinum, 61 Gold, and 99 Silver awards, along with 14 Honorable Mentions.
Winning Entrants: ARSONAL, Brunner, Célie Cadieux, Extra Credit Projects, Freaner Creative & Design, PangHao Art Studio, Partners + Napier, PETROL Advertising, ReThink, Rhubarb, SJI Associates, Sukle Advertising, and SUPERFY.
Judges: Ariel Freaner, Alan Hunter, Suzy Jurist, Ben Nessan, Andrea Por, and Christina Roche.
Content: This Annual includes amazing Platinum, Gold, and Silver Award-winning print and video advertisements from well-established firms and agencies. Honorable Mentions are also presented. Also featured in the annual is a selection of award-winning work from the competition judges and our yearly In Memoriam list of the advertising talent we've lost over the last year.

Design Annual 2024

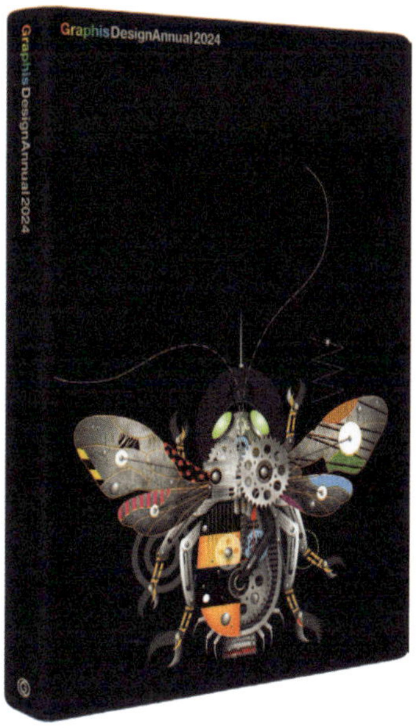

2023
Hardcover: 272 pages
200-plus color illustrations
Trim: 8.5 x 11.75"
ISBN: 978-1-954632-24-0
US $75

Awards: Graphis gave 12 Platinum, 108 Gold, and 436 Silver awards, along with 182 Honorable Mentions, to many international designers who challenged what design can do with innovative, creative works.
Winning Entrants: AV Print, The Balbusso Twins, Carmit Design Studio, Journey Group, Michael Pantuso Design, Namseoul University, Omdesign, PepsiCo Design & Innovation, Studio Eduardo Aires, Sun Design Production, Underline Studio, and Wonderlust Industries, Inc.
Judges: Antonio Alcalá, Roger Archbold, Maria Alma Guede, Mike Hughes, Byoung il Sun, and Vishal Vora.
Content: This book includes award-winning work from the judges, as well as Platinum, Gold, and Silver-winning work from internationally renowned designers and design firms. Honorable Mentions are presented, and a list of designers that we have lost this past year and a directory of design museums are also included.

Narrative Design: Kit Hinrichs

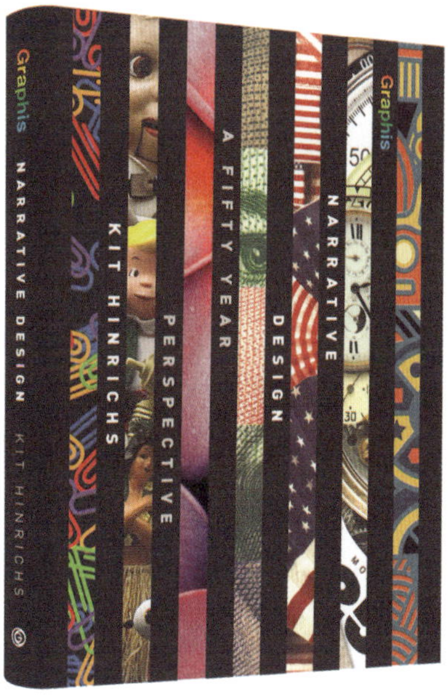

2023
Hardcover: 248 pages
200-plus color illustrations
Trim: 9 x 12"
ISBN: 978-1-954632-03-5
US $65

Narrative Design: A Fifty-Year Perspective is a collection of over 50 years of work from the obsessive graphic designer Kit Hinrichs. To the legendary AIGA medalist, author, teacher, and collector, design is the business of telling a story. It's not just about communicating a product or a corporate ethos—it's about contributing to the collective culture of storytelling. Presented in the book are not individual case studies but rather categories of work and graphic approaches to assignments that have wowed clients and dazzled viewers. The work is arranged to communicate Hinrichs' creative thinking, which always leads to a unique and effective solution to any design conundrum.

Books are available at graphis.com/publications

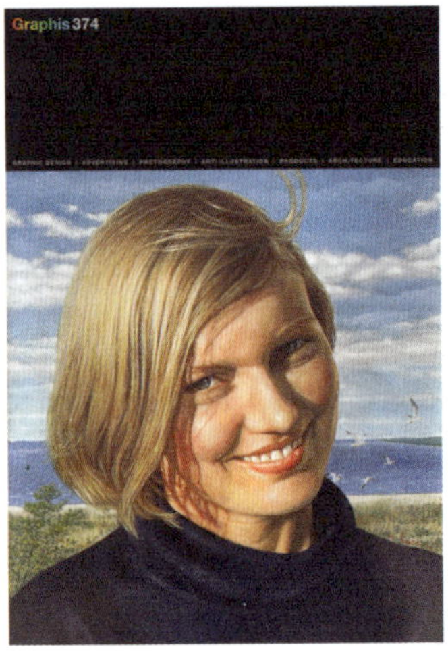
Graphis374

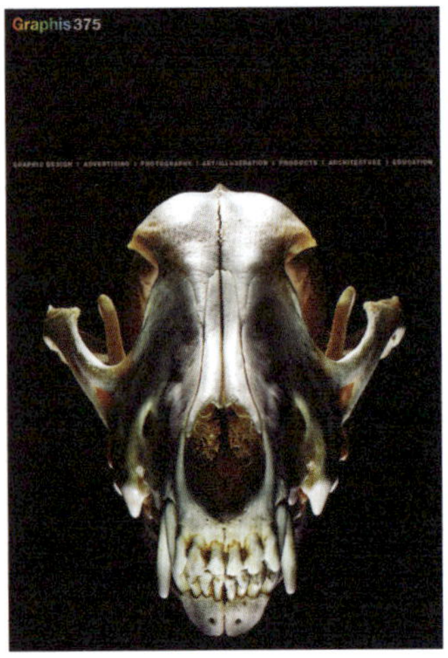
Graphis375

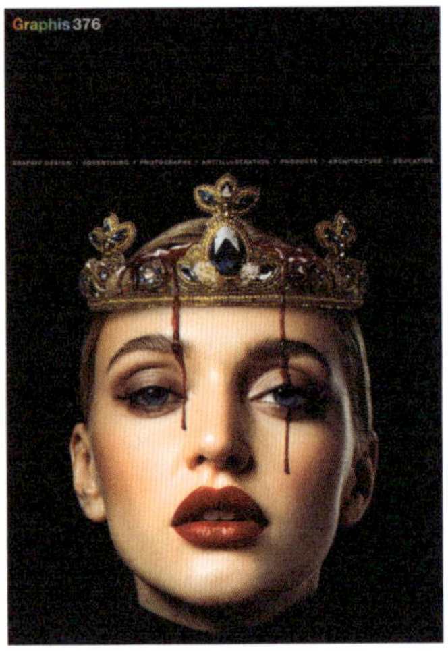
Graphis376

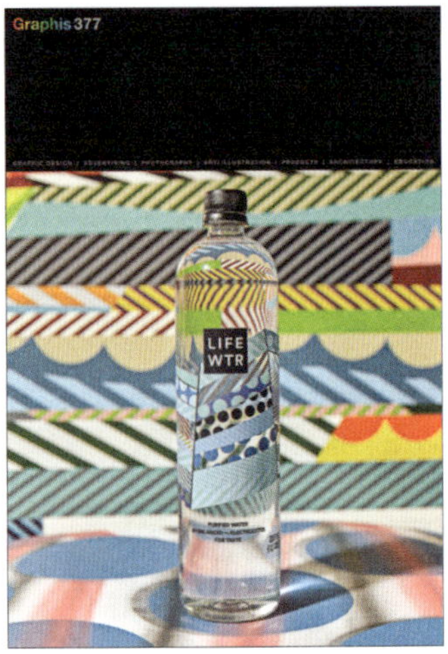
Graphis377
LIFE WTR

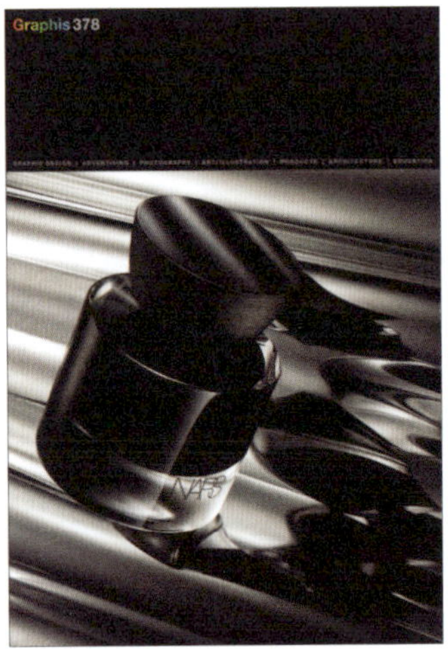
Graphis378

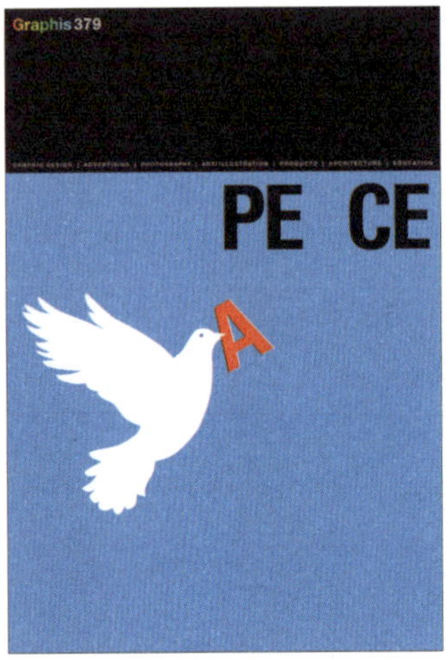
Graphis379
PE CE
A

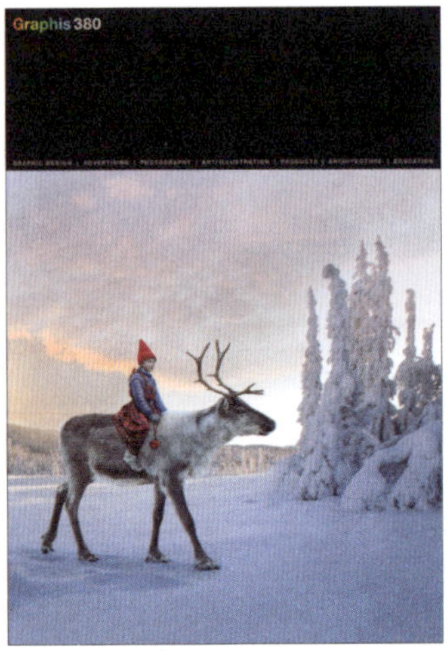
Graphis380

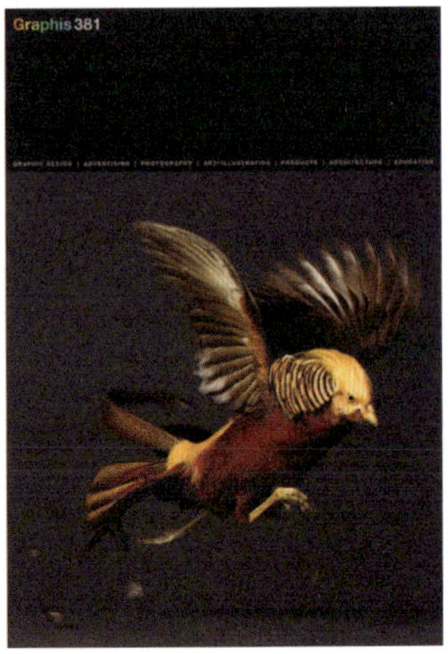
Graphis381

A

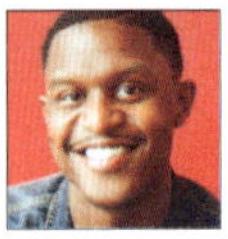

Quinnton Harris

Retrospect co-founder and chief executive officer, Quinnton J. Harris is a creative leader and entrepreneur living in Brooklyn, New York. His new venture focuses on building products and digital experiences that are radical, culturally nuanced, and more accessible for untapped or overlooked market opportunities. Previously, he served as Publicis Sapient Group's creative director within experience design as well as co-leader of global computational design, which focused on evolving the organization's design systems practice. He played a critical role in accelerating CXO John Maeda's vision for fostering a more inclusive, multidimensional, and cohesive experience design capability. He also served as head of experience for San Francisco. In early 2020, he completed a short tenure as John Maeda's chief of staff, finding much success in pushing critical CXO initiatives, implementing systems for global collaboration, and enhancing internal communication strategies. Quinnton also led the #hellajuneteenth movement and got over 600 companies committed to observing Juneteenth as a paid holiday for its employees. Prior to joining Publicis Sapient, he served as inaugural creative director at Blavity, Inc., and before that led design at Walker & Company Brands, a start-up consumer products and tech company notably acquired by Procter & Gamble. He is an MIT alum, graduating with a SB in mechanical engineering and dual minors in architecture and visual arts.

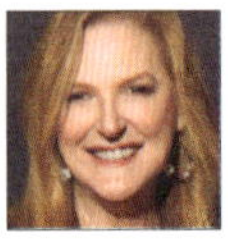

Patti Judd

Award-winning creative director, accomplished marketing and film executive, and co-founder of the San Diego International Film Festival, Patti joined Graphis as chief visionary officer. A key initiative was forming the Graphis Industry Advisory Board to promote greater industry insights and connections globally. Patti blends business savvy gained from twenty plus years at her agency with the entertainment biz acumen garnered from working in music and film. Her studio, Judd Brand Media, champions her passion for creating innovative work, receiving over 100 awards in design, advertising, and marketing. Her work includes notable global brands such as WME, Disney, Mattel, Montreux Jazz Festival, Century 21, Aramark, Service America, and Hilton, alongside numerous emerging brands, recording artists, and filmmakers. Her influence goes from helping launch a major live music venue, where she was a key player in its growth, to one of the top live jazz venues in the world, to co-founding the San Diego International Film Festival. She holds two executive producer credits for a children's TV series on Nickelodeon and a feature film in association with the BBC, which premiered at Sundance (acquired by Universal Pictures). Currently, she is in development as executive producer on an exciting new animated children's series. Patti's nonprofit work includes being a foster youth board member and a past president of an arts and culture board benefiting Balboa Park, the largest urban cultural park in the US. Recently, she was awarded as an Altruist Honoree by *Modern Luxury* magazine.

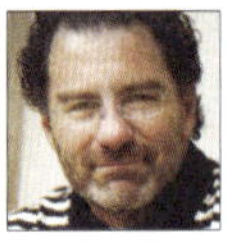

Michael Pantuso

As a multidisciplined graphic designer and artist, Michael Pantuso thrives at the intersection of creative thinking, artistic expression, and strategically inspired ideas. Throughout his career, Michael has managed his own design practice, partnered with the branding agency IDEAS360°, and held positions inside TBWA Worldhealth (formerly CAHG) and Discover Financial. Located in the Chicago area, Michael is focused on creating design and art for clients, collectors, and organizations that make a social impact—these include charities, not-for-profits, NGOs, educational and arts bodies, social enterprises, and for-profit businesses who want to do more good. Michael's practice creates all the usual outputs of a branding agency—design identities, advertising, social media, print literature, websites, email, e-newsletters, photography, etc. But he does so in the context of a bigger picture—a vision for what the brand is, and, more importantly, what it can become. It's a passion that comes from a desire to make things better. Michael's art is an extension of this passion, but it's revealed and expressed in a more visceral way. One example of this can be seen in his "Mechanical Integration" work, where he explores nature and humanity through a series of fine art illustrations that integrate natural life forms with the inner workings of mechanical components. Part of this collection was recently celebrated as a solo exhibition which began in Paris, France, followed by a tour of Europe that concluded in early 2020. Much of that work now remains in galleries and private collections.